d.

(

READERS IN CULTURAL CRITICISM
General Editor: *Catherine Belsey*

Posthumanism	*Neil Badmington*
Theorizing Ireland	*Claire Connolly*
Postmodern Debates	*Simon Malpas*
Reading the Past	*Tamsin Spargo*
Performance Studies	*Erin Striff*
Reading Images	*Julia Thomas*
Gender	*Anna Tripp*

Readers in Cultural Criticism
Series Standing Order
ISBN 0–333–78660–2 hardcover
ISBN 0–333–75236–8 paperback
(outside North America only)

You can receive future titles in this series as they are published by placing a standing order.
Please contact your bookseller or, in case of difficulty, write to us at the address below with your name and address, the title of the series and the ISBN quoted above.

Customer Services Department, Macmillan Distribution Ltd
Houndmills, Basingstoke, Hampshire RG21 6XS, England

Performance Studies

Edited by Erin Striff

palgrave
macmillan

First published 2003 by
PALGRAVE MACMILLAN
Houndmills, Basingstoke, Hampshire RG21 6XS and
175 Fifth Avenue, New York, N.Y. 10010
Companies and representatives throughout the world

PALGRAVE MACMILLAN is the global academic imprint of the Palgrave
Macmillan division of St. Martin's Press, LLC and of Palgrave Macmillan Ltd.
Macmillan® is a registered trademark in the United States, United Kingdom
and other countries. Palgrave is a registered trademark in the European
Union and other countries.

ISBN 0–333–78673–4 hardcover
ISBN 0–333–78674–2 paperback

This book is printed on paper suitable for recycling and
made from fully managed and sustained forest sources.

A catalog record for this book is available
from the Library of Congress.

Library of Congress Cataloging-in-Publication Data

Performance studies / edited by Erin Striff.
　　　p. cm. — (Readers in cultural criticism)
　　Includes bibliographical references and index.
　　ISBN 0–333–78673–4 (cloth) — ISBN 0–333–78674–2 (paper)
　　1. Theater–Anthropological aspects. 2. Performing arts. I. Striff, Erin, 1968–II. Series.

PN2041.A57 P47 2002

791—dc21   2002026750

10　9　8　7　6　5　4　3　2　1
12　11　10　09　08　07　06　05　04　03

Printed and bound in Great Britain by
Creative Print & Design (Wales), Ebbw Vale

To Megan and Alex

Contents

PERFORMANCE AND THE WORLD

PERFORMATIVITY/PERFORMANCE

General Editor's Preface

Culture is the element we inhabit as subjects.

Culture embraces the whole range of practices, customs and representations of a society. In their rituals, stories and images, societies identify what they perceive as good and evil, proper, sexually acceptable, racially other. Culture is the location of values, and the study of cultures shows how values vary from one society to another, or from one historical moment to the next.

But culture does not exist in the abstract. On the contrary, it is in the broadest sense of the term textual, inscribed in the paintings, operas, sculptures, furnishings, fashions, bus tickets and shopping lists which are the currency of both aesthetic and everyday exchange. Societies invest these artefacts with meanings, until in many cases the meanings are so 'obvious' that they pass for nature. Cultural criticism denaturalises and defamiliarises these meanings, isolating them for inspection and analysis.

The subject is what speaks, or, more precisely, what signifies, and subjects learn in culture to reproduce or to challenge the meanings and values inscribed in the signifying practices of the society that shapes them.

If culture is pervasive and constitutive for us, if it resides in the documents, objects and practices that surround us, if it circulates as the meanings and values we learn and reproduce as good citizens, how in these circumstances can we practise cultural *criticism*, where criticism implies a certain distance between the critic and the culture? The answer is that cultures are not homogeneous; they are not even necessarily coherent. There are always other perspectives, so that cultures offer alternative positions for the subjects they also recruit. Moreover, we have a degree of power over the messages we reproduce. A minor modification changes the script, and may alter the meaning; the introduction of a negative constructs a resistance.

The present moment in our own culture is one of intense debate. Sexual alignments, family values, racial politics, the implications of economic differences are all hotly contested. And positions are taken up not only in explicit discussions at political meetings, on television and in the pub. They are often reaffirmed or challenged implicitly in films and advertisements, horoscopes and lonely-hearts columns. Cultural criticism analyses all these forms in order to assess their hold on our consciousness.

There is no interpretative practice without theory, and the more sophisticated the theory, the more precise and perceptive the reading it makes possible. Cultural theory is as well defined now as it has ever been, and as strongly contested as our social values. There could not, in consequence, be a more exciting time to engage in the theory and practice of Cultural Criticism.

Catherine Belsey
Cardiff University

Acknowledgements

I began this project while working at the University of Glamorgan and I would first like to thank all my former colleagues who helped me, particularly Katja Krebs, for reading a draft of the introduction and giving supportive feedback, and Diana Wallace, for dragging me away from my office and offering sound advice over coffee. Since beginning my job at the University of Hartford I have found enthusiastic support from Catherine Stevenson and Bill Stull; their thoughtfulness has made a significant difference to me as I have completed this book.

Series Editor Catherine Belsey and Palgrave Macmillan editors Anna Sandeman and Beverley Tarquini have provided constant encouragement and guidance, and have helped make this project an exciting one. Anna Tripp and Margaret Bartley were always willing to respond helpfully to the many questions I e-mailed them. I would also like to thank the authors whose work comprises this reader, for their suggestions and assistance, and for their remarkable writing. Philip Auslander was particularly generous with his advice and his comments on the introduction.

Finally, I owe a very special thanks to Alex Cave who, as always, has provided practical and emotional support – this book is also very much his achievement. I would like to dedicate this work to Alex and also to our daughter Megan Striff-Cave, who was delivered at the same time as the manuscript and has brought so much inspiration and joy into our lives.

The editor and publishers wish to thank the following for permission to use copyright material:

Philip Auslander, for material from *From Acting to Performance* by Philip Auslander, Routledge (1997), pp. 126–53, by permission of Taylor & Francis Books Ltd; Judith Butler, for material from *Bodies That Matter: On the Discursive Limits of 'Sex'* by Judith Butler (1993), pp. 223–42, by permission of Routledge, Inc, part of The Taylor & Francis Group; Susan Leigh Foster, for 'Choreographies of Gender', *Signs*, 24:1 (1998), 1–10, 26–9, by permission of The University of Chicago Press; Paul Gilroy, for material from *The Black Atlantic: Modernity and Double Consciousness* by Paul Gilroy (1993), pp. 72–87, by permission of Verso; Lynda Hart, for material from *Fatal Women: Lesbian Sexuality and the Mark of Aggression* by Lynda Hart (1994), pp. 89–103. Copyright © 1994 by Princeton University Press, by permission of Princeton University Press; Katherine Liepe-Levinson, for material from 'Striptease: Desire, Mimetic Jeopardy, and Performing Spectators', *The Drama Review*, 42:2 (1998), 9–37. Copyright © 1998 by New York University and the Massachusetts Institute of Technology, by permission of MIT Press; Bernth Lindfors, for 'Ethnological Show Business: Footlighting the Dark Continent' from *Freakery: Cultural Spectacles of the Extraordinary Body*, ed. Rosemarie Garland Thomson (1996), pp. 207–18, by permission of New York University Press; Sharon Mazer, for 'The Power Team: Muscular Christianity and the Spectacle of Conversion', *The Drama Review*, 38:4 (1994), 162–88. Copyright © 1994 by New York University and the Massachusetts Institute of Technology, by permission of MIT Press; Vivian M. Patraka, for material from *Spectacular Suffering: Theatre, Fascism, and the Holocaust* by Vivian M. Patraka (1999), pp. 109–13, 114–17, 121–9, by permission of Indiana University Press; Peggy Phelan, for material from *Mourning Sex: Performing Public Memories* by Peggy Phelan, Routledge (1992), pp. 95–116, by permission of Taylor & Francis Books Ltd; Joseph Roach, for 'Culture and Performance in the Circum-Atlantic World' from *Performativity and Performance*, ed. Eve Kosofsky Sedgwick and Andrew Parker (1995), pp. 45–63, by permission of Routledge, Inc, part of The Taylor & Francis Group; Richard Schechner, for material from *The Future of Ritual: Writings on Culture and Performance* by Richard Schechner, Routledge (1993), pp. 45–71, by permission of Taylor & Francis Books Ltd.

Every effort has been made to trace the copyright holders but if any have been inadvertently overlooked the publishers will be pleased to make the necessary arrangement at the first opportunity.

1

Introduction:
Locating Performance Studies

Erin Striff

What constitutes a performance? To what extent are performances occurring throughout culture(s)? If a performance isn't defined by the purchase of a ticket and entering a theatre space, when and where can it be seen to begin and end? Is it still a performance if there are no spectators present? Performance is often perceived to be an activity that only takes place behind the proscenium arch or is contained within the box set. The discipline of performance studies has expanded upon this definition so that we can now see that performance is an inherent part of the customs, rituals and practices of cultures.

To consider performance is to study how we represent ourselves and repeat those representations within everyday life, working on the assumption that culture is unthinkable without performance. The theatricality of everyday activities, such as the way clothes are worn or a meal is served, can be analysed in terms of performance studies. There are also many public spectacles with similarities to the traditional theatre, such as a trial or a soccer match, which can be read as performance.

When we view performances in the theatre, what is performance and what is not may appear to be sharply delineated, even though these distinctions are not always that simple. These delineations become even more blurred when a performance takes place outside a theatre, because performance may or may not include traditional characters, acting, or a script. Performance can therefore be understood as being related to theatricality, a sense of otherness, of non-identical repetition, that can occur anywhere, at any time. It may consist of societal rituals, or it may be understood as the conscious and unconscious adoption of roles that we play during everyday life, depending on the company we keep, or where we are located at the time. The theatrical metaphor is a fundamental tool we use to understand culture. As Pelias and VanOosting write, '[t]o alter the balance between artistic and rhetorical foregrounds in the theatrical experience displays performance as an integral part of everyday life, rather than a rarefied event on the periphery of communal experience'.[1]

1

If we think of the primary constituents of theatre, we might return to the importance of audience. Is a necessary aspect of performance therefore something to do with monitoring? Of watching yourself being watched? Marvin Carlson writes that '[p]erformance is always performance *for* someone, some audience that recognises and validates it as performance even when, as is occasionally the case, that audience is the self'.[2] A performance might assume there are spectators appreciating the act *as performance*, even if we are only watching ourselves. Further, if there is no proscenium arch separating actor from audience, this can mean that the spectators are implicated as much as the performer.

Though we can perhaps give an indication of what needs to be present in order for an act to be read as performance, it is very difficult to come up with a definition of what performance actually is. Our understanding of performance is largely based on what we recognise as theatre, but performance may lack any or all of the signposts we associate with a theatre production. The object of a particular performance could be anything from proselytising to protesting, but what is the most productive way to analyse the meaning of what is performed?

In this introduction I attempt to raise some issues surrounding the discipline of performance studies, mapping what is a relatively new field, to prepare the reader for the important explorations other scholars have made in performance studies. I'm reminded of the title of the Fifth Annual Performance Studies conference I attended in Aberystwyth, Wales, in 1999, entitled 'Here Be Dragons'. This phrase, of course, was written on ancient maps to indicate uncharted territory, linking the unknown with danger. To define performance studies is to attempt to chart that border region where a map becomes mystery. With a new field, and a particularly contested one, it is difficult, and possibly reductive, to attempt any sort of definitive guide to that which lies beyond. There will always be competing maps that chart vastly different topographies to the ones I've travelled. If performance is primarily about *practice*, however, it is appropriate to let the authors in this volume speak for themselves. Maps are never drawn alone, and it is therefore through their examples that we may gain an understanding of that uncharted territory. For this reason, I will here trace briefly a history of performance studies as an academic discipline, then proceed to discuss how each of the chapters and sections in this volume may further our understanding of additional aspects of performance studies.

As performance studies has become increasingly influential, questions have been raised as to where (and to whom) performance studies belongs? Should it be situated and studied within the realm of theatre studies, or social sciences, or viewed through the lens of cultural and critical studies? Dwight Conquergood said at the first Performance Studies Conference in 1995 that 'Performance studies is a border discipline, an interdiscipline, that cultivates the capacity to move between structures, to forge connections, to speak with instead of simply speaking about or for others.'[3] Performance studies draws together many different academic fields, languages, and metaphors. It is consequently read and defined very differently depending on one's background, and this has created much debate as to how the field might be claimed/defined. Because so much of the development of the field has come about as a direct result of these disagreements, it is impossible to separate a consideration of performance studies from the genesis of the discipline, which became widely recognised internationally in the 1990s.

Most scholars agree that performance studies was initially popularised at New York University and Northwestern University. Richard Schechner was extremely instrumental in establishing the field – as early as 1979 he created a course at New York University's Drama Department entitled 'Performance Theory' and brought in visiting faculty from anthropology, psychology, semiotics and the performing arts.[4] Because of their increasingly interdisciplinary approach, the department changed their name to Performance Studies in 1980. Northwestern University's department of Performance Studies is housed within a School of Speech, and has links with a related field known as Oral Interpretation. As Conquergood explains, Northwestern takes 'performance as both subject and method of research'.[5] They perform texts such as diaries and ethnographic field notes, but do not stage traditional plays. These two institutional histories demonstrate that performance studies has had a variety of influences, adding to its interdisciplinary nature.

As its methods began to become more well known (and appealed to those scholars who were doing similar work by a different name) the First Annual Performance Studies conference was held at New York University in 1995, and took place at Northwestern the following year. Only a short time later, performance studies has become an increasingly popular subject to study, in the United Kingdom where I write this, as well as in other departments around the world.

Performance studies has had, at times, an uneasy relationship with theatre studies, partially because of the 'evangelical fervour'[6] as Philip Auslander puts it, with which some academics have embraced it. Richard Schechner, for example, in a much-quoted address he gave at the Association for Theatre in Higher Education conference in 1992, has gone so far as to say:

> The new paradigm is 'performance', not theatre. Theatre departments should become 'performance departments'. Performance is about more than the enactment of Eurocentric drama. Performance engages intellectual, social, cultural, historical, and artistic life in a broad sense. Performance combines theory and practice. Performance studied and practised interculturally can be the core of a 'well-rounded education'.[7]

Here and in a number of other pieces on performance studies he questions whether, since the raison d'être of many theatre studies programmes is to train practitioners, and since there are very few jobs to be had in the theatre, would it not be better to train students how to think about performance in a more broadly based way, which might also prepare them for other careers? This kind of dichotomy risks characterising theatre studies as an increasingly limited area, focusing on what is seen to be a rarefied art form. Jill Dolan acknowledges that some theatre departments are pre-professional institutions that have little interest in theory. However, she rightly points out that other theatre studies departments employ critical and cultural theory as a way of looking at texts and performance, so that it is reductive to view performance studies as the only field where this kind of work is taking place.[8]

The question of how theatrical texts are used within performance studies is another important issue. Performance studies acknowledges that much of world drama is created without the dramatic scripts taken as a given in what many think of as 'traditional' theatre; consequently, it has a very all-encompassing view of what might comprise a performance text. W. B. Worthen writes that '[r]econsidering how, or whether, texts are actually opposed to performances, is one way to rethink the disciplinary instruments that map the contours of drama/theatre/performance studies today'.[9] He shows concern that some will simply equate theatre studies with dramatic text and performance studies with performance, clearly a reductive approach.

Concerns have also been raised about the way in which performance studies is using the metaphors of theatre studies but simply not applying them to the theatre. Jill Dolan argues that theatre studies should be 'acknowledged and visited, rather than raided and discarded...'[10] Furthermore, considering the pervasiveness of the theatrical metaphor in performance, the question of what can be identified as a performative act can easily turn into 'what can't?' Has the theatrical metaphor become so over-determined in performance studies that it ceases to mean anything? Other critics question how useful this metaphor is in our thinking about culture. Philip Auslander writes,

> Although I recognise that just about anything can be looked at as performance, I'm not sure that it's profitable in every case to do so. It's also not entirely clear how looking at other phenomena 'as performance' is different from looking at them 'as theatre'. Generally when the uninitiated want to discuss the 'performative' aspect of some event or routine of living, they refer to it as 'dramatic' or 'theatrical'. What questions does thinking in terms of the performance metaphor raise that thinking in the theatre metaphor does not? The theatrical metaphor has a long history and is deeply ingrained in our culture, in our thinking about performance

and, arguably, in performance itself. As Herb Blau has written, 'it is *theatre* [...] which haunts *all* performance whether or not it occurs in the theatre' (1987:164–5). Much as some practitioners of performance studies would like to establish performance as an episteme separate from theatre, it may well be that our primary concept of what performance *is* derives inevitably from theatre.[11]

It is clear that, in performance studies, we are never far from the theatre, whether or not we are considering traditional theatrical productions. We must not, of course, not to assume that theatre is any less complex than performance, but that it is a particular style of performance which should not be discounted.

Dwight Conquergood argues that 'Performance privileges threshold-crossing, shape-shifting, and boundary-violating figures, such as shamans, tricksters and jokers, who value the carnivalesque over the canonical, the transformative over the normative, the mobile over the monumental'.[12] It is also important to point out that although some practitioners of performance studies choose to focus upon performances that are transgressive in some way, there are many other performances which do not violate boundaries and in fact may be reactionary in nature.[13] In the same way that there is more than one style of play, and some are more likely to wind up on theatre studies reading lists than others, some styles of performances are especially privileged in performance studies.

We have seen the way in which performance studies is closely related to theatre studies, and it is important to note that the field also has very strong links with the social sciences. I will here briefly consider three theorists working in the social sciences who have significantly influenced performance studies. Erving Goffman's work, *The Presentation of the Self in Everyday Life*, has been particularly useful in our understanding of the roles we adopt and the drama that we play out during daily life. According to Goffman, these roles can be taken on sincerely, so that the performer is 'convinced that the impression of reality which he stages is the real reality...',[14] or cynically, with the performer knowingly deluding his or her audience. In either case, Goffman emphasises the way in which we are constantly performing, whether or not we are aware of the roles we are inhabiting.

Another social scientist central to the field of performance studies is Victor Turner, an extremely influential anthropologist who worked with Richard Schechner. His work was deeply influenced by theatre studies; as Marvin Carlson writes, '[t]he language of drama and performance gave him a way of thinking and talking about people as actors who creatively play, improvise, interpret and re-present roles and scripts.'[15] In assessing human behaviour Turner employs the useful concepts of the liminal and the liminoid. These terms can be understood as differentiating activities which are often cyclical, collective, and integrated within a society, from those that tend to be idiosyncratic, fragmentary, outside a society, playful, and sometimes part of a social critique.[16]

J. L. Austin, as a philosopher whose theories relate to the field of linguistics, has had a palpable effect on many chapters in this volume. Austin's account of the performative, or the way speech acts are translated into human behaviour, has much relevance to performance studies. In their book *Performativity and Performance*, Parker and Sedgwick express the issues at stake in performativity by asking, '[w]hen is saying something doing something? And how is saying something doing something?'[17] Austin's book, *How to Do Things With Words*, derived from lectures he gave at Harvard University in 1955, put forth that the performative is a speech act that should not be judged on whether it is true or false, but on whether or not it actually occurs. Therefore, performative speech, such as christening a ship or sentencing a criminal, can be seen as inextricably linked with institutional authority.

Though there is not space in this introduction to fully trace links between performance and the social sciences, Marvin Carlson in *Performance: A Critical Introduction* does just this admirably well. In the first section of his book, he relates performance to fields such as anthropology, ethnology, sociology, psychology, and linguistics. Carlson himself explains:

[a]s performance studies has developed as a particular field of scholarly work, especially in the United States, it has been very closely associated with the various social sciences, and a complex and interesting cross-fertilisation has been the result. The study of traditional 'artistic' performance, such as theatre and dance, has taken on new dimensions and begun to explore newly observed relationships between these and other cultural and social activities, while the various social sciences have found theatre and performance metaphors of great use in exploring particular kinds of human activities within their own fields of study.[18]

Carlson's thorough approach maps the way in which many different fields have had a profound and lasting effect on performance studies. Because this reader is also specifically aimed at students of cultural criticism, however, the chapters in this volume are more inclined to look to critical and cultural theory's intersections with performance studies than to the social sciences.

Because performance studies is located between so many disparate fields it will, of course, bring about a certain degree of controversy, which we can particularly see in the spate of articles variously critiquing or promoting the field that were published in the early to mid-nineties in journals such as *The Drama Review*. However, through their disagreements, many scholars would back up Richard Schechner's point that 'Performance studies is "inter" – in between. It is intergeneric, interdisciplinary, intercultural – and is therefore inherently unstable. Performance studies resists or rejects definition.'[19] If the knowledge of this contention indicates the way in which performance studies is never one thing nor another, then we can see its potential as a mode of discourse.

Though we have seen how all-encompassing the field can be, I must here state the particular focus of my reading of performance studies. This volume does not cover the realm of traditional theatre studies; there will be no discussion of traditional plays, as such. There are chapters on music, dance and performance art, but these essays also locate performances within culture rather than considering them as aesthetic gestures alone. The chapters also tend to focus on issues of race, nationalism, gender and sexuality. Because these subjects are very often sites of contestation, reading them through the border discipline of performance studies seems particularly appropriate.

Finally, the themes that I have used to organise the chapters are intended as a possible guide rather than a definitive delineation of the book. There are, in fact, many other ways in which the chapters might have been grouped. Similarly, in the next part of my introduction, in which I will focus on themes which link the chapters and the sections together, I am attempting not to sum up each chapter, but to consider the way in which each one helps bring us closer to an understanding of performance and performance studies.

POPULAR PERFORMANCE

The first section discusses popular performance: in particular, a group of men who perform feats of strength while evangelising, British sideshows displaying Africans in the 1900s, and strip clubs. We can easily recognise these acts as performance, but we tend to think of them as 'shows', or entertainment for the masses, rather than as 'theatre', an aesthetic event. In fact, all three chapters focus on these performances as profit-making businesses, and discuss the monetary success of these gestures. Some, in defining performance studies, accentuate that performance may be more accessible than the theatre. By considering these types of performances the authors are not attempting to elevate low/popular culture into a more sophisticated aesthetic experience; rather they are arguing that they can and should be read as performances within culture.

Chapters 2 to 4, perhaps because they are dealing with performances that succeed only if they are commercially successful, drawing in the crowds, are deeply concerned with audience response and participation. Marvin Carlson writes that in performance:

> The audience's expected 'role' changes from a passive hermeneutic process of decoding the performer's articulation, embodiment, or challenge of particular cultural material, to become something much more active, entering into a praxis, a context in which meanings are not so much communicated as created, questioned, or negotiated. The 'audience' is invited and expected to operate as a co-creator of whatever meanings and experiences the event generates.[20]

Though Carlson's comments apply very well to a range of cultural activities not necessarily recognised as performance, the same is also true of the chapters in this section. For example, Mazer's 'The Power Team: Muscular Christianity and the Spectacle of Conversion' (chapter 2), discusses a performance in which the evangelical message is part of the build-up that results in the 'payoff' of a performer breaking through blocks of ice. What is curious about the production is what she calls the 'altar call' finale, where the audience members are asked to sign a card dedicating or rededicating themselves to Christ. At that point it is the audience's own religious commitment which becomes the focus of the show. Those who do not participate in this religious act are made to feel out of place, not living up to the standards that have been set by others. Mazer also makes the point that by appearing as a committed religious spectator, one's image has been captured and will be broadcast as living proof of the success of the ministry. Thus, we can see how in performance studies the audience often has a complex role to fulfil. Unlike the 'high art' of theatre, where a piece's exclusivity is sometimes seen as a marker of its good taste, in popular performance it is often the size of the crowd that counts.

Bernth Lindfors' 'Ethnological Show Business: Footlighting the Dark Continent' (chapter 3), focuses upon Africans displayed in British sideshows in the 1900s. Lindfors argues that the more 'other' these Africans seemed, the more they served to affirm British cultural superiority. Consequently, as long as the Africans appeared 'savage' to the crowds, their behaviour was acceptable, as any indication of their being civilised would mean they were not sufficiently 'other' from the audience. These racist responses give us another side to the importance of audience in performance studies – that often their reaction tells us as much about the community forming the audience as it does about that which they view and judge.

Katherine Liepe-Levinson's 'Striptease: Desire, Mimetic Jeopardy, and Performing Spectators' (chapter 4) also discusses audience relationship to performance. She describes 'mimetic jeopardy' as being the point at which the spectator takes a more active role in the strip show, whether by putting a tip in a stripper's G-string, or participating in shows staged just for them, such as lap dancing, while the other spectators watch them as well. There is a sense of danger inherent in the act as well as being able to safely act out fantasy in what is, essentially, a controlled environment. This chapter demonstrates that it is not always clear who is a performer and who is a spectator, or where a performance begins and ends.

PERFORMING BODIES/PERFORMANCE ART

The next section is specifically concerned with performance art. One of the hallmarks of performance studies is that traditional characters do not act out dramatic texts – but this should not reductively be taken to mean that performance is somehow 'more authentic' than the theatre. In performance art, the performers themselves become the text to be read. We are, in fact, encouraged to read the artist as being fundamentally present in his or her own work, frequently through the expressions of their bodies. This helps to explain the way in which the body figures so prominently in much performance art and performance in general. It is important to realise that neither of the chapters in this section simply provide an overview of performance artists' productions; rather, they contextualise the performance within culture.

Philip Auslander, in 'The Surgical Self: Body Alteration and Identity' (chapter 5), discusses performance artists who read their own body text against the grain through surgical alteration. This of course brings up the question of what constitutes a 'natural' body, and at what point it is read as an 'unnatural' one. He focuses first on the artist Orlan, who directs plastic surgeons to give her the face she most desires in the name of art, rather than the face that the doctor believes is the most medically suitable. Auslander also discusses the performer Kate Bornstein, who, as a male to female transsexual, has defied typical post-op expectations, first, by insisting that she will not now, as a woman, enter into relationships with men, and second, by refusing to identify fully with the female gender. In this way she defies gender categories, insisting that her identity remains unfixed. As both Orlan and Bornstein have altered their body through surgery, they perform their post-surgical bodies every time they walk down the street, not just while appearing on stage. Their performance continues long after the scalpel is wielded, because their bodies do not fit into the norms decided by culture.

Lynda Hart's 'Reconsidering Homophobia: Karen Finley's Indiscretions' (chapter 6) chronicles how performance artist Karen Finley was one of the four artists defunded by the National Endowment for the Arts in 1990 for what they deemed to be obscene art. Hart makes the link between Finley's defunding and homophobia, though Finley was the only heterosexual artist to have funding withdrawn. Hart asserts that because her performances were gender transgressive in terms of the body (suggesting, for example, anal penetration) Finley too became a victim of homophobia. Her 'straight' body enacting a 'queer' performance was enough to make spectators and funding bodies alike feel uncomfortable, as they were unable to separate the performer from the performance. This slippage between performer and material is another of the hallmarks of performance studies. Both of the chapters in this section call into question ideas about what is 'normal' and 'natural' about gender and the body and provide a very clear link to Butler's queer performativity, which is discussed in later chapters.

PERFORMING HISTORIES/MEMORIES

The fact that performance studies is not generally concerned with what is understood as a traditional dramatic text does not, however, mean that texts are not performed, and in this section, the texts are competing memories and histories of the same events. In chapter 7, 'Spectacular Suffering', we can see that a building can become a site of performance, designed to elicit a certain response from the spectator. In her account of the American Holocaust Memorial Museum, Vivian M. Patraka cites Michel de Certeau, an influential theorist in performance studies, to show the way in which a place may become a performance space, where the narrative is decided by the participants. Museum patrons do not expect to witness an actual performance at the museum but the very architecture encourages a particular reading of the past. Patraka also shows the way in which this museum is subject to biases and to assumptions, that it is not a value-free representation of history. She documents her experience of speaking to some museum visitors whose response to a display of a freight car (used to transport Jews to concentration camps) was very different from the one that the museum encourages. Patraka interviewed a Jewish couple who associated freight cars not with victimisation, but with the trains to the German front they blew up when they were members of the underground movement. Patraka makes the point that the building itself is capable of encouraging a certain performance narrative, which may still be resisted by spectators.

Peggy Phelan in 'Hearing Anita Hill and Clarence Thomas' (chapter 8), views the Anita Hill–Clarence Thomas sexual harassment hearings of 1991 as a performance of the gaps and elisions in narratives, memories, and the 'truth', which of course can never be uncovered. Like Patraka, Phelan focuses on the way in which memory may be performed and re-presented, but never completely 'managed'. Part of her project is to show how the law attempts to provide redress for sexual injury and trauma. Phelan shows how two competing narratives that ran throughout the hearing were based on law and psychoanalysis, but neither was adequate in terms of uncovering what actually happened. Phelan's use of psychoanalysis is also instructive in terms of performance studies, for she deals with the way the unconscious can be brought to light within a performance. The Hill–Thomas hearings were a case of unofficial knowledge, with their emphasis on rumour, whereas the Holocaust museum is re-presenting history from a particular perspective. Either way, both can be seen as performances about which we as spectators are encouraged to make a closed reading, but that we have the ability to resist.

PERFORMANCE AND THE WORLD

Through its appropriation of anthropology, performance studies demonstrates the way in which performance can be read differently across cultures. The three chapters in this section focus on performance and international exchange. They all also touch on another aspect important to performance studies: they discuss the fact that a written text is not the only way to express knowledge. This search for alternatives to writing as a basis for performed text is a point particularly important to performance studies. Dwight Conquergood discusses text in terms of ethnography: 'the mode of "discussion", the discourse, is not always and exclusively verbal: issues and attitudes are expressed and contexted in dance, music, gesture, food, ritual, artefact, symbolic action, as well as words.'[21] By not over-privileging the written text, he encourages us to consider other ways in which culture is transmitted.

Richard Schechner is an extremely important scholar in terms of applying anthropology to performance and this section begins with his, 'The Street is the Stage' (chapter 9). He focuses specifically on the way in which those participating in demonstrations and protest use physical space. In addition, his scholarship on anthropology is also in evidence. He considers the way in which the carnival atmosphere of the protesters both at Tiananmen Square and the Berlin Wall contrasted so sharply with the regimented behaviour of those in power. Schechner argues that this unofficial culture is 'liminoid', a term coined by Victor Turner, meaning that its activities are developed on the margins of society and carry with them potential for change. Schechner also shows the way in which unofficial performances can sometimes transmit information more effectively than text can. He chronicles the way in which the official media in China at the time of the Tiananmen Square protests was unreliable, but it was the moments of impromptu performance, protesters singing and dancing in the square, going on hunger strike, offering interviews to the international media, that conveyed what was actually occurring across the globe.

Joseph Roach's chapter (10), 'Culture and Performance in the Circum-Atlantic World' is about performance and collective memory, with particular focus on the way in which culture can be transmitted in ways other than literature. He looks at the performance of funerals, referring particularly to Schechner's concept of 'restored behaviour', which can be repeated with a certain distance. Or, as Schechner himself puts it, 'Performances... allow people to play with behaviour that is "twice-behaved", not-for-the-first-time, rehearsed, cooked, prepared.'[22] There is, then, a cultural script that we all follow, though, as Roach points out, the repetitions are necessarily non-identical and are therefore reinvented each time. These important points emanate from anthropological readings of performance.

Paul Gilroy's 'Jewels Brought From Bondage: Black Music and the Politics of Authenticity' (chapter 11) is concerned with the cultural exchange of music throughout the black Atlantic world and the shadows of the terrors of slavery inherent within the music. Gilroy's points are similar to those made by Roach in that he is interested in cultural exchange; this chapter traces the way in which music is adapted and developed as it migrates through and between cultures. Performance is therefore not viewed as static but as something that is enriched and enlivened through diaspora. Gilroy also makes the point that music became increasingly significant because use of written communication was punishable by death. It is a recurrent concern within performance studies that we do not over-emphasise written text and fall prey to the cultural assumptions that it is a higher form of communication.

PERFORMATIVITY/PERFORMANCE

This final section is concerned with the performative, an idea which has become extremely influential in the field of performance studies. J. L. Austin's *How to do Things With Words* has already been discussed in terms of its introduction of the performative utterance as a speech act which carries with it cultural and institutional authority. His most-cited example is the ' "I do (sc. Take this woman to be my lawful wedded wife)" – as uttered in the course of the marriage ceremony.'[23] This speech act is extremely important to a reading of queer performativity, for if the performative takes with it all the assumptions of a society ordered by systems of authority, a performative will, necessarily, re-present the status quo. Judith Butler's 'Critically Queer' (chapter 12) is a key text in our understanding of performativity. She reads J. L. Austin in terms of the heterosexual authority of the 'I do' example, and wonders what happens when the performative 'queer' operates beside it. She discusses theatrical events in which performatively naming oneself queer is a political act, as in ACT UP die-ins. Butler's argument is that the citation of gender is a repetition of convention, never perfectly performed.

Susan Leigh Foster, in her chapter 'Choreographies of Gender' (13), critiques Butler's view of performativity and makes the case that choreography is a more appropriate metaphor for gender than performance. She argues that choreographic conventions (based on cultural identities) provide the basis of a dance, and that performance is more related to how an individual might interpret those codes. Foster provides an appropriate end to this book, because in dealing with choreography, she returns us to the performing arts, and yet she is focusing on the performative, a highly theoretical aspect of performance studies. In coming full circle, we can see that performance studies can be used to read performing arts texts, but her work looks beyond the performance in and of itself, considering the culture in which it exists.

While preparing this volume, I received the tragic news that one of the authors, Lynda Hart, died of breast cancer on 31 December 2000. Her work in performance studies, queer theory and feminist theatre has been extremely influential on many scholars, myself included. Among other important works, she edited a collection on feminist theatre entitled *Making a Spectacle* and its follow-up (edited with Peggy Phelan) *Acting Out*. These ideas of 'acting out' and 'making a spectacle', are appropriate for the way performing women have been written off, but the phrases can also be applied to performance studies. Acting out unconscious desires, acting out of place, out of turn, particularly when so many in this volume are dealing with marginalised subjects in terms of race, class or sexuality, may be an appropriate gesture. Acting out questions the status quo and makes possible Judith Butler's theories of queer performativity and Joseph Roach's references to cultural liminality. Furthermore, performing in culture often involves making a spectacle of oneself. The lack of formal structure creates an element of danger, of performing without a net. And for us, as spectators, the performance occurs before we have a chance to rely on our received responses that would, perhaps, dull our sensibilities and limit the depth of our reading of what took place before us.

2

The Power Team: Muscular Christianity and the Spectacle of Conversion

Sharon Mazer

It is good that the divine is associated with the Virgin Mary and a blissful Jesus, but we can sense how different it would be for young men if we lived in a culture where the divine was associated with mad dancers, fierce fanged men, and a being underwater, covered with hair.

(Robert Bly)[1]

Jesus Christ was no skinny little man. Jesus was a man's man.

(John Jacobs)[2]

At the centre of a nondescript auditorium stage, John Jacobs, a thick-necked muscular man wearing a red-white-and-blue, stars-and-stripes nylon athletic costume, stands in a spotlight. His wrists have been first wrapped in silver duct tape and then locked into handcuffs. Another similarly dressed man – Mike Hagen – stands a step behind Jacobs and demands silence so that Jacobs can concentrate on the ordeal of breaking the handcuffs. Hagen holds a microphone to Jacobs' face. Jacobs tells us: 'I am going to flex my arms and chest and upper back and push my body to the limit.' His breathing is amplified as he strains against the handcuffs, first one way and then another, for perhaps as long as five minutes. At last, screaming, he breaks through the cuffs and triumphantly holds his now-separated hands above his head. The spectators cheer. Hagen, exultant, shouts: 'Let's give Jesus a hand! Come on!' Jacobs takes the mike and chants: 'Praise the Lord. Praise the Lord. Praise the Lord'.[3]

The 'chains of the devil' have been broken. Once again Jacobs tells the audience that his exceptional strength is both a sign of his faith in Christ and a demonstration of the power of God. The breaking of handcuffs is the final act in a series of feats of strength, testimonials and pitches for money, orchestrated and performed by John Jacobs and his Power Team as part of an evangelical crusade. Jacobs' success will be measured in the number of spectators who, moved by the performance, will decide to dedicate themselves to Christ. During the altar call, in what may be termed a spectacle of conversion, these spectators will step forward to receive a more personal blessing and to affirm their commitment to a born-again life by filling out the 'decision cards' offered by the volunteers who stand ready to embrace the new converts.[4]

PERFORMING THE WORD

Evangelical preaching has always been a highly visible form of performance in American culture, but never more so since the advent of cable television. The tradition it follows is rooted in the revival tents and medicine shows of nineteenth-century America. Today's evangelical ministers are pragmatists who extend their evangelical range with secular performance practices and the electronic media. The dramaturgy of each performance is carefully calculated to transmit the Word to large numbers of people as it finances evangelicalism's far-reaching efforts by way of the collection bucket and by mail. Through modern communications technologies, the flocks of these twentieth-century preachers have become the world at large. Many no longer lead site-specific churches or congregations; instead, they minister to what have been termed 'parachurches'.[5]

Parachurch preachers offer themselves 'for hire' to churches around the country in addition to broadcasting their 'services' via satellite from churches, tents, auditoriums and television studios. Their performances of exhortation conflate the quest for Christian salvation with a more secular brand of show-and salesmanship. According to Hadden and Shupe:

> When Johnny Carson breaks for a commercial, even if Ed McMahon is hawking the product, there is a psychological distance between the 'real' programme and the selling of a sponsor's product. For religious broadcasters, the tasks of preaching, entertaining, and selling are all intertwined.[6]

Or as another historian puts it: 'If "sin" advertised it in sensational terms, then God must be advertised still more colourfully. If the Devil offered amusement, so must the angels.'[7] Indeed, the spectacle of conversion has become theatricalised to such a high degree that we must now consider such performances as part of secular performance culture, and their followers more as audiences than as congregations.

John Jacobs and his Power Team explicitly acknowledge their calculation in conflating popular performance practices with evangelical proselytising. In Jacobs' own words, he is a 'soul-winner', a 'fisher of men' who performs feats of strength in order to attract non-Christian audiences to the evangelical message. In *People Magazine*, Jacobs explains the Power Team's 'melding of circus and religion' as 'bait'.[8] Team members reiterate this theme in their own interviews. Mike Hughes tells a reporter for the *Repository*, a Canton, Ohio, community paper: 'God doesn't care about us breaking rocks. This is just a tool. He told us to be "fishers of men". This is only the bait.'[9] In another interview, Craig Lemley echoes: 'It's a bait to hook the people who would never come to a regular church service.'[10] And John Kopta tells a reporter for the *Galveston Daily News*: 'All we do on this stage is bait. [...] People won't go to church, but they'll come to see us do these crazy things.'[11] The pastors who invite the Power Team to perform are equally comfortable with the fishing metaphor. Pastor E. C. Damiani at the Faith Assembly of God in Poughkeepsie, New York, told me that the Team's exhibition was an effective 'hook' for drawing people into the church.[12]

By buying tickets, spectators agree to listen to the Team's testimonials, to its pleas for money and its prayers for their redemption. In return, they are offered the spectacle of muscular young men ripping phone books, bending steel, lifting logs, exploding hot water bottles and breaking all sorts of odd objects, including blocks of ice, burning cinder blocks and handcuffs. These 'muscular Christians' – the phrase was first coined in the USA by baseball-player-turned-preacher Billy Sunday (1862–1935)[13] – display their bodies as a sign of spiritual power, poised against the imprecations of vice, itself defined, in large part, as society at large.[14] Their ability to break things represents the strength necessary to resist the lure of drugs, alcohol, premarital sex, gang violence and generalised despair. Members of the Team often claim a primary role in preventing teen suicides. Mike Hughes articulates the Team's position in the public schools: 'We're not able to mention the Gospel in the schools, but we warn kids against the dangers of drugs, alcohol and teen suicide.'[15] In another report, Keith Davis tells a group of young people: 'Many of you are thinking of giving up too soon'.[16] Elsewhere, Berry Handley points to 'the teen who was considering suicide but changed her mind, that makes all the hours of working out with weights and practising stunts worthwhile'.[17]

The Power Team's performances can be breathtaking at times, a testament to the potential power and grace of the human body. But these exhibitions are also deliberately designed to manipulate and sustain a highly programmatic spectator response. Everything that happens on the stage is calculated to induce large numbers of people to come forward, to leave their seats and step to the edge of the stage where they can be counted as they dedicate (or rededicate) themselves to Christ at the end of the evening.

The John Jacobs Evangelistic Association offers live performances of the Power Team across the USA and around the world. Their circuit is generally rural, but they have made appearances in more urban areas such as Tacoma, Orange County and Chicago, as well as in world centres such as London, Cape Town, Moscow and Jerusalem. They perform in civic centres, hotel ballrooms, sports palaces, fairgrounds or under tents during a week that culminates at the host church's Sunday services where members of the Team lead the worship before a now substantially increased membership.

The Power Team claims the 'power to move a generation' in most of its promotional materials, and while its audiences are, in actuality, a mixture of the faithful and the curious, old and young, its stated target is in fact young men in their teens and early twenties. To attract these young audiences, the Team positions itself in competition with, and employs the tricks of, other performance practices aimed at teens. All performances are videotaped for later broadcast over the Trinity Broadcast Network (TBN), among other places, in the Saturday line-up in direct competition with cartoons, MTV, American Gladiators, and professional wrestling. The Team also offers inspirational education programmes at no charge to public school administrators. These school programmes are necessarily stripped of explicit references to God, Christ, the Spirit, Christianity and salvation. Nonetheless, the Power Team's ostensibly secular exhibitions increase its mainstream visibility and serve as promotional events for the evening performances.

What we see in the Power Team's performances is essentially a pastiche that visibly mimics many of the most popular, most secular forms of performances. Like American Gladiators, the Team displays powerful bodies dressed in patriotic colours performing feats that ordinary people cannot. As in professional wrestling, the Power Team's presentation of its pumped-up male bodies and what those bodies can do becomes a sign for less-visible values, its televised broadcasts are in large part advertisements for live performances, and the entire set-up is calculated to attract ever-larger audiences.

To see the Team performing up close and to be seen by them, to be touched and blessed in the most literal way, is to be welcomed into a magic circle defined by the aura of celebrity that the Team very deliberately projects. Borrowing a large part of its syntax from MTV, the Power Team performs its acts against a musical backdrop, particularly in the TBN broadcasts, where breakthrough moments are collaged, replayed in slow motion and underscored with choruses of 'Gospel Rock':

Our God is an awesome God.
He reigns from heaven above.
With wisdom, power and love,
Our God is an awesome God.

At the same time, like characters in the children's cartoons against which the TBN broadcasts are pitted, each member of the Team is presented with

superhuman qualities which are proved against apparently immovable obstacles. Indeed, one newspaper headline blares: 'Move over Batman, God has
a new team of Superheroes',[18] and the Power Team markets its own comic
book. In Jacobs' words:

> America loves a hero, but the hero Americans should love most [...], a
> comeback story bigger than Rocky, that makes Rocky look like checkers
> [is Jesus Christ] who died on the cross on Friday. Jesus Christ is no little
> fairy-tale. [...] He whipped the devil on his own turf.[19]

MEN ON A MISSION

The Power Team's performances may be seen as a contemporary psycho-
machia, a morality play in which human actors stand in for virtue and vice in
the struggle for the soul of man. However, in the Team's binary, the
opposition is not human but rather inanimate, unspeaking objects which
lack voice or volition – unlike the expressive range and passion of medieval
vice figures. The confrontation is thus one-sided. The Team represents the
forces of virtue as heroic men who, glistening with the sweat of their
struggles, challenge apparently immovable objects that are variously articulated in the Team's discourse as representative of vice, the devil, or other
antichristical forces. They are, in their own self-presentation, 'Men on a
mission to reach this world',[20] crusaders who carry the signs of faith in their
bodies rather than on medieval banners.

When the men break through concrete, through cinderblocks, ice, handcuffs, etc., they symbolically defeat the obstacles to faith and clear the path
to redemption. Mike Hughes, for example, claims: 'Our programme illustrates the barriers and stumbling blocks that can be overcome through
Jesus.'[21] Or as one less-than-secular newspaper headline crows: 'Satan and
concrete beware.'[22]

The iconography and rhetoric of the Power Team's performance is explicit: the display of the disciplined male body is a stand-in for the less visible
soul. The Team's hypermasculine bodies, their bulky bodies, along with their
ability to perform what appear to be extrahuman feats of strength, are signs
both of the men's devotion to Christ and of His power made manifest in
man. In the vernacular of the Power Team, then, the male body as it is
recognised and defined by its muscularity, literally enacts a promise to
Christian men that their bodies can be likewise powerful at the same time
that it acts as a manifestation of the Spirit which would otherwise remain
invisible.

The Team's equation of masculinity with spiritual and physical power
would be unremarkable but for the degree to which Jacobs and his fellow

Team members are explicit in their repudiation of what they consider to be the 'feminisation' of Christianity. The Team's display of masculine muscularity is derived from, and provides a model of, an idealised Christian patriarchy. The battle for converts is to be fought in masculine terms, man to man, with men on earth as stand-ins for God-the-Father. They repeatedly attribute to the dominant (i.e., non-Christian) culture the idea that Christian men are somehow less 'manly' than non-Christian men and then dare non-believers to question their masculinity. In the words of Team member Mike Hagen: 'What makes me sick is when people say that Christians are sissies.'[23] Jacobs himself often elaborates upon the proclamation that 'Jesus was no skinny little man. Jesus was a man's man.' Evangelical zeal, in Jacobs' terms, becomes what 'separates the men from the boys'.[24]

In almost every appearance, live and taped, Jacobs refers to his parents' divorce when he was ten years old, to his despair at losing his father, and to the power of God to be a 'father to the fatherless'. Addressing his audience as husbands, fathers, sons and brothers, Jacobs urges men to reclaim their families' spiritual lives from the feminine realm. According to Jacobs, too many fathers have relinquished to mothers their roles as both models and authority figures for their sons. A real man takes his family to church, leads his family in prayer and devotion, and otherwise ensures that the lives of his wife and children conform to Christian doctrine. Every man in the audience, Jacobs insists, has the potential to become like God the Father. Not only is each man's body and spirit subject to control and constraint, but a truly devoted husband and father should build his family – and his community – in h/His image; he should, that is, control and constrain them as well as himself.

MAKING EVERETT 'TOO HOT FOR THE DEVIL'

In addition to scrutinising a videotape purchased directly from the John Jacobs Evangelistic Association and watching numerous Power Team broadcasts over the course of a year or more, I witnessed a live performance of the Power Team at the Civic Auditorium in Everett, Washington, on Thursday, 18 July 1991. This particular crusade was sponsored by the Living Word Christian Center with performances in the Civic Auditorium for five consecutive nights. In addition, the Team toured local schools during the days and at the end of the week led the Sunday service at the Christian Center. Each appearance was videotaped for future broadcast and was also photographed for publicity purposes and souvenir distribution. What follows primarily outlines and analyses the Power Team's performance in Everett, which was consistent with what I have learned from conversations with pastors and from watching its various programmes and videos before and since.

The audience waiting patiently on two lines outside the Everett Civic Auditorium is excited but orderly, relatively homogeneous, white and apparently lower middle class, but then this is a relatively rural town, not New York or even Everett's more urban neighbour, Tacoma. It is a warm, glowing evening, a few hours before sunset. Families predominate; casually dressed, they pile out of their cars in groups of four or five or more, join the lines and converse with their neighbours as their children dart around. Many seem to have already seen the Power Team perform, either the previous night, in school, or in earlier crusades. Many are wearing Power Team T-shirts. Some carry Bibles. Certain men stand out as body-builders. Their stance on line is somewhat self-conscious; their sculpted muscles bulge from their T-shirts; their equally sculpted, bleached, gelled and moussed hair is crew-cut short on top and punk-rock long down their backs; and their voices are raised a little louder than the others, discussing how much they can lift and what it takes to break bricks.

Admission is a remarkably inexpensive two dollars. But opportunities to spend more money are in evidence: souvenir tables loaded with posters, autographed pictures, T-shirts and other Power team memorabilia (including miniature Louisville slugger baseball bats and handcuffs) as well as flyers for future Living Word Christian Center events (one features 'Soldiers for Christ', two men of colour in shades with lots of gold, who appear to be a rap group out of Chico, California). Volunteers from the Christian Center wearing Power Team T-shirts are easy to spot. They cheerfully greet the crowd, encouraging people to purchase souvenirs even as they point the way to the auditorium and to the restrooms.

The stage is already lit as we enter the auditorium. Scaffolds of varying heights are positioned behind blocks of ice covered in blue quilts, stacks of cinder blocks and other paraphernalia. On the stage, members of the Power Team – easily recognisable in their red-white-and-blue stars-and-stripes sweats – mingle with other men wearing black Power Team T-shirts, as well as with church officials, other privileged members of the community and several uniformed police officers. Stationary television cameras are also visible about five rows from the stage at house right and left. As house lights dim, the audience comes to attention. Still and video photographers begin to circulate at the edge of the stage. Over the loudspeakers, the Power Team's theme song is played at a decibel level worthy of a rock concert:

> We are destined to win,
> Surrounded by His love,
> Guided by His power.
> Destined to win.
> We ... are ... destined ... to ... win!

A series of introductions and acknowledgements marks the shift from the secular world of the Civic Auditorium to the sacred performance of the crusade. First to appear is Pastor Frank Pina of the Living Word Christian Center. He offers a welcome and a benediction, then introduces the county sheriff. The sheriff admonishes the youth present to mind their manners, to be respectful of the performers, of their parents and the church, and to 'just say no' to drugs. Finally, Jacobs takes over as emcee. He greets the spectators and is loudly welcomed with applause and cheers. He praises the pastor and his church for their evangelical commitment, introduces Team members and reminds spectators that their reason for being present transcends the spectacle. Asserting his authority in a manner much like that of the sheriff, Jacobs then singles out a young man, who appears to have been whispering and laughing with his buddies, as a scoffer, warning him, along with the other young men in the audience, to take this performance seriously. The Power Team is here to lead spectators in witnessing, worshipping and otherwise demonstrating their devotion to Christ. To be disrespectful of the performers is to offend the Higher Power. The audience applauds this forceful demonstration of paternal authority, and Jacobs promises that, with the audience's support, the Power Team can make the city of Everett 'too hot for the devil'. The spectators roar their approval.

The Power Team's exhibition of strength is patterned in a consistent, ever intensifying cycle of anticipation, exhortation, engagement, climax and reflection. Like professional wrestling, the set-up, which is verbal, is extended to create desire for the payoff, which is action. Jacobs first points to the areas of the stage and the objects which have been readied – to the sweating ice, stacked bricks, hot water bottles, etc. – as he paints a picture of the feats the audience will soon see performed: 'With no fear he will slam his forehead into this block of ice. [...] With lightning speed, he crashes his skull straight through.' Jacobs outlines the dangers faced by the performers: 'Blowing up this hot water bottle, the air can rush back and rupture your lung.' He then initiates a sequence of testimonials which culminate in a homily and a prayer. He reiterates the promise of the spectacle to come but pauses to perform one of a variety of homiletic pitches for money in which he calls on the Christian Center volunteers to pass the collection buckets or urges spectators to purchase souvenirs or 'artefacts'. The money collected, Jacobs offers another prayer. Finally, the feats are performed. The spectators cheer. Jacobs leads them in prayer, then begins to describe the next set of feats.

'LOOK HOW STRONG WE ARE. LET US TELL YOU WHY.'

By separating words from spectacle, Jacobs stands against the inherent tensions between his mission and the attractions of his own performance.

Throughout the performance, he explicitly points to the Team's bodies –
'Look how strong we are' – and then explains the source and significance
of the men's strength. The exchange between performers and spectators
is simultaneously evangelical and economic, earthly and transcendent: in
paying attention to the Team's sermons and in spending dollars in donations
and purchases, spectators are to be rewarded both with an exciting demonstration of strength and with a chance at eternal life. The talking part of the
cycle seems to take a very long time – at least 30 minutes – while the physical
action itself is very brief – three to five minutes at most. The extended period
in which the spectacle is promised but not yet performed is clearly calculated
to elevate and sustain a high degree of suspense in much the same way, and
with about as much subtlety, as a circus ringleader teases his spectators with
the idea that they will soon be treated to the sight of a man putting his head
in the lion's mouth. The time that elapses from the first description to the
actual action, along with the constant presence on the stage of the objects to
be confronted, is designed to fuel the spectators' desire for the victory of man
over object.

That the picture Jacobs paints faithfully matches the action the Team
performs implies an equivalent correlation between words and deeds in
relation to the evangelical agenda. If what Jacobs claims is manifestly true
of the Team's power, then it must be true of God's power. That he truthfully
represents the spectacle to the audience signals the authenticity of his representation of the sacred. That the Team member performs the feat successfully without serious injury is a manifestation of God's power as it protects
him at the moment of duress. The relationship of word to deed literally
mimics the theological relationship between the eternal and the temporal:
the Word of God, it is clear, lasts far longer than any body-bound spectacle.

It is difficult to remain unimpressed by what these men can do, but it is
also difficult to resist scepticism. It is most apparent that the spectacle itself
is an elaboration upon sideshow strongman standards when one man lies on
a bed of nails while another, lying on the first man's chest, lifts a barbell.
These feats demand both brute strength and precise skill, to be sure, but
many also employ no small amount of illusion and not a little deception.[25]
Cinder blocks can be baked; ice blocks can be scored. Once the first layer is
broken, inertia takes care of the rest. Phone books, hot water bottles and
steel bars can be baked, scored, or otherwise prepared, as can handcuffs.
Breaking baseball bats is relatively simple when pressure is placed on the
proper point. It is, in fact, possible that the only genuine, non-illusory
display of strength occurs with the lifting of heavy objects – in Everett a
tree log. Even here, the impression of strength is enhanced by the apparent
effort with which two or more men, either other members of the Team or
stagehands, lift the object into place for the performer. That Team members

are strong is not in question, but neither is the degree to which the feats are staged rather than 'natural' and the effects upon the audience calculated rather than naïve.

'LOOK ME IN THE EYES!'

Audience response is explicitly controlled throughout the Power Team's performance. As with his initial confrontation with the young scoffer, Jacobs immediately and directly attacks any outburst of laughter or talking out of turn. He stops in mid-sentence, points to the offender, challenges him to admit the truth of the homily in progress and to acknowledge both the power of the preacher and the power of God. It is an effective technique for commanding renewed attention from everyone in the audience. From where I sit in the balcony, I am never quite sure that there has been a real infraction – I never see the disruption, never hear the laughter or the chattering – but I can feel spectators around me straightening up, perhaps wanting to avoid being singled out, or perhaps in what is simply a sympathetic, reflexive response to hearing someone being scolded. The message is unambiguous and not unlike Christian doctrine in general: behave according to the script or risk exposure and censure.

Beyond this directly confrontational, explicitly authoritative stance, Jacobs also deploys a wide range of strategies for structuring and containing our responses to the performance and to his message. Many of these strategies, particularly his mode of direct address, are recognisable from evangelical preaching practice present and past. The lights in the auditorium are constantly being raised or lowered, so that the audience moves from high visibility to relative invisibility. Jacobs puts spectators on the spot, frequently asking us to concur with repeated, generally rhetorical questions, which invariably begin with 'How many of you know...?' as in 'How many of you know that to have your father walk out on you when you are only ten years old is a terrible loss?' He explicitly directs spectator response throughout to segments of the performance, telling us when to cheer and when to be silent, when (and how) to pray, when to put money in the plate, when to be impressed and on what terms, and so on. Moreover, he frequently demands that spectators 'look [him] in the eyes', in a manner that recalls the vaudeville hypnotist, as he repeats the crux of his homily.

Spectator response to the Power Team's performance is situated within a closed system in which no alternate or outsider position is visible. The live performances employ a group of ten or more stagehands, men who are less muscular than the Team and who sit around the edges of the stage when not shifting objects. They reflect and model audience response throughout the performance, much as a church choir might. What spectators see, if they happen to be looking instead of praying, are rapt, devoted faces, eyes shining with inspiration or humbly closed in prayer.

Throughout the Everett performance, Jacobs echoes the sideshow talker as he teases: 'In a few minutes, Berry will use his arms to destroy two six-foot high walls of ice, while Mike breaks twelve feet of ice with his head.' Later: 'In just a minute you will see John, Keith and me bend these pieces of steel, each an inch in diameter, with our teeth.' Closing his tease with an implied or actual, 'But first', Jacobs begins to testify or introduces another member of the Team to tell his story. The narratives explain why the members of the Team are there to be looked at and why we are looking at them. The enactment of personal revelation justifies each man's participation in the performance as missionary rather than exhibitionistic. The spectacle of manly men sharing their feelings, fears and ideals perhaps runs contrary to clichés of manhood, but beyond the customary born-again narrative of 'I was lost and now I'm saved' is a performative strategy for creating a sense of immediacy, intimacy and authenticity.

DESTINED TO WIN

What we see may best be described in terms of the heroic or epic ordeal: at once a test of faith and proof of God's power made manifest in the men's straining, sweating bodies. They concentrate, strive and break through barriers which are both concrete (literally) and abstract, simultaneously a demonstration of actual physical strength and a confrontation with spiritual danger. The courage and determination with which each performer confronts the onstage obstacle represent the force with which each spectator should face the more ephemeral obstacles to faith and salvation. The feeling of release that comes with the moment of breakthrough is a model of the release, the breaking through of everyday cares, that the person who dedicates himself, or herself, to Christ is sure to experience. Then too, the seriousness with which Team members confront the physical obstacles on the stage is staged explicitly to mirror the sincerity of their message. The moment of breakthrough is, on their terms, a predicate for victory in the struggle for souls.

Given the Team's emphasis on masculinity and patriarchy it is clear that the struggle for dominion over the flesh is also a struggle to reassert the dominance of a man-centred ethic. What is presented and sustained is a series of interactions between men, and between men and objects, in which the feminine 'other' is introduced only at very precise, carefully circumscribed moments, and the Team's few references to women are primarily attached to its ongoing plea for funds: 'We need $40,000 beyond what our sponsors have contributed so that our wives and children can continue to travel with us.' In this presentation, wives and children are clearly depend-ants, representative of the Team members' hidden yet virtuous lives, an assertion that these are indeed 'real' – that is, heterosexual – men.

In Everett, Mike Hagen's five-year-old daughter is brought out to re-inforce this plea for donations. Her diminutive size and squeaky, girl-child voice are overshadowed by the bulk of Jacobs' body and his deeper adult male voice as he gently questions her: 'Do you love your Daddy?' 'Yes!' 'Do you love Jesus?' 'Yes!' These are, after all, men who can restrain their violence and direct it only toward deserving opponents. The only other appearance of the feminine in the performance is when two teenage girls are invited to come up onto the stage where, in exchange for Power Team T-shirts, they are invited to touch Mike Hagen's chest through his light T-shirt to verify that he is not wearing any armour as protection from the bed of nails on which he is about to lie. Giggling, they poke at the man. Literally, they represent what he is not.

BREAKING THE CHAINS OF THE DEVIL

The final feat in the Everett performance, and frequently in the broadcasts, is also the Power Team's signature: the breaking of handcuffs. It is astonish-ing both because of its apparent impossibility and because it is rhetorically and performatively paradoxical. The feat is said to have originated in 1979 when Jacobs was preaching in prison.

> John Jacobs had been preaching the Gospel back in 1979 to about 10 prisoners each week when he tried something new. After a guard had showed him the technique of breaking out of the handcuffs, it was an-nounced to the entire prison that he would be demonstrating just that. Instead of the usual 10, about 800 prisoners came out and heard the Gospel being preached. Nearly all of them raised their hands in response to the altar call that he gave.[26]

The same county sheriff who began the evening with a lecture about respect for authority returns to the stage and handcuffs Team members one to another so that they form a human chain. Once handcuffed, Jacobs tells the audience that the Team will now strive to break the 'chains of the devil'.

> Chains. Chains. Chains. How many of you know that before you become a Christian the devil can put you into chains? Chains of bitterness, lust, hate, guilt. The devil leads you around by these chains. Let's break the chains. Let's break the chains. Let's break the chains.[27]

This rhetoric converts the handcuffs, which conventionally represent the righteous restraint of the law, into a marker for anti-Christian forces. There is no homily attached to this iconic shift, no explanation. It simply happens.

By considering that Jacobs initially learned the trick while proselytising in a prison and by remembering his repeated urging that young men become 'rebels for Christ', it is possible to come to terms with the ambiguous positioning of the handcuffs – and the sheriff – in the Power Team's discourse. According to Jacobs, to be a Christian is to step outside mainstream American culture, to risk the censure and taunts of one's non-Christian peers. A young Christian man is, in essence, the James Dean of the '90s. The ambiguity of the handcuffs, along with the emphasis of the performance on acts of destruction, allows Jacobs to stand between authority and rebellion. At the same time, the handcuffs literally bind the men together in an unnatural way. In the Jacobs' lexicon, men must stand together but individually; they must seek the community of the Spirit, but find the Spirit in their own hearts. Then, too, for these heroes of virtue to be handcuffed together is clearly an injustice; breaking the cuffs reasserts the world order.

THE SPECTACLE OF CONVERSION

The curtain call is, in effect, an altar call. Jacobs urges those who have been moved by the Holy Spirit to approach the stage. In this final, and crucial, test of the Team's powers in Everett the majority of the audience steps forward to receive a second, more intimate, hands-on blessing directly from the Team. These acolytes print their names, addresses and phone numbers on decision cards, checking a box that indicates either that they are dedicating themselves to Christ for the first time or that they are rededicating themselves to Christ. They are told that they will soon receive a congratulatory letter from the Power Team. Many will return on subsequent nights, and by the end of this crusade, many will have become members of the Living Word Christian Center.

Those of us who do not come forward at the altar call are effectively excluded from the culmination of the performance. All evening, we have been made to feel highly visible and necessary to Jacobs and his Team. Now, at the moment of closure, we are ignored. No one is looking at us. No one is demanding acknowledgement or asking for concurrence. No one is telling us what to do or shaping our experience. What we do, whether we remain seated or leave the auditorium, has become irrelevant. We are in the shadows. They are in the light. We have become onlookers to the spectacle of conversion.

From the balcony, I can see members of the Power Team, along with Pastor Pina, standing at the edge of the stage greeting, embracing and praying with the masses assembled there. It is difficult not to feel desperately left out, difficult to resist the desire to be a part of the community that is forming on the main floor. I can see small groups of people scattered throughout the auditorium: some beginning to stand and gather their things, some still seated. For a long, disconcerting, uncomfortable stretch of time, my companion and I debate what to do, whether we should leave or stick around and see what happens next. The penalty for not stepping forward is clear. We are literally stranded. To be unmoved by the Spirit is to be at a loss, without direction, cut off from the loving embraces of Jacobs and his Team-mates.

To exclude the unconverted is, in the end, the Power Team's most powerful trick. They offer their audiences born-again Christianity as the reassurance of divine order, firm boundaries and eternal victory against the imprecations of contemporary, temporal gratifications. The secular world is, conversely, represented as chaotic, purposeless and inclined to decay and despair. Like the performance, the evangelical world is well mapped, sharply focused on Christ and the Word of God, and inclined toward reclamation and celebration. Outside the auditorium, each individual must struggle to create and sustain a place for him/herself, to make countless decisions with little guidance and few guarantees. Inside, the individual is offered a clearly circumscribed role to play, with explicit guidance and fervent guarantees. Outside, attachments to others are precarious and provisional; an individual is constantly at risk of being cut loose, left to drift alone and uncomforted. Inside, the bond is absolute; the individual who dedicates him/herself to Christ, who enters into the contract with the Power Team by signing a dedication card and becoming a member of the sponsoring church, is assured of a perpetual communal embrace, inoculated against isolation, confusion and disorder.

What was promised has been delivered. Bricks have been broken along with audience members' resistance to the Spirit. What began as an echo of popular performance now claims its place as an act of worship. In the Team's own terms, the bait has been taken, the trap snapped shut. The dedication cards will be counted, and the numbers used both to assure the Living Word Christian Center that it has gotten its money's worth and to promote future crusades.[28] The Power Team's display of strength and devotion has been superseded by a spectacle of conversion, directed by Jacobs and performed with the spectators. My image has been captured along with those of other spectators by the Power Team's lenses. The live performance, which I have paid for and in which I have participated, will be archived, edited and integrated with other such performances into the Power Team's broadcasts and promotional materials. It will become part of an ever-growing überspectacle, a testament to the power of the Team's performance.

In a final bit of irony, even my choice to remain outside the benediction fixes me within the Team's spectacular and discursive frame. My role becomes that of the unconverted, defined in the Team's homilies and pressed upon me by the fact of my exclusion. Furthermore, by attending to the apparent conversion of hundreds of others and, later, recounting what I have seen, my description of the event, I am bearing witness. I have been cast within the Power Team's rhetoric which is comprehensive and relentless in its mapping of believer and sceptic.

Indeed, I am as necessary to the culmination of the performance as are the 'saved'; it is my resistance that makes their yielding all the more moving, more dramatic. When I choose to remain in my seat, the choice of others to step forward is made more visible. In sensing my exclusion, the moment of inclusion can be more strongly felt by those at the edge of the stage. All they have to do is turn and look back. But unlike Lot's wife, these men and women will be called again and again by Jacobs and the Power Team. For the next week, the 'born again' can return every night to the scene of their redemption. When the crusade is over they can continue to participate actively in the programmes offered by the Living Word Christian Center. If over time their faith weakens, it can be restored through the interventions of the church, by another such spectacle, or even by a return performance of the Power Team. Or they can drift away, in the evangelical vernacular, becoming lost once more, once more awaiting redemption. But by then the decision cards and donations will have been tallied, incorporated into the church's annual report and into the Power Team's promotional materials. For now, in Everett, John Jacobs and the Power Team appear to have won.

3

Ethnological Show Business: Footlighting the Dark Continent

Bernth Lindfors

Ethnological show business – that is, displaying foreign peoples for commercial and/or educational purposes – has a very long history in Europe, and it became an increasingly common form of enterprise after advances in navigational technology half a millennium ago put Europeans in touch with human communities all over the globe. As the world shrank, traffic in all kinds of exotic goods grew. One reads of live Eskimos being exhibited in Bristol as early as 1501, of Brazilian Indians building their own village in Rouen in the 1550s, of 'Virginians' on the Thames in 1603, and of numerous other native human specimens from the New World, Africa, Asia, Australia, and the Pacific Islands being conveyed to European cities and towns as biological curiosities in the centuries that followed.[1] In a sense, this trade in odd human bodies was little different from an earlier practice that has continued right up to modern times: the commercial exhibition of *lusus naturae* – human and animal freaks, dead or alive. There appears to be a healthy natural interest in unusual and unnatural beings. Indeed, the stranger the creature, the stronger the draw.

By the end of the nineteenth century ethnological show business had grown into a major form of public entertainment in the Western world. The Wild West shows of Buffalo Bill Cody, the foreign spectacles and sideshows of the Barnum and Bailey Circus, and the national displays at various world's fairs and colonial exhibitions are examples of gigantic international enterprises that catered to this insatiable appetite for savouring the wonderful variety of the human species. The whole wide world was now available for scrutiny – for a small fee. The armchair traveller was in his heyday.

In an interesting essay in a book entitled *Exhibiting Cultures: The Poetics and Politics of Museum Display*, Barbara Kirshenblatt-Gimblett makes the point that:

Exhibitions, whether of objects or people, are displays of the artifacts of our disciplines. They are for this reason also exhibits of those who make

29

them, no matter what their ostensible subject. The first order of business is therefore to examine critically the conventions guiding ethnographic display, to explicate how displays constitute subjects and with what implications for those who see and those who are seen. ... The question is not whether or not an object is of visual interest, but rather how interest of any kind is created. All interest is vested.[2]

It is in this reflexive context that I would like to look at the conventions governing the exhibition of Africans in the British Isles in the nineteenth century, a century that opened with extensive European exploration of the African continent and closed with wholesale European expropriation of that continent. This was the same era that saw the abolition of one system of economic exploitation – the slave trade – and the concurrent institutionalisation of another – imperialism. In such a century, how were African peoples represented to the British public? In whose interest was it to see them this way? What subliminal messages lurked beneath the skin of these exhibitions?

Let's start with one of the most notorious figures – namely, Saartjie Baartman, a San woman who was exhibited in London in 1810–11, billed as the 'Hottentot Venus'. The name was a joke, for in physique she little resembled any European notion of classic beauty. Like many San women, she had steatopygia, a greatly enlarged rump, which appears to have been the single feature of her anatomy sensational enough to bring out crowds to see her. She had been conveyed to England from the Cape by a Boer farmer and a British naval surgeon who had first tried to sell an interest in her to an antiquarian who owned a museum of art and natural history. When this deal fell through, she was put on display in a hall near Piccadilly Circus, which, according to a London *Times* reporter, had

a stage raised about three feet from the floor, with a cage, or enclosed place at the end of it; that the Hottentot was within the cage; that on being ordered by her keeper, she came out, and that her appearance was highly offensive to delicacy. ... The Hottentot was produced like a wild beast, and ordered to move backwards and forwards, and come out and go into her cage, more like a bear in a chain than a human being. ... She frequently heaved deep sighs; seemed anxious and uneasy; grew sullen, when she was ordered to play on some rude instrument of music. ... And one time, when she refused for a moment to come out of her cage, the keeper let down the curtain, went behind, and was seen to hold up his hand to her in a menacing posture; she then came forward at his call, and was perfectly obedient. ... She is dressed in a colour as nearly resembling her skin as possible. The dress is contrived to exhibit the entire frame of her body, and the spectators are even invited to examine the peculiarities of her form.[3]

Some of the spectators accepted this invitation by touching her rump and searching for evidence of padding or some other artifice beneath her skimpy, skin-coloured dress. A woman who saw the show reported that 'one pinched her, another walked round her; one gentleman *poked* her with his cane; and one *lady* employed her parasol to ascertain that all was, as she called it, "*nattral*". This inhuman baiting the poor creature bore with sullen indifference, except upon some great provocation, when she seemed inclined to resent brutality, which even a Hottentot can understand. On these occasions it required all the authority of the keeper to subdue her resentment.'[4]

Another spectator told a similar tale of what had transpired on the night he had seen her perform:

> She was extremely ill, and the man insisted on her dancing, this being one of the tricks which she is forced to display. The poor creature pointed to her throat and to her knees as if she felt pain in both, pleading with tears that he would not force her compliance. He declared that she was sulky, produced a long piece of bamboo, and shook it at her: she saw it, knew its power, and, though ill, delayed no longer. While she was playing on a rude kind of guitar, a gentleman in the room chanced to laugh: the unhappy woman, ignorant of the cause, imagined herself the object of it, and as though the slightest addition to the woes of sickness, servitude, and involuntary banishment from her native land was more than she could bear, her broken spirit was aroused for a moment, and she endeavoured to strike him with the musical instrument which she held: but the sight of the long bamboo, the knowledge of its pain, and the fear of incurring it again, calmed her. The master declared that she was as wild as a beast, and the spectators agreed with him, forgetting that the language of ridicule is the same, and understood alike, in all countries, and that not one of them could bear to be the object of derision without an attempt to revenge the insult.[5]

It is clear from these remarks that not everyone in the audience found this kind of entertainment amusing. Within a few weeks, letters of protest began to appear in the London press complaining not only of the degraded nature of the exhibition but also of the state of servitude in which the woman apparently was being kept.[6] Since slavery had recently been abolished in Britain, why was the keeper of this unhappy woman being allowed to profit from her misery? Such a display was both immoral and illegal.

Members of the African Institution decided to take the matter to court, but the case was dismissed after the Hottentot Venus, interviewed in Low Dutch, testified in behalf of her managers, saying she had freely consented to exhibit her person in England, was earning good money, and wanted the show to go on.[7] There was some doubt that she fully understood the nature of the contract she had entered into, but the presiding magistrate at the Court of the King's Bench felt he had no alternative but to release her into the care of her keeper.

What most impressed ordinary people about this case was not the high conscience of the gentlemen of the African Institution who had brought the action, but the low cupidity of the Hottentot. Her insistence upon her right to make a spectacle of herself, like any profitminded dwarf or giant in the exhibition trade, became the subject of countless jokes, cartoons, and newspaper doggerel. Here is a sample from a ballad that began to circulate after the court ruled that she could return to the stage:

Oh have you been in London towne,
Its rareties to see:
There is, 'mongst ladies of renown,
A most renowned she.
In Piccadillie streete so faire,
A mansion she has got;
On golden letters written there,
'The Venus Hottentot'.
But you may ask, and well, I ween,
For why she tarries there;
And what, in her is to be seen,
Than other folks more rare.
A rump she has, (though strange it be,)
Large as a cauldron pot,
And this is why men go to see
This lovely Hottentot.[8]

Saartjie Baartman's story does not have a happy ending. For the next few years she appears to have continued performing at fairs, festivals, and rented halls throughout the British Isles, and in 1814 she finally wound up in Paris, where she excited the attention of professional zoologists as well as sightseers. When she died there in 1815, her body was dissected by Baron Georges Cuvier, the leading naturalist of his day, who promptly published a scientific paper on the peculiarities of her posterior and private parts.[9] He also arranged for various bits of her body – brain, skeleton, skull, body hair – to be preserved for further scientific scrutiny, and he made waxen moulds of her genitalia and plaster casts of her body, one of which stood on display in Case 33 at the Musée de l'Homme until as late as 1982. So Saartjie Baartman has had a career in science as well as in popular culture, having been reified not only as a comic figure of outlandish voluptuousness, but also as a durable set of physiological reference points in biometric discourse. For scientist and lay person alike, she became a somatic cliché, a coarse stereotype of female primitivism. Because she was displayed, treated, and conceptualised as little better than an animal, the Hottentot Venus remains even today a potent symbol of Africa's supposed degraded backwardness. Cuvier compared her to a monkey and an orangutan,[10] scientifically dehumanising her and her kind. It was this sort of biological slur that reinforced European beliefs that Africans were closer to the lower order of brutes than to human beings.

Essentially the same reaction was registered a generation later when a group of five 'Bosjesmans' (i.e., San) – two men, two women, and an infant – were exhibited for five years throughout Europe. One of the first notices of their arrival in Liverpool in 1846 stated that the Bosjesmans showed 'how very nearly sentient beings may sink to, or rather have never risen above, the condition of animals endowed with reason to guide or govern their instinctive propensities. ... They are supposed to belong to one of the numerous tribes of their benighted country which have not yet emerged from absolute barbarism.'[11]

Aside from their diminutive size and odd features (which did not include pronounced steatopygia), what appears to have made the Bosjesmans particularly fascinating to British spectators was their rudimentary life style: they owned very few possessions, used only the simplest tools, built no permanent structures, and wore hardly any clothing. All these traits could have been traced to the fact that they were a hunting and gathering people and therefore had no need for possessions or paraphernalia that would impede their mobility, but the British interpreted a lack of things as a lack of culture and thought less of the Bosjesmans as a result. Commentators tended to agree with the oft-quoted assessment offered by the learned traveller Dr M. H. C. Lichtenstein that 'there is not perhaps any class of savages upon the earth that lead lives so near those of the brutes as the Bosjesmans; – none perhaps who are sunk so low, who are so unimportant in the scale of existence; – whose wants, whose cares, and whose joys, are so low in their nature; – and who are consequently so little capable of cultivation.'[12] In short, the Bosjesmans were presumed to be an utterly hopeless lot.

Yet, the very extremity of their 'degradation' made them all the more interesting to British audiences, for whenever these visitors deviated even slightly from accepted standards of cultivated behaviour, their 'foolish' actions were construed not only as further proof of Bosjesman barbarity, but also as clear confirmation of British cultural superiority. The more different the Bosjesmans appeared, the more comfortable the British felt. It was when the 'savage' betrayed some sign of common humanity that the 'civilised' expressed surprise and a little concern. John Bull did not fancy seeing himself reflected in this monstrously misshapen mirror.

One can find this kind of British cultural prejudice displayed quite openly in statements made by newspaper reporters about the Bosjesmans' most

undeniably human characteristic – their language. The Bosjesman phonological system happens to contain a set of implosive consonants, commonly
called 'clicks', which do not exist in the English phonological system. Since
'well over 70 per cent of words in Bushman languages begin with a click
consonant',[13] this is a very prominent feature in Bosjesman speech. The
number and variety of these click consonants, complicated still further by
subtle vowel colourings and significant variations in tone, make Bosjesman
languages, according to a contemporary authority, 'from the phonetic point
of view... *the world's most complex languages*'.[14] All of this complexity was
lost on Victorian British auditors, who heard only the unfamiliar clicking
and popping noises and drew their own conclusions.

The greatest temptation was to compare these sounds to those made by
non-human creatures. The *Liverpool Mail* said that 'their language – if the
singular sounds by which their conversations are conducted can be termed a
language – completely puts our alphabet *hors de combat*. It is not unlike the
chirps of birds, and is supposed to consist of about twenty words, whose
meanings are varied by the pronunciation.'[15] The *Liverpool Chronicle*
reported, 'It is a perfect novelty to hear them talk, their language resembling
more the "click" of turkeys than the speech of human beings.'[16] The *Birmingham Advertiser* described the phenomenon as a 'singular compound of
inharmonious articulations, copiously interspersed with a kind of chirp or
click... and bearing no remote analogy to the babel of the smaller birds and
animals in a menagerie.'[17] Other papers drew comparisons to 'the clucking
of a hen',[18] 'the chucking of fowls or the motion of machinery',[19] or the
sound 'used by ostlers to urge their horses'.[20]

The *Spectator* offered the fullest and most perceptive linguistic description
of the clicks, but concluded with an unflattering comparison:

> Three of the consonants, we observed, consisted of these sounds – the
> noise made by the lips in slightly kissing, as when you kiss your hand; that
> made by smacking the tip of the tongue against the palate, as you do when
> tasting a flavour, or as some women do when they express petty vexation;
> and the clucking noise made with the hinder part of the tongue against the
> palate to urge a horse or assemble poultry; these three sounds, especially
> the two former, are consonants of rather frequent occurrence. A vowel
> sound, often repeated, resembles the French *eu*, but uttered from the chest
> with the coarse singsong drawl of a boy driving away birds. The language
> is as rude and undeveloped, in sound at least, as the physical conform-
> ation of the people [who as adults] are undeveloped children, stricken with
> senility while their forms are still immature.[21]

There was a similar tendency in other papers to associate unusual phon-
ology with a lack of adequate physical, mental, moral, cultural, and/or

linguistic development. The *Era* described the Bosjesman language as 'wholly incomprehensible, for nobody can interpret it. . . . Their words are made up of coughs and clucks – such as a man uses to his nag – anything more uncivilised can scarcely be conceived.'[22] According to the *Manchester Guardian*, this language was 'singularly barren, exceedingly harsh and unpleasant to the ear . . . its most remarkable feature [being] some inarticulate clicks and clucks'.[23] The *Glasgow Examiner* reported that such language consisted of 'a series of *clicks* stuck together in some curious philological way, to represent their few and simple ideas'.[24] The *Manchester Express* called it 'rude and harsh in the extreme';[25] the Dublin *Warder* said it was 'an unintelligible jargon';[26] and the *Plymouth Times* found it 'so imperfect that its sounds can hardly be rendered in writing by any syllables we can frame'.[27] The Bosjesmans obviously were not simply a hopeless lot; their ridiculous language betrayed them as a singularly inarticulate hopeless lot.

Some commentators were unwilling to consider them better than dumb brutes. London's *Morning Post* asserted that 'They belong . . . to the lowest class of humanity; and the power of speech being excepted, there are many of the inferior animals possessing a greater development of the higher faculties than this savage specimen of human kind.' The only example cited to support this dismissive generalisation was the beaver, who 'possesses the faculty of constructiveness to a very marked extent'. The rest of the article was devoted to illustrating the 'marked resemblance' between the Bosjesman and the baboon, orangutan, chimpanzee, and monkey.[28] A reporter for the *Cork Southern Reporter* also felt that in their 'brutelike indistinctness of language' as well as in a number of other traits, the Bosjesmans 'come so near the Monkey tribe, as to make us almost question their humanity'.[29]

Of course, a number of journalists were quite prepared to give the Bosjesmans the benefit of the doubt, principally because these grotesque children of nature were able to speak a language, albeit a simple and somewhat beastly tongue. But no reporters of that day believed that a Bosjesman's rudimentary linguistic competence made him the intellectual equal of a European. That would have been carrying liberal ideas much too far. A correspondent for the *Observer* put it this way: 'Their distinguishing characteristic . . . as men is the use of language, but besides that they have little in common – either those now on view, or their brethren in the bush – with that race of beings which boasts of a Newton and a Napoleon – of a Fenelon, a Milton, and of Dante.'[30] No one would dare to attempt to make monkeys out of such distinguished men.

The arrogant ethnocentrism underlying British responses to the Bosjesmans appears to have been typical of European attitudes toward African peoples during the age of imperialism, but sometimes it is shocking to come across racist remarks made by Victorian gentlemen one might otherwise have assumed to be among the most enlightened observers of the human scene. David Livingstone, for example, speaking specifically of the Bosjes-mans, noted that 'the specimens brought to Europe have been selected, like costermongers' dogs, on account of their extreme ugliness. That they are, to some extent, like baboons is true, just as these are in some points frightfully human.'[31] Charles Dickens, in a humorous essay devoted to debunking the romantic myth of the Noble Savage, had equally uncomplimentary things to say of this troupe of mini-savages:

> Think of the Bushmen. Think of the two men and the two women who have been exhibited about England for some years. Are the majority of persons – who remember the horrid little leader of that party in his festering bundle of hides, with his filth and his antipathy to water, and his straddled legs, and his odious eyes shaded by his brutal hand, and his cry of 'Qu-u-u-u-aaa!' (Bosjesman for something desperately insulting I have no doubt) – conscious of an affectionate yearning towards that noble savage, or is it idiosyncratic in me to abhor, detest, abominate, and abjure him? I have no reserve on this subject, and will frankly state that, setting aside that stage of the entertainment when he counterfeited the death of some creature he had shot, by laying his head on his hand and shaking his left leg – at which time I think it would have been justifiable homicide to slay him – I have never seen that group sleeping, smoking, and expector-ating round their brazier, but I have sincerely desired that something might happen to the charcoal smouldering therein, which would cause the immediate suffocation of the whole of the noble strangers.[32]

Here, in a voice which has come to be regarded as quintessentially Victorian, is one of the first overt suggestions in England of a final solution to the Bosjesman problem. Such genocidal urges, of course, had already been translated into action in the Cape, where British and Boer settlers had felt compelled to deal ruthlessly with such small, ugly, possessionless, monkey-like, clicking, clucking savages. The visceral reactions of Dickens and other spectators to the Bosjesmans were only a confirmation and validation of attitudes that guided British colonial policy.

When ridiculing the notion of the 'Noble Savage', Dickens did not confine his remarks to the San. In fact, his principal target was a larger troupe of South African performers who had been transported to London in 1853 by A. T. Caldecott, a prosperous merchant from Natal. These thirteen 'Zulu Kaffirs' turned out to be a profitable speculation, for they attracted huge crowds and even won an invitation to appear before Queen Victoria and her children at Buckingham Palace. What helped to make this exhibition more popular than other ethnographic displays was the fact that it was an ex-tremely dramatic performance, not a static sideshow. The performers acted out incidents said to be typical of Zulu life and did so with great fervour. The advertisement placed in the London *Times* on the day the show opened stated that the exhibition would illustrate 'in an extensive and unexampled manner this wild and interesting tribe of savages in their domestic habits, their nuptial ceremonies, the charm song, finding the witch, hunting tramp, preparation for war, and territorial conflicts'.[33] To explain some of the scenes, Caldecott's son served as an interpreter and master of ceremonies, lecturing briefly on Zulu customs and traditions before they were enacted on the stage.

The earliest review of the 'Caffres at Hyde-Park-Corner' (as they came to be called) appeared in the *Times* two days after the premiere. It is worth quoting at length because it is typical of the response of British theatre critics to this novel entertainment:

Eleven men, with a woman and a child, are assembled into a company, and instead of performing one or two commonplace feats, may be said to go through the whole drama of Caffre life, while a series of scenes, painted by Mr. Charles Marshall, gives an air of reality to the living pictures. Now the Caffres are at their meal, feeding themselves with enormous spoons, and expressing their satisfaction by a wild chant, under the inspiration of which they bump themselves along without rising in a sort of circular dance. Now the witchfinder commences his operations to discover the culprit whose magic has brought sickness into the tribe, and becomes perfectly rabid through the effect of his own incantations. Now there is a wedding ceremony, now a hunt, now a military expedition, all with characteristic dances; and the whole ends with a general conflict between rival tribes. The songs and dances are, as may be expected, monotonous in the extreme, and without the bill it would be difficult to distinguish the expression of love from the gesture of martial defiance.[34]

In his essay, Dickens elaborated on each of these scenes by emphasising the Zulus' comically picturesque barbarity. Here, for example, is how he described their preparations for battle:

When war is afoot among the noble savages – which is always – the chief holds a council to ascertain whether it is the opinion of his brothers and friends in general that the enemy shall be exterminated. On this occasion, after the performance of an Umsebeuza, or war song – which is exactly like all the other songs – the chief makes a speech to his brothers and friends, arranged in a single file. No particular order is observed during the delivery of this address, but every gentleman who finds himself excited by the subject, instead of crying 'Hear, Hear!' as is the custom with us, darts from the rank and tramples out the life, or crushes the skull, or mashes the face, or scoops out the eyes, or breaks the limbs, or performs a

whirlwind of atrocities on the body, of an imaginary enemy. Several gentlemen becoming thus excited at once, and pounding away without the least
regard to the orator, that illustrious person is rather in the position of an
orator in an Irish House of Commons. But, several of these scenes of savage
life bear a strong generic resemblance to an Irish election, and I think would
be extremely well received and understood at Cork.

Dickens followed this up with a paragraph playfully suggesting other
parallels between the ceremonies of the noble savage and the practices of
civilised man in Europe, but he returned to his main theme in his concluding
statement: 'My position is, that if we have anything to learn from the Noble
Savage, it is what to avoid. His virtues are a fable; his happiness is a
delusion; his nobility, nonsense . . . and the world will be all the better when
his place knows him no more.' Here we are back at the genocidal imperative.
Dickens did not explicitly advocate that Zulus, Bosjesmans, and other non-
Western peoples be physically exterminated; he may have been too much of
a gentleman for that. Instead, he recommended that they be 'civilised off the
face of the earth' – in other words, subjected to cultural, not literal, genocide.
But this may have been only a manner of speaking. Dickens was intent on
demolishing a romantic myth of the nobility of uncivilised mankind, and if
he employed verbal overkill to accomplish his purpose, he was only behaving
as he may have imagined a proper, pragmatic Victorian should to destroy a
pernicious illusion. A few laughs at the expense of the Zulus would do his
English audience a world of good.

The Zulu Kaffirs of 1853 were only the first in a long procession of Zulu
performing groups to appear in the British Isles in the following years. Their
novelty value increased during the Anglo-Zulu wars when regiments of
Cetewayo's warriors twice massacred British troops in pitched battles.
Such proven prowess in combat generated a great deal of curiosity in Europe
and the United States about these fierce, courageous, and militaristic people.

Circus entrepreneurs tried to take advantage of this curiosity by recruiting
Zulus for their shows. P. T. Barnum even went so far as to offer Queen
Victoria's government $100,000 for permission to exhibit the captured Cete-
wayo for five years, a petition that did not amuse the Queen.[35] A rival
showman outdid Barnum by putting on display three of Cetewayo's nieces
(whom he billed as the chief's daughters, true 'Zulu princesses'),[36] a baby,
another Zulu chief, and twenty-three warriors who had surrendered to
British authorities in South Africa; it has been reported that 'their arrival
in London was greeted by over one hundred thousand people on the docks
and as far up the street as the eye could reach'.[37] Other showmen could not
ignore such palpable signs of popularity, and soon spears, shields, feathers,
and war paint could be found in abundance in every sideshow and even in
circus 'specs', or opening pageants.

Needless to say, many of these Zulu performers were frauds. More than one circus veteran has commented on this in his memoirs: 'I recollect at the time of the Zulu war how one showman conceived the idea of exhibiting a number of Zulu warriors. There was only one drawback – not a single Zulu was at that moment in the country. But drawbacks do not exist for the born showman and a party of ordinary niggers were easily made up into Cetewayo's savage soldiery.'[38] An American showman recalled:

> In the side show we had a big negro whom we had fitted up with rings in his nose, a leopard skin, some assegais and a large shield made out of cow's skin. While he was sitting on the stage in the side show, along came two negro women and remarked, 'See that nigger over there? He ain't no Zulu, that's Bill Jackson. He worked over here at Camden on the dock. I seen that nigger often.' Poor old Bill Jackson was as uneasy as if he was sitting on needles, holding the shield between him and the two negro women. Fortunately for him, about this time the audience was called to another portion of the tent.[39]

But in the years following the war authentic Zulus became more plentiful in both Britain and the United States, and fewer Bill Jacksons had to fill their sandals. The programme for Barnum's show at Madison Square Garden in April 1888 advertised 'Two Real African Zulus',[40] and a naturalist writing in 1885 on ethnographic exhibitions at dime museums declared that

> The idea that the Dime Museum Zulus were manufactured to order is false. There have been Zulus. These are not, as some of the journalists have wickedly insinuated, Irish immigrants, cunningly painted and made up like savages. They are genuine Zulus; and though we need not believe the lecturer's statement that they fought under Cetewayo at Isandhwalo *[sic]*, and displayed prodigies of valour in order to free their country from British rule . . . there is no doubt that they would prove terrible enemies in battle. Looking at their leaps and bounds, and listening to their yells and whistles and the rattling of their assegais against their shields, no one can wonder that English cavalry horses were at first afraid to face them.[41]

Some showmen were afraid to face them, too, and found it more convenient to continue to employ pseudo-Zulus who could be more easily controlled and disciplined. When James Lloyd engaged a dozen bona fide tribesmen for a show that toured Ireland, he found that 'their wildness [in performing dances] was disturbingly genuine; this being one of the disadvantages encountered by showmen who, with more honesty than aesthetic perception, prefer Nature to Art. Nature, it has been said, is pulling up on Art; but she has still a long way to go before she produces savages who are equal to the other for show purposes.'[42]

That most circus showmen preferred Art to Nature is evident in their use of the term 'Zulu', which in American circus jargon gradually expanded its field of reference to include any Negro who participated in the 'spec'.[43] A black labourer or musician employed by the circus could earn a 'Zulu ticket' (a credit slip for more pay) by donning a costume and parading around the hippodrome track in the grand opening pageant. 'Zulu' thus became synonymous with artifice and disguise. Pseudo-Zulus proliferated, emerging as a stock character type that eventually entered the standard vocabulary of ethnic imagery projected by such powerful media as Hollywood films.

In the nineteenth century British notions of Africanness acquired a resonance that radiated to other parts of the Western world, where they often became amplified into grotesque caricatures that took on a life of their own, perpetuating themselves as durable stereotypes of barbarism. It may have served British colonial interests to portray subjects in Africa as freaks and savages, but these negative oversimplifications and distortions also served the vested interests of those in the New World who sought to deny basic human rights to black people. It was one thing for Dickens to lampoon what he construed as the eccentric ignobilities of the Zulus. However, the circus entrepreneurs who employed poor old Bill Jackson and others of his kind to 'act Zulu' took ethnological show business to a new extreme of theatrical misrepresentation, using a real victim to promote a patently false mythology that to a large extent was responsible for his victimisation. The Hottentot Venus, the Bosjesmans, the Zulu Kaffirs, and all the other true and false Africans who literally gave body to such lies were unwitting collaborators in their own exploitation, agents of their own dehumanisation. Putting them in the footlights in this fashion was one method of ensuring that in the Western mind, Africa would remain unillumined, an irredeemably Dark Continent.

4

Striptease: Desire, Mimetic Jeopardy, and Performing Spectators

Katherine Liepe-Levinson

Jay Bildstein, an owner of Scores, the Manhattan sports and strip bar, presented a workshop at the exclusive St Moritz Hotel in New York City entitled 'How to Own, Manage, Run or Even Dance in a Topless Bar' (1992).[1] His presentation was sponsored and advertised by the Learning Annex, a traditional adult education centre. Early on in the session, Bildstein told his rapt and overflowing audience that female strippers can earn anywhere from $200 to $2000 in tips per night. One of the workshop members raised his hand and blurted out that he could not understand why topless bar patrons would spend that much money 'just to look at naked women'. 'What really goes on in those clubs?' he asked. Bildstein immediately reassured his audience that prostitution was a rare occurrence in middle-class and upscale strip establishments, specifically because most dancers earn far more than hookers and under much safer conditions. He admitted he wasn't exactly sure why his customers were willing to empty their wallets for what seemed to be relatively little in terms of traditional ideas about sexual satisfaction. 'But, whatever the reason,' Bildstein smiled, 'it makes for good business.' He and his audience then shook their heads in wonder over the mystery of the striptease industry – and the questions remained hanging in the air: What exactly are patrons buying – or buying into? What is going on between the spectators and the performers?

A few years ago, I embarked on a study of white, middle-class, heterosexual (or mimetically heterosexual) female and male striptease events that took place in eight cities, and in more than 70 different strip bars, clubs, sex emporiums, and theatres in the United States and Canada.[2] As a former professional dancer and actor (from the Zurich Opera Ballet to *OH! Calcutta!* on Broadway), I have been keenly interested in live performances that centre on the body, nudity, and sexual display, and in the theories that seek to explain them. During the three years of field research for this project, I attended gay, lesbian, and transsexual strip events as well.[3] The eventual

41

decision to limit the study to primarily 'white, heterosexual, and main-stream' strip shows[4] was the result of a provocative, reoccurring discussion that took place during the Women and Theatre Conferences from 1990 to 1992. In this forum it was suggested that women who fall into the various categories of white, middle-class, and straight should attempt to make their own personal and political spheres 'strange' – especially with regard to the concepts of 'whiteness' and 'heterosexuality'. To make dominant hetero-sexuality strange in this sense became one of the major goals of the project. In light of the above, the most striking feature I encountered during the field research was the many ways in which the various strip shows simultaneously upheld and broke traditional female and male sex roles and other related cultural rubrics as an integral part of the performance. This article focuses on the strip show's concurrent upholding and breaking of conventional sex roles in terms of the participation of the spectator. And, in the process, it interrogates several of the prevailing theories about sex, gender, representa-tion, and the dynamics of desire.

It almost goes without saying that striptease events (also referred to as exotic, nude, topless, and bottomless dancing shows by trade papers such as *Exotic Dancer, Canadian Stripper, Mentertainment*, and the *Go-Go Gazette*) reproduce many stereotypical aspects of our culture's sex roles through their intertwined rituals of performer nudity, spectator gazing, and patron tip-ping. In the scheme of most of these events, men pay women to perform sexual acts, to play what is commonly called the sex-object role. In the dramatic, sartorial design of the show, the male spectators are protected by their dressed state, while the nudity of the female performers suggests the cultural and physical vulnerability and accessibility of women to men. The far fewer exotic dance shows that feature men stripping for women fre-quently present the performers in the conventional action roles of masculin-ity. Gladiators, policemen, military officers, business executives, and the like strut their sexual stuff onstage in performances of physical strength and social authority. Only a few clubs for women present completely nude male dancers. However, because of the status of men in our society, and because so many male strippers emphasise physical prowess in their acts, their nudity may refer less to the vulnerability of the body than to additional demonstra-tions of power and sexual expertise. As an adjunct to this scenario, female spectators often appear to be more interested in soliciting the gaze of the male stripper – by dancing, yelling, and wildly waving dollar bills – than in taking up the roles of sexual scrutinisers themselves. Women also tend to laugh during male exotic dance acts. This behaviour may suggest that female patrons are less serious about sexual consumption than men, or that they are entertained or even embarrassed by such spectacles rather than aroused. But this is only part of the strip show's performance of gender and desire.

[...]

While members of Bildstein's Topless Bar Management class worried that spectators patronise strip clubs to have 'real' sex with the dancers, traditional feminist and gender studies interpretations of female strip shows for men usually claim, as Jill Dolan puts it, that male spectators 'pay to see the image of the stripper as commodity; they buy control over the gaze'.[5] In other words, men go to strip shows for the erotic pleasure of controlling women by paying to participate in rituals of tipping and looking that embody our culture's patriarchal commodification and objectification of females. Conversely, such interpretations also contend that no matter how long a female spectator looks or how much money she is willing to spend during the event, the male dancers still retain their social and sexual positions of control. This is a truism because men enjoy greater social and economic power than women in real life, and because men categorically take up the positions of the active desires (and gazers), while women as a class are taught only to 'desire to be desired'. It follows, then, that female patrons attend strip events for the fantasy of being seen and being desired by the male dancers. And in this way, these shows, too, cannot help but reproduce and reinforce the social power and authority of the penis-phallus.[6]

However, as the introductory sampling of striptease tipping rituals and activities suggests, using such a system of analysis to explain ecdysiastic performance is problematic at best because both female and male spectators not only pay to gaze at strippers, they also pay, and even tip extra, for the commodity of their own stage time – for moments in the spotlight where they can be seen by the dancers and their fellow spectators, where they can become the object of the gaze. Many strip events for both women and men also include activities in which patrons can play at being coerced into mimetic sex acts initiated by dancers, MCs, and even other patrons. These scenes of induction range from the old 'handcuff the patron to a chair or pole' routine to raffle contests and hustling schemes that not only shift the direction of the gaze, but also alter the balance of sociosexual power by underscoring the vulnerability and accessibility of the spectator's body (and pocketbook).

Contemporary strip shows are similar to the category of entertainments that Erving Goffman describes as 'the final mingling of fantasy *and action*'. They feature scenes for hire where 'the customer can be the star performer'.[7] Patrons purchase these activities, not to gain control over others, but as a way to experience the thrill of 'jeopardy during a passing moment'.[8] This thrill consists of voluntarily exposing oneself to some sort of perceived external danger, such as standing up in front of an audience and being scrutinised by the group. It is the possibility of being carried away or done in by the event; it is the pleasure produced by a mixture of fear, the hope for a positive outcome, and the exhilaration of having experienced 'danger'.[9]

Depending upon the particular bar, club, or theatre, thrill-seeking strip-tease patrons can step into the spotlight through several means: they can pay extra for ringside seating that places them simultaneously within the sight-lines of the strippers and their spectating peers; they can tip dancers to perform 'tip "n" kiss'. 'table dancing', and 'lap dancing' acts that shift the site of the performance into the audience areas; and they can purchase the right to leave their official audience seats to perform in footlight tipping ceremonies, minidramas, and photo shoots that take place next to or even on the stage with the strippers. These 'acts for hire' are played out in concert with the various scenes of induction that often appear to sweep spectators into the spotlight against their will. The balance of this essay describes the starring roles and jeopardy positions that female and male spectators perform as a part of the different strip events. This kind of spectator participation foregrounds *both the intersections of and the gaps between* the social imperatives of everyday life and the mimetic propositions of an event that rests on theatre and sexual fantasy.

RINGSIDE SPECTATORS
BIG SPENDERS, TIPPING RITUALS, AND SEXUAL SURRENDER

Female patrons at Chippendales New York pay an outright $10 tariff, on top of the $20 to $25 admission or cover charge, for seats that are literally onstage. Male and female striptease devotees in Montreal are expected to tip the maître d' for the privilege of front-row seating. In most other clubs there is an unspoken rule that the spectators positioned nearest the performance areas must tip more extravagantly and more frequently than those seated further away. If patrons do not comply with this expectation, they risk public censure. On one occasion, the manager of Flash Dancers in New York City quietly requested an entire row of male patrons to change seats because they were not tipping enough. Such precautions not only ensure the dancers the greatest economic rewards possible, but also guarantee all the patrons in the club the most 'exciting' show. Front-row spectator tipping activities create continuous sex scenes of patron–performer interactions that are viewed by the rest of the audience. These activities may involve strict no-touch exchanges, intricate tipping rituals, and even scenes of intimate touching for female and male patrons alike.
[...]
Clubs that feature more intricate tipping rituals for their front-row spectators also constitute desire through the device of 'mimetic jeopardy'. Patrons of Rick's, the Men's Club, and La Bare in Houston, and String-fellows Presents Pure Platinum in New York City, are expected to tip the dancers by placing dollar bills, in the correct fashion, into their G-strings,

Speedos, underwear, or thigh garters. According to the house rules of the Houston clubs, female and male spectators are only allowed to tip the dancers at the sides or hip areas of the G-strings, bikinis, and Speedos. In Washington, DC, male patrons are not allowed to place money anywhere on a female stripper's body while she is moving. As a result of the latter custom, the topless and bottomless female dancers of J.P.s in our nation's capital invented a performance feat that consists of holding on to an overhead bar placed above the stage and swinging back and forth so that when they fly forward their exposed genitalia almost, but not quite, graze the upturned faces of the men who must remain immobile and unflinching. In all of the above activities, the strippers have the option of making the tipping game relatively easy or more difficult for the participants. The dancers may pause during their performances and help direct the spectator's money into the proper place; they may continue to move and tease, forcing the patrons to wait in attendance; or they may pretend to stop dancing and accept tips, but then suddenly begin to move again causing the would-be tippers to fumble in front of the group.

[...]

While a person may enter into an activity or an event with the expectation of achieving mastery and control over the situation, such a drive is mediated by the participant's need to first surrender to the rules at hand. As Nelson Foote notes, 'any kind of play generates its own morality and values. And the reinforcement of the rules of play becomes the concern of every player because without their observance, the play cannot continue'.[10] To agree to abide by the rubrics of any game implies from the outset a certain amount of risk because one is usually dependent upon other players, and because there is always the possibility that one may fumble or otherwise make a mistake.

Most modern middle-class strip clubs forbid the audience participation practices of some of the strip joints of bygone years, which occasionally included oral sex and coitus between patrons and performers. However, a few contemporary strip shows for male spectators, and many events for female spectators, combine ringside tipping procedures with legal scenes of intimate touching. Show World's Triple Treat Theatre features female performers who encourage front-row patrons to fondle their naked breasts as part of the strip act. The Harmony Theatre allows spectators to touch the exposed pubic area of the nude dancers as well, as long as they do so at the dancer's discretion and only when the performer is onstage and the spectator in his or her audience seat.[11] It is notable that very few of the spectators, in both of these theatres, actually participated in the intimate acts with the dancers. The majority of front-row patrons were content to tip for the exchange of looks and verbal 'niceties'. The spectators who did perform in this sex play rarely grabbed or aggressively handled the dancers' bodies. Instead, they carefully followed the directions of the strippers as they tentatively, fleetingly, and even delicately performed their tasks. This pattern of spectator behaviour suggests that these acts of intimate touching are not only thrilling because of their obvious tactile appeal, but because they are scripted as transgressive even from within the confines of the strip shows. [...]

Intimate touching games in strip events conspicuously script patrons as coperformers in public sex acts. Because intimate scenes for hire are culturally more taboo than the exchange of money, gazes, and verbal expressions of desire, their participants are expected to be bound even more closely to the rules that support those performances – rules that both uphold and break traditional sex roles. While female patrons usually demonstrate a sexual aggressiveness that is alien to most settings outside the strip show, many male patrons tend to take on what has been dubbed as a 'submissive' pattern of behaviour.[12] Lawyer Keith McWalter, shocked by these goings-on, wrote an article for the *New York Times* denouncing the Texan strip shows he had seen for producing 'a vengeful inversion of the old Victorian injunction. "Ladies don't move". Now the men were inert, slouched in their couches and the women were mobile'.[13]
[...]

PERFORMING IN THE AISLES
THE TIP 'N' KISS, TABLE DANCING, AND LAP DANCING

In some strip events, spectators can pay dancers to make 'seat call', not only in the front rows of the theatres, but throughout the other audience areas as well. These acts temporarily shift and split the site of the performance and the gaze of the participants. The 'tip "n" kiss' or 'orchestrated dollar bill wave' is found exclusively in clubs for women. This activity, usually under the direction of an MC, is in keeping with the outward design of containment projected by many strip events for females. After the male dancer completes his formal strip routine onstage, the MC announces that the performer is ready to exchange sexual favours with the audience members for additional tips. The dancer roams around the spectator seating areas as the MC proclaims the rules and expectations of the event. He (or occasionally she) shapes and directs the actions and desires of the spectators with such lines as: 'Ladies, do you like what you see?' 'Then wave those dollar bills!' 'Come on – don't be bashful – have some fun!' 'Ladies, wave those bills – the dancers will show their appreciation for your appreciation!' 'Put those bills anywhere on your body and the beefcake will retrieve them with his lips!' 'One dollar for a kiss!' The dancer's travels are frequently accompanied by a follow spot that highlights the momentary starring roles of the tipping spectators as they kiss and fondle the stripper. While the role of the MC suggests one more manifestation of the ways female sexuality is socially manipulated and controlled, it simultaneously functions as a signifier of transgression. The MC plays the part of a challenger who, like the barkers of the amusement parks, dares and encourages the participants, goading them into action by pointing out the extraordinary qualities of the entertainment. This challenge adds to the thrill of the experience by underscoring the taboo aspects of the roving lust scenes. At the same time, the MC continually reminds the audience that the social and economic hierarchies have been restructured in the world of this play. Such a convention allows the female patrons the freedom to publicly request sexual exchanges without the stigma of 'bad girl' labelling, because they do so as part of a game decorum. This obvious orchestration of desires is not a symbol or sign of female passivity, but rather a mimetic conspiracy, produced by both women and men, to get around the cultural pressures of the double standard.

The table dance, a more elaborate variation of the dollar bill wave, is available in many clubs for men and a few clubs for women.[14] The table dance is a complete mini-strip act performed alongside of the tables and chairs of patrons seated in the audience at a cost of $5 to $20 for a two- to six-minute routine. It is not uncommon for several of these acts to take place in the audience at the same time, while the traditional strip show continues on the formal stage. Individual female and male spectators often hire separate table dances for themselves, but the majority of patrons seem to engage in these activities as shared experiences between two or more spectators. In most clubs, patrons can also hire several dancers to perform together at one table. That is, a spectator party of four can engage four strippers to table dance for them simultaneously. In these situations, the different spectator roles of seeing and being seen become even more pronounced and complex. Individual tables or parties of patrons vie with each other for the attention of the larger audience – almost as if they were competing theatre companies cast with traditional stock characters (i.e., the group clown, the group sweet gal or guy, the group leader, etc.). Each member of a table-dancing group interacts directly with the dancers and the patrons of their immediate circle. Same-sex dancers may glance at and speak to each other, just as same-sex spectators may glance at and speak to each other. The circulation of sexual interest and sexual power can be both hetero-and homoerotic; both are reserved for erotic fantasy and indicate sexual preference in real life, even though the larger dramatic situation is stated as heterosexual.
[. . .]

In all of these scenes, table-dance activities produce numerous subgroups of female and male patrons who sigh together, shake their heads in unison, collectively roll their eyeballs, giggle, and pretend to slide under the tables or off their chairs. As they perform for one another, the spectators murmur or exclaim statements such as: 'I can't stand it!' 'I can't take it!' 'I don't believe this is happening'. Yet, they continue to engage more 'up close and no-touch', 'bound massages', 'air-kissing', and 'clothing rack' scenes for themselves and their friends. The role of 'I can't take it', for female and male patrons alike, more than suggests that the issue of 'control' for many striptease aficionados may have far less to do with discrete and gendered positions of dominating and being dominated than is usually theorised, and much more to do with the spectators' wish to play at being sexually overwhelmed or to play at jeopardising *self-control* through the performance scenarios they at once hire and abandon themselves to. Karl Toepfer, recalling his experience of a group orgiastic performance event for men led by two women (the goddess Sylvia and her nameless attendant), makes a similar point:

> My whole body felt exquisitely taut with an intense pressure to exceed an unprecedented threshold of pleasure, but proof of my strength seemed to depend on sustaining this tautness for as long as possible. It was a matter of *self-control*.[15]

While the table dance often spotlights a complete cast of characters, the lap dance, the ultimate seat show, foregrounds the individual. Brought to the general attention of the public by the film *Show Girls*,[16] this event allows spectators to hire performers to literally rock and roll on their laps for a charge of about one dollar per minute. Strip shows for women regularly present male dancers who bump and grind on the laps of patrons, but none of them offer the explicit and prolonged lap-dancing entertainments found in some clubs for men. New York City's Harmony Theatre, and the Mitchell Brothers' O'Farrell Theatre, the Market Street Theatre, and the New Century Theatre in San Francisco feature lap-dancing entertainments in conjunction with elaborate mainstage strip shows. The dancers perform complete, individual exotic dance acts on the stage and then redress or partially redress, and stroll up and down the aisles of the audience to indicate that they are available for lap-dancing requests while the formal strip show continues. During a lap-dancing act, the patron must remain dressed and seated in his chair at all times, while the dancer must wear underpants. Hand to genital, genital to genital, and oral-genital contacts between performer and spectator are not allowed, but dancers are permitted to caress patrons by 'dry humping' or dancing through their clothing.

On the West Coast, lap dancing is also called *mardi gras*. Considering the game plan and visual appearance of these events, the term makes some sense. The traditional mardi gras or carnival was, and still is in some places, a festival that features parodies, mockeries, and role reversals of the prevailing social order. It commonly includes culturally condoned excesses of drinking, eating, and sex. Since the Market Street and the New Century theatres have retained their original movie house designs, the lap-dancing performances take on a Felliniesque appearance, with the multiple make-out scenes lit by the glow of the big stage. Spectators star in explicit, private-moment sex scenes that are exciting because they occur in public places and because the physical constraints and rules of the event produce a sea of women on top.

CROSSING THE FOOTLIGHTS
STAGE SIDE TIPPING, MINIDRAMAS, AND PHOTO SHOOTS

Spectators can also costar in formal striptease acts that take place onstage by temporarily leaving the relative safety of their audience seats and stepping up to, or even onto, the main performance areas of the bars, clubs, and theatres. The most common of these experiences involves footlight tipping where the spectators leave their seats and move alongside the stage to tip the dancers in front of the entire audience. The female patrons of the Sugar Shack II, however, can make spectacles of themselves in the very act of going to and from the stage. In this nightclub, women tip the male hosts (ushers and waiters) to physically pick them up and carry them from the audience seats down the aisles to the main stage. The male hosts cradle the women in their arms, sometimes jogging and twirling as they make their way down the aisles to join the line of tippers at the stage. Once stage-side, the ushers lift their charges aloft so that the rest of the viewers can watch their fellow spectators tip and caress the male strippers. This event allows female participants to enjoy two male sex partners at the same time – one who holds them in his arms and another whom they kiss and caress. Sometimes there are so many requests for the hunky-man taxi ride that the club uses a traffic manager, complete with walkie-talkie, to prevent accidents. The rest of the spectators watch, not only the tipping show onstage, but the commotion that takes place up and down the aisles. These dramatic encounters may suggest the traditional sexual surrender position for women through the motif of 'being carried off'. But such scenes also indicate the extent to which female desire and economic control over sex acts can be carried.

Other strip clubs and theatres invite spectators to cross the footlights and play leading roles in actual minidramas that take place centre stage. Scenes for male patrons usually involve action fights, while those for females feature themes of courting and romance. Such scenarios obviously play on gendered stereotypes, but they include narrative twists and character developments that thwart traditional sex-role norms as well. Many of the larger clubs for men offer regular 'lady wrestler' or 'foxy boxing' presentations. [...]

The minidrama 'courting scenes' for female spectators duplicate the strip show in miniature. At Chippendales New York and Chippendales Los Angeles, the biggest spender of the evening is beckoned onto the stage by the MC and is seated in the middle of the performance area. From this vantage point, the onstage patron watches a dancer strip directly in front of her as he lip-syncs and mimes a love song. Variations of this routine include multiple sets of spectators and dancers performing the scene onstage together, and patrons and strippers using the basic design to act out specific dramatic situations, such as candlelight dinner dates and bondage games.

The Chippendales New York version of the bondage game courting scene opens with three female spectators seated in chairs in the middle of the stage. One male dancer moves from woman to woman as he takes off his clothes. He stares into their eyes, sits on their laps, strokes their bodies, and strokes his own body. In several different viewings of this show, some patrons sat quietly by and allowed the male dancer to take control over the interactions; other participants actively caressed the dancer and, sometimes, directed or limited his behaviour. After the lead dancer completes his routine, three more bikiniclad male strippers enter and wrap crepe-paper streamers around the women's bodies so that they look as if they are tied to their chairs. The trio of strippers then alternately dance for and caress their bound amours. In contrast to the first half of the scene, the women remain motionless. The play concludes with the strippers kissing the captives and then releasing them. The symbolic and practical use of *paper* bondage in this scene demonstrates the importance and underlying mutual consent necessary for the playing out of such erotic encounters. To be in bondage is presumably to be controlled and therefore to be placed in real jeopardy. But here, the 'bonds' are conspicuously under the command of both the dancers and the tied-up spectators. If the male sex and courting show isn't up to par, the captive women (even though they may be subject to peer pressure and the intimidation of the theatrical scene) can still get up and walk away. While such courting scenes typically represent the male as the initiator of romance and sex, they simultaneously feature women in the process of gazing at sex acts that have been presumably designed for their pleasure. That is, these dramas *stage* scenes of female sexual looking and desiring. As Dolan suggests in her discussion of the economy and the visibility/invisibility aspects of female gazing, desire, and hegemonic control, 'the aim is not to look like men, but to look at all'.[17]

A number of clubs for both women and men offer their spectators the opportunity to become the centre of attention by having their pictures taken with the dancers while their peers gather around to watch. Photo shoots provide patrons with stage time as well as with mementos of the show that extend the act of looking and being seen beyond the initial theatrical encounter.[18] In clubs for men, these activities follow the performance of each featured stripper. They can take place on the stage or in the lobby at a cost $5 to $10 per Polaroid. Male spectators are allowed to request how they would like to be pictured with the dancer. Many of the spectator–stripper poses have become so established that patrons can ask for them using a common vocabulary (e.g., 'a lap pose', 'a wide lap pose', 'breasts on the head', 'head on the breasts', 'ear muffs', etc.). Because of this standardisation, there is the additional pressure on the participants to 'correctly' perform the designs they, themselves, select. While some of the accepted positions place the nude or near-nude strippers in the laps of patrons in Penthouse-like 'spread' shots, many others situate the dancers behind patrons. This focuses the audience's attention on the spectator and also points to the male author-ship of a medley of stereotypical sexual fetishes. In most cases, the dancer and her male supporting player gaze toward the camera and the studio audience in a deliberate solicitation of the gaze as they parody the sexual interests and fetishes of men through their performance of physical exaggeration and comedy (e.g., the dancer holds her breasts on top of a patron's head or manipulates them to cover his ears).

[. . .]

No matter how expensive the ticket, how generous the tip, or how 'porno-graphic' one may deem the material, photo-shoots, minidramas, hunky-man taxi rides, table dances, and all other striptease rituals featuring the exchange of money for erotic acts suggest that it is virtually impossible for any participant, male or female, to buy control over all the gazes that can occur in a theatrical encounter. Schechner sums up this complication that is foregrounded in ritualistic events such as striptease but intrinsic to all live performance situations:

A person sees the event: he sees himself; he sees himself seeing the event; he sees himself seeing others who are seeing the event and who, maybe, see themselves seeing the event. Thus there is the performance, the perform-ers, the spectators; and the spectator of spectators; and the self-seeing-self that can be performer or spectator or spectator of spectators.[19]

While it is also impossible for theatrical situations to constitute spectator gazes, identifications, and differentiations that are completely fluid – that is, berefit of political signification – such exchanges are likewise never absolutely monolithic, gendered, or classed. Encrusted as the representational apparatus may be with dominant signification, it cannot be construed as an inherently male or hegemonic device, since its very structure encourages many kinds of bi-gender, cross-gender, and cross-cultural identifications (albeit mediated by the social and personal positions of the viewers). In the words of Barbara Freedman, 'if theatre has offered men a chance to identify with the place of a mother's look, to imitate the mother's desire, and to control the woman's looking back, theatre also offers the opportunity to reframe that moment from a point of view alien to it'.[20] For Freedman, the strip show is, in fact, 'quintessential theatre, its stage the battle place of one's look'.[21]

[...]

CONCLUSION
BEYOND DESIRE IN 2D

What do spectators buy or buy into when they attend strip shows? What is going on between patrons and dancers? Spectators pay to participate in highly regulated rituals about sex and desire both as viewers and performers. The performances of the spectators and the dancers discussed throughout this essay clearly indicate that the positions of seeing and being seen in live strip shows (and in erotic-sexual play) are not discrete, nor are they absolutely connected to the respective positions of control and surrender, even in the most hegemonic of arenas. It is possible to theorise, then, that positions of 'desiring', 'wanting to be desired', and 'being desired' are likewise interwoven and inseparable for female and male participants in heterosexual contexts – even though aspects of these parts may be played out in forms that reflect the indoctrination of cultural gender norms. For, in all the instances described, while the strippers are assuredly designated as the sex objects, the spectators, male and female, frequently desire and attempt to take up those roles as well – roles that our culture persists in labelling as inherently female and passive.

[...]

A number of sociological and psychoanalytical interpretations of the 'being ravished' fantasy propose that these scenarios exist because they allow 'good girls' (and good boys) to try out all kinds of sexual experiments and still retain their 'pure and good' status because they were forced into the acts. However, such critiques still regard the 'being taken' role as one of passivity – which is inaccurate. As the rituals of the striptease illustrate, one of the lures, risks, and even hoped-for outcomes on the part of spectators who gaze at desired sex objects is the sex objects' immense power to render the beholders 'helpless slaves of passion'.[22] Implicit in erotic-sexual play (that is, specifically in situations of mutual consent or fantasy), the roles of the desirer and the one who is being desired, the experiences of being sexually overwhelmed and sexually in command, are double states that each include the aspects of erotic surrender and control.

The Dworkin–McKinnon,[23] Marxist-materialist, and psychoanalytic critiques of sexual difference and social inequality have revealed much about the roots and structures of sexism and other kinds of bigotry in our culture. However, these theories are problematic because they rest on two-dimensional formulations of desire, which the strip show, being a performance specifically about desire, foregrounds. Whether such critiques analyse explicit and non-explicit sexual representations by equating them with actual physical violence and rape, socioeconomics, or Oedipal narratives, they all break down the experiences of erotic desire in hegemonic discourse into two discrete, oppositional, and immutably gendered categories: the 'active, "male" desirer-controller', and his companion, the 'passive, subordinate, "female" object-of-desire'.

In the most general and practical sense, 'Desire in 2D' theories of gender and representation cannot thoroughly interrogate how sociosexual symbols are used in the construction of female and male sex roles because their formulations eliminate so many of those uses. In terms of performance theory, since men are said to desire only positions of control, such paradigms foreclose on the spectator's experience of being 'moved', 'swept away', 'taken in', or even 'manipulated' by the mimetic scene. They disregard, as Berkeley Kaite puts it, the spectator's desire to look until his 'eyes pop out of his head' and the 'subject' of his desire has 'got him by the eyeball'.[24] To have one's eyes pop out of one's head – to be grabbed by the eyeballs – is one of the great pleasures of the mimetic experience. While such spectator desires and pleasures – for both males and females – have been acknowledged in many other theatrical venues, they are usually ignored in the analyses of sexual representations and pornographic-erotic entertainments because they do not link male desire ultimately to a position of domination.

There is no question that powerful links between sexual representation and the machinations of our sexist society exist, sometimes in glaringly visible ways. However, social sexism and sexual representation do not function as a single seamless system of oppression because they are not perfectly matched terms. Sexuality, in the 'real life' of our current society, continues to be viewed with a mixture of horror and awe. But if we analyse the stuff of erotic desire, adult fantasy, and representation exclusively in terms of our social dictates and inequities, we deny sexual agency to all. We reinvent and promote the double standard that insists that explicit sexual expressions are inherently harmful to women. We categorically condemn the male sex and the fantasies of men as oppressive by falling into the trap, as Williams warns, of simply reversing the 'dreadful patriarchal ideas that sex is evil and that the evil in it is women'.[25] And, by resting our critiques of sexual representation and gender on either/or evaluations (whether coming from the far Right or the far Left), we promote varying concepts of a 'good' or an 'authentic' sexuality – an idea that threatens to become evermore a part of legislation.

5

The Surgical Self: Body Alteration and Identity

Philip Auslander

The problem of theorising the body, which is always central within performance theory and criticism, has taken on a new urgency in light of ever-
accelerating technological interventions. Computer bulletinboard users
take full advantage of the opportunity to create and sustain disembodied
identities and discourse in cyberspace. Virtual reality technologies promise
an even more developed version of disembodied experience in which the
participant's body will become a somatic synthesiser whose primary function
will be to produce 'real' physical responses triggered by artificially created
sensory stimuli. To an ever greater extent, medicine, too, takes the virtual
body as its object. An MRI (magnetic resonance image) is, after all, an image
of a digitised, videated body;[1] a surgeon may then operate on that body
guided by its mediatised image on a video monitor. The object of both
diagnosis and treatment is a virtual body thoroughly penetrated and constructed by imaging technologies. Even as developments such as the AIDS
crisis and the appearance of a flesh-eating virus remind us of the body's
fragile materiality, that body is increasingly dematerialised by the medical
practices designed to help it withstand destruction.

This ongoing technological dematerialisation of the body has generated
counter-responses, both in performance and in the culture at large. The
editor of a collection of New Age-ish essays on the body writes that
'We no longer listen to our bodies directly, but only to what modern science
tells us about our bodies. ... [T]he somatically felt body...and the tactile-
kinesthetic body...are all but repudiated.'[2] Andrew Murphie notes that
performative responses to the advent of the technobody range from the
anxiety expressed or implied in much of the Body Art of the late 1960s
and 1970s – the last-ditch celebration of 'Meat Joy' even as the 'meat' itself
was slipping into obsolescence – to the cyborgian ecstasy expressed to
different degrees in the work of Laurie Anderson and Stelarc.[3] Neither
response seems satisfactory: the ecstatic celebration of the technobody is
insufficiently critical, while critiques that want to restore to the body a
prelapsarian integrity are merely nostalgic. Too often, performance practices

that have sought to reclaim the body without denying technology have succeeded only in 'making the body docile for its tasks in the technological age'.[4]

A relatively small, but intriguing, trend within performance art in the 1990s has been the performance of the medical body. Examples include my two subjects here: French performance and multi-media artist Orlan, whose current project contextualises cosmetic surgery as performance, and Kate Bornstein, who presents her post-operative, transsexual body as the object of her performances. Given the extent to which the body is subjected to, invaded, and, ultimately, produced by technologies while under medical treatment, it may be that the medical body is the ideal vehicle for performances concerned with the fate of the body, self, and identity in a technologised and mediatised postmodern culture. Both Orlan and Bornstein evade the problematic Murphie identifies, that of performance's merely preparing the body for its subjugation by technology, by balancing celebration of technology's potential for body alteration through plastic surgery with a critique of the ways that body technologies may be used to serve dominant ideological interests. The site on which both the celebration and the critique take place is the relation of what can only be called the 'self' to the body.

The relation of self to body is the central theme of popular medical discourse on plastic surgery. The author of a book entitled *Cosmetic Surgery for Women* asserts that 'most people have two images of themselves: the person they see when they look in the mirror, and the ideal of who they would like to be'.[5] Similarly, the author of *Liposuction: New Hope for a New Figure through the Art of Body Contouring* summarises the procedure by saying: 'the "miracle" of liposuction has given you a second chance to have the kind of body you've always wanted'.[6] These statements, and many others like them, presume that what might be called the self (understood here as the functions of intellect, personality, and psyche separate from the body) constitutes the definition of the individual to which the body should be made to conform. This self is imagined as transparent to itself, stable, and essentially static: it knows what type of body it wants and it has *always* wanted that type. Once that body type is achieved through surgery, the self has found its perfect outward representation.

This concept of self underpins the discourse not just of cosmetic surgery, but of all forms of elective plastic surgery, including gender-reassignment surgery, popularly characterised as a way of correcting nature's mistakes, of liberating the woman-trapped-in-a-man's-body or the man-trapped-in-a-woman's-body. In these cases, the gender identification of the inner self is represented as 'correct', and the body is represented as the errant exterior that must be brought in line with the desires of that self. Bernice Hausmann's description of the discourse of gender-reassignment surgery applies to plastic surgery generally. 'To advocate hormonal and surgical sex change as a therapeutic tool', she writes, '... it is necessary to acknowledge a certain autonomy of the psychological realm; in other words, it is necessary to make psychology the realm of stability and certainty, while the body is understood as mutable.'[7] I want to argue here that both Orlan and Bornstein use the technology of plastic surgery in ways that challenge the rhetoric of the stable self intrinsic to the surgical discourse. Rather than being the means by which an integral inner identity achieves its appropriate physical representation, plastic surgery, as used by both of these artists, contributes to the definition of a posthumanist self, a self for which identity is mutable, suspended, forever in process.

THEATRE OF OPERATIONS I: ORLAN

Orlan's conceptual performance project since 1990, entitled 'The Reincarnation of Ste. Orlan', consists of her undergoing a series of cosmetic surgeries intended to reconstruct her facial features to resemble those of female figures in well-known works of art. She plans to give herself 'the nose of a famous, unattributed School of Fontainebleau sculpture of Diana, the mouth of Boucher's Europa, the forehead of Leonardo's Mona Lisa, the chin of Botticelli's Venus and the eyes of Gerome's Psyche'.[8] She has produced a computer-generated image with these features superimposed upon her own and sometimes claims that she will continue to have operations until her face resembles the composite. Orlan had her first six surgeries in France and Belgium; her seventh operation took place in New York City in November of 1993. It was relayed by satellite to the Sandra Gering Gallery in New York's Soho and other points around the world where audiences gathered to observe the event in progress and to communicate with the artist by phone, fax, and videophone.

Orlan stages her operations as performances, with texts, props, music, dancers, and costumes (both for herself and for the medical personnel). She also documents them on video. In order to be able to supervise these performances as director/choreographer, she accepts only a local anaesthetic for operations normally performed under general anaesthesia. In her gallery shows, Orlan displays and sells videos of the operations, photographic installations that trace her recovery from surgery and her changing appearance, and art objects incorporating vials of the bodily materials removed during her surgeries.

Unlike such earlier body artists as Chris Burden and Gina Pane, who positioned themselves as outlaws or, at least, as marginal figures performing antisocial acts in obscure corners, Orlan mounts her critique of a widespread cultural body practice from within the terms of that practice itself.[9] In this respect, her work exemplifies resistant postmodernist political art, demonstrating what Craig Owens calls 'the impossible complicity' of postmodernist political art, 'the necessity of participating in the very activity that is being denounced *in order to denounce it*'.[10]

It is important to be clear about just what is being denounced in Orlan's work. A statement Orlan circulates declares that 'Orlan brings into question the standards of the beauty [*sic*] imposed by our society. The standardisation of images inscribe themselves principly [*sic*] in women's flesh through the immediacy of plastic surgery...'.[11] Orlan's performed critique of physical standardisation as the premise of cosmetic surgery echoes a similar emphasis in feminist accounts of cosmetic surgery as 'a form of cultural significa-tion'.[12] As Anne Balsamo makes very clear, the discourse and practice of cosmetic surgery serve to reinforce a culturally determined canon of beauty imposed by men on women, belying the claim that the purpose of cosmetic surgery is to 'enhance a woman's "natural" beauty'. The 'ideal face' depicted in one surgical textbook 'is of a white woman whose face is perfectly symmetrical in line and profile'.[13] '[A]s a cultural artifact, the "aesthetic face" symbolises a desire for standardised ideals of Caucasian beauty'.[14] Even the author of a book called *Cosmetic Surgery: A Consumer's Guide* unwittingly suggests the status of plastic surgery as a tool of patriarchal domination through standardisation when she suggests that it and Chinese foot-binding are equivalent forms of 'personal enhancement'.[15]

Kathryn Pauly Morgan has raised the question of what might constitute a politically valid feminist response to the practice of cosmetic surgery and proposes what she calls the Response of Appropriation. Morgan suggests that 'healthy women who have a feminist understanding of cosmetic surgery are in a situation to deploy cosmetic surgery in the name of its feminist potential for parody and protest'.[16] She proposes that women might have themselves altered surgically to look older and 'uglier' (i.e., to defy their culture's standards of female beauty). In Morgan's view, multilating oneself to prove a point is no worse than the normal, socially accepted practice of allowing oneself to be surgically multilated in order to conform to cultural standards of beauty.[17]

Although Orlan does not follow Morgan's proposal to the letter, it seems to me that her project is in the spirit Morgan envisions. Orlan's mix-and-match approach to selecting her new features challenges cosmetic surgery's claim of naturalism. Her new features are drawn from different periods and styles of art and show, therefore, that the concept of 'natural beauty' is a matter of history and fashion, a discursive construct, not a natural phenom-enon. Although Orlan has not set out to make herself look older or uglier (she insists, in fact, that she does not want to do anything to herself that will result in social rejection), her current appearance is in defiance of cultural canons of beauty. During a visit to Atlanta in 1994, her face was described repeatedly (and rather rudely) as evoking that of a space alien on *Star Trek*.

The features that contribute most to her alien appearance are forehead implants intended to replicate the appearance of the Mona Lisa's famous brow. These implants are distinctly unnatural in appearance and come close to achieving Morgan's programme of intentional uglification, yet they also refer to a culturally accredited icon of female beauty. (If, as is sometimes supposed, the Mona Lisa is in fact a self-portrait of Leonardo in drag, this icon is not just a standard of female beauty created by a man, but an icon that actually uses a man as its standard of female beauty.) The fact that Orlan's unconventional physiognomy is the result not of defiance of her culture's standards but, rather, of an effort to conform to canonical models of beauty is an irony not to be overlooked. The work's critical edge derives from the *failure* of the subject to become the desired image.

Orlan's critique is given historical depth by the connections she implies between cosmetic surgery and the visual arts as cultural discourses that shape ideas of female beauty. Lynda Nead observes that 'Art and medicine . . . [are] the two disciplines in which the female body is most subjected to scrutiny and assessed according to historically specific norms'.[18] Orlan marks the intersection of the discourses of art and medicine in their historical relationship to women by proposing to have herself inscribed with the image of the 'ideal' woman as imagined by historically accredited, white male European artists through the contemporary male-dominated medical practice of cosmetic surgery. Orlan thus literalises the concept of 'aesthetic surgery' (another name cosmetic surgery goes by) and implicitly points to the parallels between the principles employed by artists and surgeons in their (re)construction of the female body. From this point of view, it becomes clear that cosmetic surgery is simply a recent arrival in a long line of aesthetic and representational practices that mould the female image to a fictional, male-imposed standard and thus objectify and commodify the woman. Orlan is becoming a sort of living palimpsest demonstrating the complicity of aesthetics, fashion, and patriarchy with the representational practices that define and enforce cultural standards of female beauty (e.g., painting, sculpture, surgery).

In one of her documents, Orlan stresses: 'I am not against plastic surgery, I'm against the standard way it is used . . .'.[19] In this respect, too, her performance is in accord with some feminist accounts of cosmetic surgery. Both Balsamo and Morgan, for example, make the same distinction as Orlan between the *technique* of cosmetic surgery and the oppressive ideological uses to which that technique can be put. Morgan raises the question of whether cosmetic surgery constitutes 'a potentially liberating field of choice' for women and goes on to observe that 'the technology of cosmetic surgery *could* clearly be used to create and celebrate idiosyncrasy, eccentricity and uniqueness . . .'.[20] In light of the critique of cosmetic surgery adumbrated in Orlan's performances, it seems clear that she opposes the use of technical intervention on the body to further ideological domination of that body, but she is not opposed to intervention on the body *per se*. She neither sees technological intervention on the body as necessarily oppressive, nor considers the body as in any sense foundational or inviolable. Quite the contrary; far from expressing concern over 'distortions of nature' attendant upon advanced technological intervention, she dismisses the ideas that 'the body is sacred and magical' and 'that we must accept ourselves' as 'primitive'.[21]

Whereas many body artists implicitly or explicitly emphasise the amount of pain they sustain in their work, Orlan categorically denies that she experiences pain in the course of her performances. (Her denial is, of course, strategic: there is no question but that she experiences considerable pain as a consequence of the operations.) Inasmuch as pain has often been used by feminist performance artists to represent the cultural and political oppression of women,[22] Orlan's denial is perhaps unsettling in the context of a defence of her work as feminist. It is, however, consistent with her refusal to treat the body as foundational. Body art that foregrounds the reality of the pain the artist experiences (or risks) in the production of the work often posits the body's material presence as irreducible.[23] Orlan's work, by contrast, valorises the dematerialised, surgically altered, posthumanist body, a body that experiences no pain even as it undergoes transformation because it has no absolute material presence; its materiality is contingent, malleable, accessible to intervention.

For Mark Dery, Orlan's 'professed feminism and her manifest posthumanism cancel each other out: Those who declare war on "what is natural" are in no position to bemoan the unnatural "standards of beauty imposed by our society" ... '.[24] I would argue that the contradiction Dery has detected in Orlan's project exists only in his description of it. For one thing, Orlan critiques cultural standards of beauty because she perceives them as oppressive to women, not because they are 'unnatural'. Furthermore, the notion that feminism and posthumanism are mutually exclusive implies that feminism is necessarily based on an essentialist view of the female body. In fact, there is no intrinsic contradiction between Orlan's critique of the way women's bodies are inscribed by a patriarchal society and her (perhaps techno-utopian) vision of a body that is open to other inscriptions.

Orlan's strategy of resistance is apparent not only in her manipulation of the iconography of cosmetic surgery but also in the nature of her participation in the operations. All medical practices and discourses place the patient in a position of inferiority to the practitioner. In the case of cosmetic surgery, the inequality of this relationship is inflected by the typical genders of the participants. Referring to the way in which pre-operative consultations are staged, Carole Spitzack writes: 'the male physician, the "other", is both knowledgeable and "centred". He, unlike the fragmented female patient, is in a position to render an a priori judgment.'[25] Orlan's refusal to play the role of the passive patient is very important in terms of the gender politics of medicine. Far from being the passive body on which the surgeons perform, she is an active participant: the surgeons are as much performers in her theatre of operations as she is the object performed upon in their operating theatre. While I cannot claim that Orlan completely turns the tables of the power relations that define the surgical scene in her performances (she is, after all, the patient undergoing surgery), I might venture to claim that she gives as good as she gets. Just as Orlan, as patient, is inscribed within the medical discourse of cosmetic surgery, so the surgeons are inscribed within the artistic discourse of Orlan's performance: they operate against sets, wear costumes, share the operating room with dancers, take direction from a conscious patient, and so on. Arguably, they are the artisans who execute Orlan's aesthetic project, much like the fabricators who cast statues in bronze or pull prints for other artists.

Spitzack characterises the situation of cosmetic surgery as governed by the *surveillance* of the female patient.[26] In this matter, too, Orlan's levelling of the medical playing field is evident. The features with which she is inscribed are chosen by her from works of art, not in consultation with a surgeon. In an exact reversal of the usual procedure, she provides the surgeons with computer-generated images of the features she wants; usually, it is the surgeon who uses sophisticated imaging technologies to offer options to the patient. Orlan is not exempt from surveillance by the Foucauldian 'medical gaze', but neither are the surgeons and their work exempt from surveillance by the aesthetic gaze represented by Orlan's video and still cameras. Surgeons use impressive 'before and after' photographs in consultations with patients. Orlan takes her own 'before and after' photos; in a wry comment, one of her 'after' images shows her with three new features, glamorously made up, and wearing a Bride of Frankenstein wig (Frankenstein Meets *Vogue*!). The photos and videos Orlan makes of the operations and their after-effects fill in the gaps between the conventional 'before' and 'after' images, showing the bloody reality that intervenes between what cosmetic surgeons represent as 'pathology' and 'health'. Through these photographs and her videos, Orlan exposes and demystifies the surgical discourse. As Tanya Augsburg puts it, Orlan presents a 'very public parody of plastic surgery as covert event, as a secret yet highly valued cultural performance'.[27] Orlan's exhibition and publication of these images constitute a form of surveillance to which most medical practitioners probably would prefer not to be subjected.[28] Indeed, an ostensibly humorous comment by a psychiatrist who was asked to write on Orlan betrays the challenge her posture poses to the authority of medical practitioners: 'The subject–object Orlan is manifestly afflicted with an insidious form of artistic monomania. [. . .] She could present a danger to society in the case of an epidemic of this sort of monomania' (i.e., if more patients took control of the medical interventions and representations to which they are subject!).[29]

I have detailed the way in which Orlan's performance project constitutes a feminist critique of cosmetic surgery because I find that critique cogent and powerful, particularly as it is inscribed in the flesh of the critic. My interpretation of her work is problematised, however, by many of Orlan's own pronouncements on the relationship between self and body in her project, statements which seem, at first glance, to echo the official rhetoric of cosmetic surgery. She has frequently said that her desire is to bring her external appearance more in line with her inner sense of self by transforming a masculine appearance into a more feminine one. The following is a statement of that desire, extracted from an interview with Orlan that appeared in the *Washington Post*:

> This is a meticulous attempt, little by little, to find a more fragile, reflexive, less sensual person. It's a transsexual operation – from woman to woman. I was always very timid, very tender, fragile. I was like that as a young girl. But when I wanted to do things in society I had to create an aggressive, hard personality. An external sensuality. [T]he idea is to find what I think is most deep, most elusive in me. ... A more vulnerable person, who allows herself to show that vulnerability, tenderness and timidity. ... It's not a question of putting on a mask, but of taking one off. ... I think we can bring appearance around to reality.[30]

Orlan's suggestion here that she hopes to use cosmetic surgery (literally) to cut through the rough, masculine social mask in order to reveal her true, vulnerable, tender, feminine essence seems disturbingly to play right into the hands of cosmetic surgery as an oppressive, gender-political cultural practice.

As someone who wants to justify an argument that Orlan's work has positive political value, I was initially distressed by these statements. Upon further reflection, I have come to see them as Warholesque provocations in which Orlan mimics the conventional discourse of the cosmetic surgery patient. There is more than a touch of irony in her description of her project as 'a transsexual operation – from woman to woman'. The implication that the masculine woman Orlan considers herself to be and the feminine woman she hopes to become actually belong to different sexes suggests a politically inflected reading of gender roles that belies the conventionality of Orlan's claim that she is a feminine woman waiting to be released from the prison of a masculine appearance.

Orlan's choices of iconography are also inconsistent with her expressed desire to become more feminine. According to Barbara Rose, Orlan's reasons for selecting certain artistic images as the basis for her new appearance 'go beyond the appearance of their "ideal" features...: she chose Diana because the goddess was an aggressive adventuress and did not submit to men...and the Mona Lisa because of her androgyny...'.[31]

Aggressiveness and androgyny are hardly qualities conventionally associated with the tender, vulnerable, timid feminine that Orlan describes.

Although I have suggested that Orlan's description of her project as a transsexual operation be understood as cultural criticism, it can also be taken more literally in that Orlan does exhibit the 'polysurgical attitude' that Hausmann considers 'constitutive of transsexual subjectivity'. Hausmann's argument is that transsexual subjectivity 'is organised around a demand for sex-conversion surgery. Once this surgery is achieved, this subjectivity of demand coalesces around a new surgical goal.' Therefore, many post-operative transsexuals undergo subsequent cosmetic surgeries to enhance their new gendered appearance.[32] Like a typical cosmetic surgery patient, Orlan has stipulated that the series of operations she is undergoing is intended to realise a certain image. Her statements about the exact number of operations her project entails are wildly inconsistent, however; she has sometimes said seven, sometimes twenty, sometimes as many as it takes to make her appearance match the computer composite. Orlan, it seems, is never a finished product, never definitively post-surgical.

Hausmann's controversial reading of transsexual subjectivity[33] can help us to understand Orlan's polysurgical attitude as something other than the scalpel-slavery it is sometimes said to be. Like transsexual subjectivity, the subjectivity Orlan adumbrates through her art is constituted by its relation to surgery. But whereas, in Hausmann's view, the transsexual exhibits a polysurgical attitude because identity *qua* transsexual is realised through surgery, Orlan's open-ended surgical programme leaves her identity indeterminate. Whereas the transsexual uses repeated cosmetic surgeries to confirm a new identity established by the initial gender-reassignment surgery, Orlan's new identity is never established but always deferred until the next operation or that unspecified moment when the surgeries will end. Orlan has said that when the surgical project is complete, she will hire a public relations firm to choose a new name for her and work within the French legal system to have her new name and face legally accepted as her identity. (The fact that Orlan is not, of course, her given name is already a displacement and deferral of identity.) This plan suggests a lack of desire on Orlan's part to close off the mutability of body and identity her surgical explorations have made possible. Once the medical phase of her project ends, the legal phase begins; once the face is in its final form, the name will be put into play.

THEATRE OF OPERATIONS II: KATE BORNSTEIN

If Orlan can be described as a sort of figurative transsexual, that designation applies literally to actor/performer and author Kate Bornstein, a post-operative man–woman transsexual. In her book *Gender Outlaw*, Bornstein identifies gender as the single most oppressive socio-cultural discourse and advocates a programme of active resistance to gender categories and their normative force. Like Judith Butler, Bornstein points to the moment of 'gendering' at birth by a doctor as the subject's initiation into the system of oppression.[34] Like many feminist writers, Bornstein rejects essentialism, particularly the essentialism of what she calls 'biological gender', the belief that gender is a 'corporal or chemical essence'.[35] (Bornstein's attack on essentialism is, in part, a response to feminists who have rejected her for not being a 'real' woman.) Whereas sociologist Claudette Guillaumin claims that society takes males and females and makes them into 'men' and 'women' by forcing adherence to physical and behavioural norms,[36] Bornstein argues that society constructs 'males' and 'females' by forcing adherence to biological norms. For Bornstein, the self is gender-amorphous, holding within itself the potential for many different and changing gender and sexual identities. To settle for a singular gender is an act of self-denial: 'it's something we do to avoid or deny our full self-expression'.[37]

Hausmann points out that the discourse of gender-altering surgery displays a 'reproductive bias' in its approach to intersex subjects (i.e., hermaphrodites) which translates into a heterosexual bias in its approach to transsexual subjects:

> It is well known within the transsexual community that to admit the possibility of a homosexual post-operative life is to risk losing the possibility of admission to a surgical programme. An expression of disgust toward homosexuality and a representation of one's own desire as authentically heterosexual (only trapped in the wrong genital structure) are established points in the official etiology of male transsexualism.[38]

Bornstein's relationship to gender-reassignment surgery parallels Orlan's relationship to cosmetic surgery: she simultaneously echoes the conventional surgical discourse and resists that discourse from within its own terms.[39] Bornstein reproduces the conventional discourse by stressing how much happier she is with the 'surgically-constructed, hormonally-enhanced woman's body' she now has than she was with a man's body.[40] She resists the surgical discourse's reproductive bias in her assertion of a lesbian identity. In her play *Hidden: A Gender*, Bornstein addresses this issue through a dialogue between the autobiographical character Herman and Doc Grinder, a burlesque representative of the medical establishment. To Doc Grinder's insistence that Herman cannot become a woman and continue to love women, Herman replies that 'My gender identity has nothing to do with my sexual preference. ... My being a woman does not mean I must love men. These are two separate issues.'[41] This is a pointed rejoinder to the surgical discourse described by Hausmann, a discourse that refuses to treat gender identity and sexual orientation as *separate* issues but demands that the desire for transsexual surgery be linked with a reconfigured heterosexual identity.

Bornstein enacts perhaps her most radical critique of the surgical discourse by asserting that her new female body is not the final expression of her inner self. In a poetic monologue entitled 'The Seven Year Itch', she explains that she underwent gender-reassignment surgery with the conventional expectations all plastic surgery patients are supposed to have – that she will finally have the body she's always wanted:

> when I went through with my gender change,
> when I had the surgery,
> when they raised and lowered the knife,
> when they cut through the blood and bone and nerve,
> I thought to myself now I'm gonna know some peace of mind ...
> I said to myself the war is over,
> let's build a memorial to the dead.
> But it didn't work out that way.
> There were still wars going on in my brain.[42]

Bornstein's resistance to the surgical discourse is manifest in her inability to consider her male self as simply 'dead' and her refusal to 'become' a naturalised woman by suppressing the fact that she was once a man and constructing a new biography for herself as a woman, as her doctors have encouraged her (and all other gender-reassignment patients) to do.

Contradicting the popular perception of the male–female transsexual as originally a woman-trapped-in-a-man's body and challenging the discourse of plastic surgery as the technology that enables the self to construct its own best external representation, she asserts: 'I know I'm not a man ... and ... I'm probably not a woman either ...'.[43] Observing in 'The Seven Year Itch' that the human epidermis ostensibly replaces itself fully every seven years, Bornstein asserts that her current body is a 'home-grown' female body, but challenges essentialism by warning us not to assume that her identity is therefore now fixed: 'by the time the next seven years have come and gone/I'm gonna be new all over again'.[44] She imagines transsexualism not as a crossing over from one side of the gender binary to the other but as 'the in-between place ... a place that lies outside the borders of what's culturally acceptable'[45] whose occupants possess fluid gender identities: 'Gender fluidity is the ability to freely and knowingly become one or many of a limitless number of genders, for any length of time, at any rate of change.'[46] Indeed, the only time when Herman and Herculine, the two transsexual characters in *Hidden: A Gender*, are shown to be truly happy is when they achieve a state of gender-amorphousness as a transitional moment in their respective transsexual transformations, and are given the non-gender-specific character designations of 'One' and 'Another'.[47] Once their gender transformations are completed, they can no longer even remember this euphoric state.[48]

Clearly, Bornstein valorises 'the explosive possibility of... multiply signifying sex and sexuality' that the protocols of gender-reassignment surgery seek to contain and suppress.[49] Bornstein imagines surgery as a means for achieving a partial and temporary physical identity rather than a definitive external expression of a stable inner self. Rather than seeing the psychological as the realm of certainty to which the body must be made to conform, Bornstein sees the psychological as inherently unstable and indeterminate, at least where gender identity and sexual preference are concerned. The body can be made to conform to the self's changing sense of gender and sexuality but that process never yields a final product.

SURGICAL SELVES

Plastic surgery plays a central role in both Orlan's and Kate Bornstein's performance work, and both resist the surgical discourse's deterministic characterisation of the relationship between self and body even as they present themselves as products of that very discourse. Orlan claims to want to bring her external appearance in line with a clearly articulated and stable sense of self but her project actually consists of an endless deferral of the moment at which that new identity will be fixed on her body. Although Bornstein is, at least for the moment, a finished surgical product, she sees surgery as an inadequate tool for the expression of an inherently indeterminate self which, like the body, must always be seen as subject to radical transformation.

In proposing a body that is continually available to surgical intervention, Orlan and Bornstein court the problematic identified by Murphie: there certainly is a danger that the net effect of their performance work could be to model a body that is so comfortable with surgical alteration that the performance ends up merely 'making the body docile for its tasks in the technological age'. By interrogating plastic surgery as an ideological practice, Orlan and Bornstein suggest that their performances should not be taken as uncritical celebrations of technological intervention on the body. They nevertheless embrace the surgically constructed body and refuse to ground their respective critiques of plastic surgery in a foundationalist concept of the 'natural' body, a body prior to technological inscription that can somehow be reclaimed. A body that is understood to be discursively produced and ideologically encoded can also be seen as a site of resistance where hegemonic discourses and codings can be exposed, deconstructed, and, perhaps, rewritten. Though the balance between critique and complicity thus achieved is fragile and precarious, I think Orlan's and Bornstein's performances present realistic and progressive insights into the negotiations over the technological construction of the body in which we will all undoubtedly have to engage to an increasing extent as we enter the twenty-first century.

6

Reconsidering Homophobia: Karen Finley's Indiscretions

Lynda Hart

Karen Finley wants to get even. She believes that 'revenge can be art'. As for forgiveness, she does not 'necessarily believe in forgiving at all!' She 'feels that forgiving is: *never letting go . . . a myth* by which you in actuality think you can still maintain control over someone'.[1] Not very 'ladylike' of her, is it?

When Finley was embroiled in the National Endowment for the Arts (NEA) debates as the centre target of the 'NEA Four', C. Carr provocatively suggested in the *Village Voice* that it was a 'short step from rude girl to rude queer'[2] in the censorious fantasies of the New Right. Among the four performance artists whose grants were rescinded after recommendation by the NEA peer panel, Finley received by far the most media attention as well as the greatest number of direct attacks on her art. The other three artists – Holly Hughes, John Fleck, and Tim Miller – all openly claim lesbian or gay identities, and their work is heavily marked with homoeroticism. Finley was the 'token' heterosexual, yet her work seemed to elicit more opprobrium than the performances of a self-identified lesbian like Holly Hughes. The argument that homophobia was at the heart of the obscenity charges was thrown something of a curve by Finley's inclusion in the group.

The movement from rude to queer is, I think, a large leap rather than a 'short step'. But a woman who is perceived as aggressive carries with her the shadow of the lesbian. My project in this chapter is to track the steps that led to Finley's singular positioning within the NEA controversy, and along the way to reconsider how insidiously homophobia operates in these cultural debates.

Identity politics haunted the NEA debates just as they continue to ghost the rhetoric of feminist politics and poststructuralist theory. Although the NEA has quietly dropped the anti-obscenity pledge,[3] and the 'NEA Four' have won their lawsuit, this history is worth returning to as it opened up a juridical space where identity politics collided with coalition building. David Leavitt argued that homophobia was the constitutive impulse behind NEA chair John Frohnmayer's July 1990 decision to deny funding to the four performance artists. In so doing, Leavitt emphasised Finley's singularity: 'Ms. Finley was the only heterosexual among the four performance artists whose grants were retracted.'[4]

However, homophobia is a more complex mechanism and produces more subtle reality effects than can be read simply in the targeting of self-identified *or* ideologically interpellated gays and lesbians. I want to argue that Finley's ostensible exceptionality exposes rather than impedes a reading of this decision as homophobic, and expands our understanding of homophobia as a broader and more pervasive discourse. Just as we have come to understand a pluralism of homosexualities, so we must contemplate a multiplicity of homophobias, some of them elicited by the performances of a heterosexual feminist.

The conclusion that sexual anxieties permeated these debates is inescapable. From the Mapplethorpe and Serrano censorings – the former explicitly in reaction to the artist's depiction of gay and sadomasochistic sexual practices, the latter in response to a representation of the body of Christ submerged in urine – to the defunding of the four performance artists, the NEA controversies were explicitly concerned to police displays of the body. As Simon Watney points out, sexual anxieties necessarily respond to 'our attitudes to our own bodies and one another's'.[5] The sexualised body is always a body in relationship to others, and this body is the site where 'identities' get constructed. Because the signifiers of lesbian and gay 'bodies', as opposed to racial, ethnic, or gendered bodies, are less secure, harder to read, presumably less fixed in a visible economy, the gay and lesbian affirmative slogan 'we are everywhere' must indeed seem ominous to the paranoid gaze that seeks identifiable objects.

The dilemma about identity politics is ongoing, for when identity becomes radically indeterminate, as it may in the classic deconstructive mode, it risks replacing stable, immobilising identities with idealised transcendent subjectivities.[6] Linda Alcoff poses the problem when she writes, 'In their defence of a total construction of the subject, poststructuralists deny the subject's ability to reflect on the social discourse and challenge its determinations.'[7] This crisis in the politics of representation has been met with proposals such as Gayatri Spivak's 'strategic essentialism': 'a strategic use of positivist essentialism in a scrupulously visible political interest'. But such a strategy is risky, for, as Spivak recognises, it shares the 'constitutive paradox' of humanism 'that the essentialising moment, the object of their criticism, is irreducible'.[8] Even as a tactical manoeuvre, essentialism is difficult, if not impossible, to implement when the subjects are defined by their sexualities. We could argue that Fleck and Miller were defunded because they are gay, or that Finley and Hughes were denied funding because they are women. But then we would erase Hughes's lesbianism, which she insists upon emphatically. Even momentarily, it has been all but impossible to construct a coherent category for gays *and* lesbians, or even for gays *or* lesbians. The onto-logical instability of sexualities troubles political affirmations within existing legislative frameworks. But the strength of sexuality politics lies in their *already* mobilised status. More than ever we need ground to stand on together; but constructing that ground on the basis of identity risks reifying an ontology of race, gender, and sexuality that creates 'objects' vulnerable to the conservative assaults.

While there is certainly some validity to Leavitt's emphasis on the overt targeting of gays and lesbians, the limits and dangers of isolating groups based on identity alone are apparent when Leavitt implies that situating the word 'homoeroticism' next to 'a taboo extreme of sexual behaviour few would be willing to argue in favour of'[9] (sadomasochism) detracts from the defence of homoeroticism. Such rhetoric reinscribes the same system that has brought us to this historical moment. Leavitt writes, 'Female in a world of men, Jewish in a world of gentiles, black in a world of whites: it's the same difference.'[10] But certainly it is *not* the same difference. These comments demonstrate how homogenisation always reduces by excluding.

One of the most important things that queer theory has to contribute to discussions of subjectivity formations is that not only are identities fluid across and between categories but they are also always unstable and shifting *within* the categories themselves. There are no targeted 'objects' of hostility at different historical moments. On the contrary, creating the illusion that such objects exist is precisely the anxious effort of groups that depend on making these categories to shore up the fiction of their own impermeability. It is those performers who explode the seamless body of humanist discourse and slip out of such naturalised categories who pose the greatest threat. Lesbian and gay 'content' does not have to enter the specular field according to the dominant culture's rules of recognition in order for us to read that culture's efforts to silence these representations as homophobic. Indeed when lesbians and gays enter into the 'visible' from the dominant spectator's position, it is on terms that practically guarantee a homophobic reaction. Hence homophobia becomes virtually synonymous with homosexuality, a realisation that has spurred efforts to discard the term 'homophobia' in favour of 'heterosexism'. Joseph Neisen, for example, puts forward the argument that substituting 'heterosexism' for 'homophobia' shifts the em-phasis from the latter's suggestion of something inherently abhorrent to the former's stress on the constitution of the oppressor. Neisen points out that homophobia is not a 'true phobia' anyway, for a 'phobic reaction is one in which the object that provokes anxiety is avoided'.[11] Neisen's point is well-taken. However, I would caution against discarding 'homophobia' for precisely the reasons that Neisen makes clear. That is, I think we are always witnessing a *displaced* response. For the 'object' under attack by the homophobe is the presumed stability of his/her *own* identity. Certainly homophobia targets self-identified gays and lesbians. But as evidenced by the defunding of these four performance artists, all of whom challenge the containment of the human body by dominant ideologies, policing the boundaries of the body is forcefully instituted by the naturalisation of heterosexuality. Homophobia might be more broadly understood as a diffuse and pervasive psychic mechanism that reacts to the adulteration of all binary constructions which reinscribe sameness *by* positing oppositional differences.

Jonathan Dollimore has addressed the political problematics of both the psychoanalytic and materialist accounts of homophobia. From a psychoanalytic perspective, 'homophobia might well signal the precariousness and instability of identity, even of sexual difference itself', whereas in the materialist version, homophobia 'typically signals the reverse, that sexual difference is being secured'.[12] Dollimore finds fault with the psychoanalytic understanding of homophobia for leaning toward a polymorphousness that might abet the loss of sociohistorical specificity, hence producing such radically deconstructed subjects that identity becomes entirely meaningless. This is the familiar complaint against psychoanalysis's 'ahistoricism'. On the other hand, the materialist reading could produce a functionalism reinstating the hierarchical oppositions that empower the dominant order. Between the two accounts, Dollimore finds an uneasy alliance in that they both propose that identities are formulated through exclusion and negation. What I find most intriguing about Dollimore's argument is his claim that homophobia most often works to secure a dominant cultural definition of masculinity, and only incidentally to target gay men. Since his emphasis is on masculinity, Dollimore does not mention that homophobia is also used to keep women within the confines of a historical construction of femininity. And surely the opposition femininity/homosexuality has produced a discursive and material violence as virulent as the opposition masculinity/homosexuality.

These oppositions, however, have not produced parallel effects. When men are excluded from the category 'masculinity', they *fall* into the 'degenerate' category of femininity, which is where lesbians, as women, always already were. Gay men become recognisable to the heterosexist spectator as they are 'seen' to enter the feminine. In contrast, lesbians are invisible precisely as they are contained within representational apparatuses that depend on Woman as the ground while simultaneously constructing women as the elusive enigma. When lesbians enter the field of visibility as it has been constructed within gender dimorphic parameters, the threat that they pose to the dominant order is seen as a usurpation of masculine privilege. Peggy Phelan has pointed out that 'gay men implicitly "feminise" all men which is why they arouse so much hatred. Lesbians are not as overtly hated because they are so locked out of the visible, so far from the minds of the N.E.A. and the New Right, that they are not acknowledged as a threat.'[13] In both cases, there is no simple switching back and forth between categories permitted by the dominant order of sexual difference. Both the male and the female homosexual are positioned by the naturalisation of heterosexuality in a space that is abject – the non-human. But this is a space that is not 'other' than masculinity or femininity. On the contrary, as exemplified by gay men who fall into this space and lesbians who are always already there, the abject is *consonant* with the very oppositional hierarchy masculine/feminine. However, I am not convinced that lesbian invisibility arouses less hatred or poses less of a threat to the homophobic spectator. As I have indicated earlier, historically the 'indifference' toward lesbians masked a series of projections and displacements that reveal a threat perceived as virtually apocalyptic. That the 'lesbian' could *not* be seen might mean that she is nowhere; but it could also indicate that she is *everywhere*; and her more pronounced unidentifiability therefore phobically renders her invisibility omnipresent.

Her very absence could thus make her implied presence even more terrifying. If in the materialist account the homophobe reacts with hostility to the 'otherness' of the homosexual, and in the psychoanalytic account it is the 'sameness' that produces the phobic reaction, this opposition indicates the impasse of the sameness/difference binary itself. We might turn to consider the operation of homophobia from the perspective of colonialist discourse. As Homi Bhabha argues, what is 'English' in the discourse of colonial power 'is determined by its belatedness', not by its fullness or 'presence'. Like the meaning of 'English', the meaning of heterosexuality is acquired *after* the scene of difference is enacted. Bhabha brings together a materialist and a psychoanalytic way of understanding the enunciation of colonialist discourse that is productive for an analysis of heterosexism/homophobia as well. He proposes 'two disproportionate sites of colonial discourse and power: the colonial scene as the invention of historicity, mastery, mimesis, or as the "other scene" of *Entstellung*, displacement, fantasy, psychic defence, and an "open" textuality.' These two scenes are not exclusive. They operate together to produce an authority that Bhabha calls 'agonistic' rather than antagonistic. And this authority achieves its domination through a disavowal that 'denies the *différance* of colonialist power – the chaos of its intervention as *Entstellung*, its dislocatory presence – in order to preserve the authority of its identity'.[14] If heterosexism and homophobia can be understood not as separate discourses but as effects of a double inscription that is mutually reinforcing, then the ambivalence can become ground for interventionist strategies launched from the very uncertainty that makes possible the conditions for domination.

While 'lesbian' has been located as an eccentric position from which the paradox of 'Woman' can be exposed in order to construct alternative fields of vision,[15] one need not claim a lesbian 'identity' in order to locate the reification of gender in the heterosexual contract. In other words, one can perform 'lesbian' *acts* without 'being' a lesbian. Indeed, women do so with or without intention. If we understand homophobia as the fear that the homo-sexual/heterosexual dyad is *already* adultered, a performance artist like Karen Finley is just as likely to produce a homophobic response, even though and perhaps even more so *because* she claims a heterosexual identity. In Karen Finley's work and in her position within the NEA debates, I think we can read the absent presence of the lesbian spectre, which haunts the entrance of the aggressive woman into representation.

Long before the NEA denied her funding, Finley became notorious for a performance called 'Yams up My Granny's Ass'. C. Carr covered her work in a *Voice* article entitled 'Unspeakable Practices, Unnatural Acts: The Taboo Art of Karen Finley'.[16] In our heterosexist culture, the reference to 'unnatural' acts invariably evokes homosexuality. In this case, the unnatural act performed by Finley was the smearing of canned yams on her buttocks. Carr's article was followed by a deluge of letters to the *Voice*, which consti-tute a gloss on the borderline that Finley crossed. Even the usually liberal *Voice* readers were outraged. Two themes dominate the letters – filth and madness. Some examples: one 'greatly disgusted' reader threatened to send 'a lump of shit in an envelope' to make *Voice* editors 'feel more at home'. The same writer referred to the editors as 'a pack of crazies'. Another reader equated Carr's 'rationalisation' of Finley's work with 'those who justified receiving their entertainment at Bedlam and Charenton'. One drew an analogy between Finley's art and a man on the street relieving himself under a billboard advertising tequila. This debate continued for several weeks in letters debating whether or not Finley inserted the yams into her anus, whether the yams were cooked or uncooked, and whether it was possible to insert uncooked yams.[17]

As ridiculous as these letters seem, I think they are a text worth contem-plating seriously. For this was the moment when Finley's work became linked in the public imagination with bodily orifices and the boundary between what is inside and outside the body. And it is important to notice that it was not just any bodily orifice, but the anus, the opening to the body that historically has been most associated with 'unnatural sexuality'. It is particularly worth noting that respondents read this performance not only as dirty and disgusting, but also as *gender* transgressive. As Eve Sedgwick has pointed out, the only part of a woman's body that has been singularly *unmarked* by cultural inscriptions is the anus. Whereas anal eroticism has been virtually conflated with gay male sexuality, Sedgwick remarks that after classical times '*there has been no important and sustained Western discourse in which women's anal eroticism means*. Means anything' (author's emphasis).[18] By rendering public what is necessarily privatised in order to uphold the reign of the phallus, Finley's emphasis on anality created strong associations with (male) homosexuality and thereby also constituted an attack on heterosexual supremacy. As Guy Hocquenghem explains:

> The desires directed toward the anus are closely linked to homosexual desire and constitute what can be described as a group-mode of relations as opposed to the usual social mode. The anus undergoes a movement which renders it private; the opposite movement, which would make the anus public, through what might be called desirous group-formation, provokes a collapse of the sublimating phallic hierarchy, and at the same time, destroys the double bind relation between individual and society.[19]

Finley's indiscretion was thus not only a violation of the 'purity' of womanhood, but also a wilful crossing over into a domain that has been preserved for gay men in homophobic discourse. Hence in one performative gesture, Finley not only violated the boundaries of gender but also transgressed the hetero/homo binary. And in doing so she forced a response that revealed how the latter is necessary to shore up the fictive coherency of the former.

Whether her supporters are valorising her or her detractors are vilifying her, Finley's 'indiscretions' have been persistently described as prior to or outside of culture. Here we can see the double operation of any discourse that depends on inside/outside oppositions. On the one hand, Finley's performance was considered 'obscene' because it was perceived as 'dirty' on the level of gender (she was 'outside' the category of womanhood). At the same time, the obscenity could be accounted for by her association with an act that connoted gay sexuality. Thus she was, at once, not properly 'discreet' as a woman and 'indiscrete' – not separate and distinct but mixed, adulterated. It is, of course, the former connotation that has dominated the discourse of womanhood. But it is the latter indiscretion that troubles the binary opposition of heterosexuality/homosexuality. It was this separation that was muddied when Finley performed 'Yams up My Granny's Ass', and it was the beginning of her association with homophobic constructions of homosexuality.

In addition, Finley's performances have an unusually aggressive edge in the history of women's performance art. Her shows might be likened to the 'complaint' tradition that Lauren Berlant describes as a paradigm of public female discourse. The complaint is a 'discursive deployment of ... rage, a litany of injuries', a discourse that Berlant perceives as holding little possibility for change since it is deterministically vulnerable to phallic discourse.[20] Berlant's use of the word 'witnessing' to describe the complaint seems especially appropriate for Finley, who is often described as a performer with a calling and who describes herself as a 'medium' for a collective message. Also, Finley often delivers her monologues with evangel-ical fervour: her voice – something like a cross between a televangelist's and a game-show host's – uncannily resonates with the twinning of theology and capitalism.

Certainly Finley complains. She rages incessantly about the unjust treat-ment of women, children, the homeless, the working class, and ethnic, racial, and sexual minorities. These 'themes' are well within the tradition of Ameri-can feminist performance art. And her demands are within the rhetorical parameters of liberalism. For decades partial nudity and strong sexual content have been used by feminist performers. And yet Finley has been perceived as particularly threatening in her transgression of the limits that other feminist performers have crossed without garnering much attention.

Rather than having been hysterised by phallic discourse, as Berlant's paradigm would suggest, Finley's complaints seem to have rendered her spectators hysterical. Catherine Schuler finds, for instance, that most of the male spectators she interviewed could not even *remember* having seen or heard Finley's 'Cut Off Balls' monologue in *The Constant State of Desire*. Rather than concluding, as Schuler does, that Finley's performances depend too much on an understanding of feminist theory to reach mainstream audiences,[21] I would say that what Schuler has observed is a bit of male hysteria.

Like all feminist performers, Finley struggles against the presentation of herself as an already-eroticised object. While the persistence of the Oedipal configuration and its concomitant heterosexual mandate permit little move-ment outside of the ideology of gender, Finley's performances do accomplish radical critiques of patriarchy, bourgeois culture, and sexual difference. Gender, as a social construct, and psychoanalytic sexual difference are both relentless repetitions in her work. As a gendered subject, Finley con-sistently presents herself in the roles of housewife, mother, rape victim, or incest survivor: the daughter whose father rapes her with vegetables from the icebox bin; the woman tormented by her decision to abort a fetus conceived through incest; the girl whose gang rapists throw her under the wheels of a train when they discover that she was born without a vagina. But Finley deploys these positions with a violent humour that does not play to the spectators' sympathy for the victims, as radical feminist performers often do. Rather, her graphic enactments of sexual abuse and her scatological rage assault the sex/gender system that produces these damaged female bodies by historicising it.

For example, Finley frequently locates herself within the Oedipal family structure where the female body functions as a closed system opened only by the penetration of a man or the birth of a child. But Finley manipulates her own body, calling attention repeatedly to her bodily orifices and what enters and leaves them. This autoerotic work threatens the heterosexual contract.

For in a culture that has made so thoroughly available the public display of nude female bodies to be looked at, touched, and penetrated by men, what could be so disturbing about Finley's performances? I would suggest that it is their autoeroticism that makes them threatening; and, furthermore, that the historical conflation of autoeroticism and homosexuality is still operative in perceptions of these performances.

In addition, Finley's rituals and metaphors of filth and waste cross the borderline that secures sexual difference. As self-proclaimed 'Queen of the Dung Dynasty', Finley calls attention to the abject female body. But she does not merely imitate the body in pain. Rather, she *mimics* the psychosocial structures that describe, theorise, and construct the patriarchal female body. Her performances enlist the possibilities for multiple, shifting identifications that psychoanalytic discourse permits without abandoning a materialist critique. In the gaps between her rhetoric and performance, she negotiates the psychic/social split that troubles the feminist project of enlisting psychoanalytic concepts in a materialist critique.

Unremittingly, the media have focused on Finley's excretory actions – defecating, spitting, urinating – as well as the application of various substances to her body: eggs, chocolate, glitter, sprouts. It is, in other words, the rendering of her body as indiscrete, a violation of the female body's naturalised seamlessness and a manipulation of her body as malleable, that has aroused so much controversy. In her performance, *We Keep Our Victims Ready*, the single gesture foregrounded by the conservatives who pushed to deny her funding was the smearing of chocolate on her nude body.[22] The materials that Finley applies to her body are always viscous – eggs, Jell-O, ketchup – products that are in themselves ambiguous, liminal, occupying an intermediate zone between solid and liquid.

As something of a signature, Finley's engagement with waste cannot but conjure abjection. In abjection, Julia Kristeva writes, 'as in true theatre, without makeup or masks, refuse and corpses *show me* what I permanently thrust aside in order to live. These body fluids, this defilement, this shit are what life withstands. ... Such wastes drop so that I might live' (author's emphasis).[23] Abjection is not about a lack of cleanliness or health; rather, it is an act that 'disturbs identity, system, order ... what does not respect borders, positions, rules.'[24] If the 'I' is produced through the expulsion of waste products, this process can be understood as a kind of elemental 'othering', a construction of subjectivity based on excluding or expelling the 'alien' within. The body makes waste in order to constitute itself as autonomous, sovereign, pure. The formation of subjectivity is thus a process that occurs not between discrete subjects but rather through the concealment of differences that exist within the subject.

Finley's performances might be read as inhabitations of the abject, but she does not challenge the master from this banished zone. Rather, her insistence that spectators reflect on waste launches violent assaults on a binary system that maintains its metaphysical closure by constructing the illusion of discrete terms. Finley strikes a nerve by touching the boundary that reveals what this culture's ordering system cannot tolerate. Her public display of waste products adulterates the boundary between interior and exterior. As Mary Douglas argues, maintaining a discreteness between what is properly inside and what is outside constructs a system, for 'ideas about separating, purifying, demarcating and punishing transgressions have as their main function to impose system on an inherently untidy experience'.[25] Hence to violate borders is to *reveal how a system is constructed*. Thus I would argue that Finley's excremental performances do not merely reproduce the female body's victimisation but rather perform the cultural operations that render victims and perpetrators distinct. She puts pressure on the contradictions that make such dichotomies invisible.

One of Finley's most memorable defiling rituals occurs in *The Constant State of Desire* when she strips down to her underpants, puts unboiled coloured Easter eggs in a plastic bag, and slams the bag on the floor until all the eggs are broken. She then takes a stuffed Easter bunny and uses it to sponge her body with the sticky mass. Over this she applies glitter and paper garlands. Layering her body with these substances produces a narrative of the construction of the female body as an impossible object. First we see the nude female body; then it is covered with sticky waste products that might have been reproductive; then the glitter and frills only partially cover the waste products beneath them. The final effect is a palimpsestic body that is both seductive and repellent. The destruction of the eggs is a crucial signifying gesture in this performance. From a patriarchal perspective, Finley is Woman and thus always already Mother. But here she enacts the destruction of the raw materials of reproduction, layers them on her body, and thinly disguises them with seductiveness. By making the application of this process visible, she demonstrates the contradictory inscriptions of the female body in dominant discourse.

Similarly, in *We Keep Our Victims Ready*, Finley smears melted valentine chocolates on her body, covers them with sprouts (which she announces should be read as sperm), and then layers on brightly coloured paper icicles. This is a body that at once allures and disgusts – a courtship ritual manqué. If the iconic body of the reproductive woman is always there for the scopophilic gaze, Finley brilliantly alienates that body by historicising it. Like the Brechtian social gest, Finley plays this body 'as a piece of history'. Elin Diamond has pointed out that 'the gestic moment in a sense explains the play, but it also exceeds the play, opening it to the social and discursive ideologies that inform its production'.[26] The hidden reproductive body of woman as the allure of the sexually seductive female is unveiled as a governing construction in these stunning gestic moments.

This representation also counters the perpetual return of the maternal body as a site for celebrating the essential female that relegates women to the reproductive economy. In one sense, Finley re-creates herself in patriarchy's image – as both mother and whore – but in the contiguity of the signifiers Finley performs the construction of this doubling, thus historicising it, setting it in motion to imply its mutability, and instigating an alternative: that women can destroy and reject reproductivity. Whereas patriarchy persists in reducing women to mothers by controlling their bodies through material interventions as well as perpetuating an ideology of the sacredness of motherhood, Finley performs the female body as topography for enforced fertilisation, then desecrates and defiles it so that it cannot be recuperated. Her laminations recall the patriarchal construction of Woman/Motherhood, but in their 'seaminess' they show the rough, unfinished edges of this seemingly smooth surface. Her gestures are thus situated within this history and excessive to it.

Less directly, Finley addresses the primary site where the woman/mother is perpetually reinscribed – the heterosexual dyad. One highly charged moment in *The Constant State of Desire* bears close attention. In this performance a four-tiered wedding cake remains upstage for the entire show. Finley destroys all the other emblematic props but saves the cake until the end of the performance. It is the one item that appears to escape her rage. Following a monologue in which she lists a number of strategies for social change, each item followed by an emphatic 'Nothing happened!' she wheels the cake to centre stage, lights the candles, and in the dim light that frames her face as she peers over this emblem of heterosexual union she ominously intones: 'But something's gotta give / Something's gotta give / Something's *gonna* happen.'[27] The implacability of this prop is ambiguous. But accompanied by the rhetorical shift from 'it has to' to 'it is going to', Finley suggests at the very least that heterosexuality is the site where resistance is most necessary.

Finley continues her anti-Oedipal critique in *The Theory of Total Blame* in a performance that most overtly targets the maternal body as the site of abuse and co-optation. Whereas the pain of the victim remains foregrounded in *The Constant State of Desire*, it is the laughter of a mother grotesquely inscribed as such that dominates *The Theory of Total Blame*. Much more conventional than her earlier one-woman shows, *The Theory of Total Blame* has a full cast of characters (a nuclear family), and it is set in a fairly realistic lower-middle-class American living room that is grossly overcrowded with cheap material possessions, circa late 1950s and early 1960s. This shift in form necessitates a diffusion of the voices that Finley usually performs solo. The ritualistic quality of her earlier work, in which she takes on and performs the suffering of a collective, becomes 'individualised' as she historicises the nuclear family as an ideological social unit. In a sense, Finley rejects the internalised pain of her former performances by displacing it onto the family. This movement is duplicated by Irene, the mother played by Finley, who expels her entire family from her house, including her husband whom she must arouse from a coma in order to do so. Irene plays out her imposition as a Mother with a parodic vengeance.

Defilement remains an important strategy in this play, here represented as food loathing. Beginning with a benignly comical scene in which Irene digs Jell-O out of a mould with her hands, the play accumulates images of the nurturing mother that are increasingly sinister. Playing self-consciously on the American domestic drama, Finley presents a family that has returned home to partake of mother's meal. Irene dutifully treads back and forth between the refrigerator and the table carrying armloads of food, none of which is palatable. Irene's meatloaf is a disgusting mass of raw beef slathered with ketchup, which she manipulates with her hands and shoves in one son's face. Bits of raw beef dangle from Irene's nose and lips; ketchup runs down her arms and stains her face. Irene almost merges with the meatloaf; it becomes difficult to tell where she begins and it ends.

Instead of nurturing meals, Irene serves up fantasies of the devouring mother and voices the culture's matrophobia: 'I made you and I can unmake you',[28] she threatens, boldly proclaiming the issue of the mother's responsibility for castration anxiety. If, as Freud argued in 'Femininity', the woman's remembrance of the father's incest is a fantasy of seduction whereas the mother's seduction has some basis in reality, Finley's Irene plays this game in hilarious mockery. Irene tells her children that she made them all sleep with her so they could not masturbate; she openly acknowledges lust for her children; she stands on a chair and shoves her genitals in one son's face. Irene is the phallic mother unleashed in diabolical fury. 'I'm in living hell and I intend to keep my devil *out*', she warns them.

This exorbitant mimicry does not, of course, simply dismiss the power of the nuclear family and its Oedipalisation. If it is 'the father in all of us' that haunts the monologues of *The Constant State of Desire*, it is still the Father who menaces and maims the family in *The Theory of Total Blame*. Classically absent in the former performance – a dead father who killed himself because his daughter was insufficiently attractive – the father in the latter performance is a marginal presence, lying comatose on the living room sofa for most of the play. Persistently, Finley makes and unmakes the Father. If in earlier shows the Father was the irremediable return of the repressed, in the later work Finley moves toward the suggestion that intervention is possible. Irene shakes her comatose husband awake and forcibly ejects him from the house. If the Father/phallus is the original lost object that constructs desire as a ceaseless urge for that which can never be found, Irene 'finds' the phallus, shakes him out of his deathlike sleep, and pushes him offstage in a brilliant parodic capture of the Lacanian transcendental signifier. What remains are waste products, spat out, regurgitated, excreted. Irene will not permit any corpses to take up space in her living room.

Finley cannot, of course, simply step outside of the Symbolic Order and discard the Law of the Father. According to the psychoanalytic narrative 'there can be nothing *human* that pre-exists or exists outside the law represented by the father; there is only either its denial (psychosis) or the fortunes and misfortunes ("normality" and neurosis) of its terms'.[29] In order, then, to read Finley's performances at all, one may have to understand them as limited responses of a woman who strives to disrupt that order. That is, Finley would become the hysteric. But Finley's performances directly address the paradoxical positioning of Woman within that order. Certainly for her children, Irene's maternal body is the hysterical body, 'a theatre for forgotten scenes',[30] onto which they project their anxieties. Irene, however, refuses the terms of that contract, and like the sorceress she claims the ironic status of her marginality.

Michelet's hysteric 'resumes and assumes the memories of the others',[31] much as Finley does in the collective voices of her monologues. But the sorceress-mother Irene holds tenaciously to her own memories in order to repossess them, cut them up, dismember them, and remember them. The hysteric keeps absorption and craving to herself; but the sorceress 'cooks up her affects . . . mix[es] up in dirty things; . . . has no cleanliness phobia . . . handles filth, manipulates wastes'. The sorceress-mother turns her banal family dinner into a sabbat where she 'is completely exposed – all open skin, natural, animal, odorous, and deliciously dirty'.[32] Irene is the Freudian mother unleashed from the unconscious in travesty – powerful, devouring, terrifying, seductive – and, most important, self-consciously performed rather than unwittingly inhabited. Produced from her children's nightmares, she refuses to stay there. Instead, she corporealises, taking on a body that assaults the model from which she was constructed. Her wild presence permits her to speak another story, the story of her own making and unmaking, the production of her image through a theory that becomes unsettled when confronted with her unrepressed materiality.

Finley ends *The Theory of Total Blame* by stepping outside the realistic frame of this play into one of her more characteristic monologues: the 'Black Sheep' monologue is an expressly anti-family tract in which she counts herself a member of a community that the family cannot contain. The black sheep transgress the limitations of the nuclear family. Refusing to be enclosed by it, they bond with other 'outcasts' in alternative communities. This monologue is also the finale to her piece *We Keep Our Victims Ready*. Here it is juxtaposed resonantly against a scene in which Finley portrays herself as a friend keeping vigil by the bedside of a person with AIDS. Having already been well-established as a performer whose work involves the manipulation of bodily fluids as well as anal eroticism, Finley has undoubtedly elicited AIDS hysteria as well. Indeed it may well be within this context that she has been perceived as dangerously aggressive, even as a 'fatal woman'. As Leo Bersani has so astutely argued, there is a correspondence in the minds of conservative fundamentalists between the 'promiscuity' of gay men and female prostitution. In this heterosexist imaginary, 'those [who are] being killed', gay men and persons with AIDS, 'are killers'. Bersani elaborates:

> Promiscuity is the social correlative of a sexuality physiologically grounded in the menacing phenomenon of the nonclimactic climax. Prostitutes publicise (indeed, sell) the inherent aptitude of women for uninterrupted sex. Conversely, the similarities between representations of female prostitutes and male homosexuals should help us to specify the exact form of sexual behaviour being targeted, in representations of AIDS, as the criminal, fatal, and irresistibly repeated act. This is of course anal sex.[33]

We Keep Our Victims Ready begins with a monologue about Jesse Helms's attacks on the NEA. 'It's Only Art' projects a future in which America has no museums, television, newspapers, or performances of any kind. Sculpture has been banned because it is too much like handling waste products. Hot dogs at Coney Island are outlawed because they are phallic symbols. Museums display only announcements explaining why the artists' work has been removed: Mary Cassatt for painting nude children, Jasper Johns for desecrating the flag, Michaelangelo for being a homosexual, Georgia O'Keeffe for painting cow skulls.

By beginning this performance with an assault on the New Right's censorship efforts and ending it with a monologue addressed to a person with AIDS, Finley constructs a frame of reference that connects the desire to censor with the fear that the 'black sheep' will unite in an understanding of shared oppressions, that the discreteness of constructions of subjects conceals constitutive indiscretions, that the sexual subjugation of women, gays, and lesbians depends on the prioritising and naturalisation of gender.

While Hughes, Fleck, and Miller were undoubtedly made immediately suspect and vulnerable to what Frohnmayer called the 'political realities', it is important to recognise just how pernicious homophobia is in this culture. It is not a phenomenon that oppresses only those who have named themselves lesbian and gay. Without question gays and lesbians are targeted as quintessentially unstable, unseamless bodies. But Finley's performances and the responses to them are texts that expose homophobia as a much broader and more complex psychic mechanism. Homophobia is not fear of the same, nor is it fear of difference, just as homosexuality is not reducible to same-sex object choice or to difference from heterosexuality. More productively, we could think of homophobia as a reaction to the visibility of sexualities that expose the fallaciousness of the sameness/difference binary itself. Rendering those terms indiscrete produces an instability in sexual difference that points to the heterosexual/homosexual binary as always already undone.

7

Spectacular Suffering: Performing Presence, Absence, and Witness at the US Holocaust Memorial Museum

Vivian M. Patraka

No historical referent is stable, transparent in its meaning, agreed upon in its usage, or even engaged with in the same way by any large group of people.[1] One way of contextualising the current movement of the term Holocaust is by invoking Michel de Certeau's distinction between a place and a space in his application of spatial terms to narrative. For de Certeau, the opposition between 'place' and 'space' refers to 'two sorts of stories' or narratives about how meaning is made. Place refers to those operations that make its object ultimately reducible to a fixed location, 'to the *being there* of something dead, [and to] the law of a place' where the stable and 'the law of the "proper"' rules. Place 'excludes the possibility of two things being in the same location. . . . Space occurs as the effect produced by the operations that orient it, situate it, temporalise it, and make it function in a polyvalent way.' Thus space is created 'by the actions of historical *subjects*'. These actions multiply spaces and what can be positioned within them. Finally, as noted in the train-car example later in this chapter, the relation between place and space is a process whereby 'stories thus carry out a labour that constantly transforms places into spaces or spaces into places'.[2] De Certeau's distinction between a place and a space is crucial to my argument in the way it clarifies the differing strategies of attempting to move people through a landscape whose meanings are uniquely determined in contrast to providing an opportunity for contestation and multiplicity of association.

I want to employ this distinction between place and space in considering how the referent of the Holocaust is configured by contemporary American Jews.[3] Indeed, for generations of American Jews born in the 1940s and after, it can be said that the Holocaust is constituative of our 'Jewishness' itself, sometimes operating at the expense of other Jewish traditions and histories. So despite the very palpable differences among us, both culturally and politically, it is still the case that many of our responses to the images, objects, and words connected to the Holocaust are 'hardwired', provoking automatic emotional meanings and an attitude of reverence. This widespread response makes it hard to get beyond a consensus on the agony, the loss, and the mindful viciousness that produced them so we can discern the actual discourse generated about the Holocaust and how it functions. Some of the strategies of this discourse are manipulative; they solicit our anguish, horror, and fear as the grounds for asserting larger meanings to which we may not wish to assent. But neither avoidance of the places in which these 'fixed' narratives reside nor simple dismissal is, I think, useful. For this would risk separating us from our own emotions about the Holocaust, entombing them in these monumental stories so that they are no longer available for either examination or change. Instead, we have to create spaces for critique within and among those seemingly inevitable emotional hardwirings and the places to which they get connected.

The following discussion is a step in that direction. I explore how the referent of the Holocaust is configured at a site in the United States where a cultural performance of Holocaust history is being staged for public consumption – the US Holocaust Memorial Museum in Washington, DC. My purpose in doing so is to honour this history, but also to renegotiate its effects by rethinking the set of practices set up by this important museum for the sake of both the present and the future. I also want to view the museum against the background of its mass-mailed fund-raising letters to explore some of its ideological underpinnings. Finally, my intent in the discussion that follows is to enact a performative, de Certeauian space by not fixing the museum in advance within particular Holocaust narratives, so I can continue a process of discovery for both myself and my readers.

The fund-raising letters of the museum claim the term Holocaust in its Jewish specificity by enlarging its applications to include or relate to other oppressed groups. The announcements of the museum reveal how it, perhaps inevitably given the desire to memorialise, oscillates between space and place – between the desire to provide spaces where museum-goers can perform acts of reinterpretation as historical subjects and the need to insist on the more public modality of inscribing over and over on a more passive audience the logic of a place conveying the monumental meaning of the Holocaust.

THE US HOLOCAUST MEMORIAL MUSEUM: NARRATIVES OF LIBERATION AND DEMOCRACY

We had downstairs [in the museum] waiting in line a lady being asked by a little child, what is the difference between freedom and liberated? And the mother, I couldn't butt into the middle, couldn't give that child the difference. But when you say liberated, you have to be enslaved first in order to be liberated, but freedom doesn't matter, wherever you are you can be free.

(Mr Harold Zissman, member of the Jewish resistance and survivor of the Holocaust, spoken to the author at the United States Holocaust Memorial Museum, 1993)

In order to elicit donations, the fund-raising materials for the United States Holocaust Memorial Museum in Washington, DC indicate what the museum promises to accomplish – a self-presentation that represents the main thrust of this institution[4] and prefigures many of the strategies designed for the museum itself. I believe the target audience for these fund-raising letters is, primarily, the American Jewish community, while the letters identify the target spectatorship for the museum as the public at large. A captioned photograph locates the museum by its proximity to the Washington Monument as a means of validating it spatially as a national project. Quotations by Presidents Carter, Reagan, and Bush about the Holocaust further authenticate this undertaking, along with a 1945 statement by Eisenhower – not as President, but as General and liberator – asserting that he could give 'firsthand evidence' of the horrors he saw 'if ever there develops a tendency to charge these allegations merely to "propaganda"'. Also included on the flyer is an official-looking image of the 1980 Public Law to create an independent federal establishment that will house 'a permanent living memorial museum to the victims of the Holocaust' (only 'a short walk from our great national memorials' and hence, implicitly, connected to them). The effect of this link is deliberately to blur the boundaries between the privately sponsored and the governmentally mandated as a way to inscribe the museum as much as possible within the legitimising discourse of its host country.[5]

Of course, any Holocaust Museum must enter into a dialogue with the country in which it is located and with the positioning of that country in Holocaust events, but the museum's emphasis on its geographies of announcement is insistent. A clear anxiety about denials of both the events of the Holocaust and its moral significance for Americans is embedded in these recurrent claims for legitimacy, even if some of the hyperbolic language can be chalked up to the discourse of fund-raising, which in itself constitutes a kind of melodrama of persuasion. Inevitably, an American Holocaust museum is caught on the cusp of happened here/happened there, a conundrum, as James Young formulated it ('America's Holocaust'), over whether American history means events happening here or the histories Americans carry with them. But given the large proportion of Jews living in America compared to Europe, this museum has a context of survival, of a 'living memorial' *by* the living (as framers, funders, visitors) that those in the devastated landscape of Europe can never possess. This, too, is part of American history.

Presumably, then, learning about the events of the Holocaust, *precisely* because they didn't happen here, creates what one newsletter calls a 'meaningful testament' to the values and ideals of democracy, thereby inscribing the museum within the history of American democracy and our rituals of consensus about what that democracy means, if not within American history per se. It could be argued, then, that in this museum the Constitution is to be viewed through the prism of Jewish history as much as Jewish history is to be viewed through the prism of the Constitution. Thus one of the central strategies of the museum is to assert the way in which American mechanisms of liberal democratic government would prevent such a genocidal action from occurring in the United States, as well as partially to overlap, for the US viewer, the perspective of the victims of genocide with that of the victors of World War II. This latter aspect would enhance what Philip Gourevitch describes as the museum's project to reinforce 'the ethical ideals of American political culture by presenting the negation of those ideals' as well as our historical response to them.[6] In fact, images of American troops liberating the concentration camps constitute part of the final exhibit of the museum as well as the opening tactic of the Holocaust exhibit proper, where all that is seen and heard is presented through the eyes and ears of the liberating soldiers. Even the survivor testimony played for us in an amphitheatre at the end of the exhibit prominently includes one narrative by a Holocaust survivor who eventually married the soldier who liberated her. Indeed, this marriage emplotment seems to embody a crucial strategy of the whole museum, with Jews and Jewish history (the feminised victim) married to American democracy (the masculinised liberator). Recalling that the American liberator in this survivor testimony is Jewish as well, I must note another, more implicit enactment in the museum, that of consolidating an American Jewish identity by marrying the positions of liberator and victim.

If what is critical for the museum's project is to extend our fictions of nationhood by the premise that a democratic state comes to the aid of those peoples outside its borders subjected to genocide, then the conferring of liberation becomes the story of American democracy. To assert this story entails backgrounding the masses of people who died before liberation (as opposed to the pitiful remnant left). It entails foregrounding the assumption that waging war can actually accomplish something and, more precisely, that saving Jews, Gypsies, leftists, Catholic dissenters, homosexuals, and Polish forced labour from the Nazis was one of the goals of WWII, rather than a by-product of winning the war by invading the enemies' territory. I could dismiss the museum's overall strategy as a simplistic appeal to hegemonic structures of governance. But to do so would be to deny that the museum *must engage* United States viewers with an ethical narrative of national identity in direct relation to the Holocaust. The alternative is to risk becoming a site for viewing the travails of the exoticised Other from elsewhere ('once upon a time'), or, even worse, 'a museum of natural history for an endangered species'.[7]

[...]

The fund-raising materials promise us another narrative context for making meaning out of the exhibits – one which is less palpable in the actual museum. They describe the museum's Identity Card Project, a kind of interactive theatre of identification. Each museum visitor is to receive a passport-sized ID card similar to the one a victim of the Holocaust was 'forced to carry in Nazi Germany'. At first the card is only to show the photograph of an actual person, with a brief background; then the card can be 'updated' at 'regular computer stations' for a fuller account. Most interesting is the actual list of victims from which these identity cards are drawn: they include Jews, Gypsies, homosexuals, Jehovah's Witnesses, and the handicapped, as well as others the Nazis labelled 'undesirables'. Thus, while still emphasising the specific reference to Jews, the canon of the Holocaust victims has been reinterpreted and expanded, most pertinently to include homosexuals, whose desire for institutionalised recognition in the past had often been met with silence or resistance. This could offer us one means of considering the relationship of Jews to Other(ed) differences.[8] Moreover, if the actual coloured badges of these groups were to become part of the representation, they could convey the way the Nazis visually constructed categories of colour upon religious, ethnic, sexual, political, and physical differences, thereby creating a racialised spectacle of visible difference where none existed. Such colour coding could also complicate the monolith of European 'whiteness' by exemplifying the ease with which that racial strategy was and continues to be manipulated for ideological and economic gain. The goal would be not to instil a passive 'white terror' in white spectators, but to demonstrate the constructedness of 'whiteness', its instability as a category, and the undesirability of relying on it for either self-knowledge or protection.

In the actual museum, the number of computers is inadequate to allow the enormous number of museum-goers to update their identity cards periodically, so we are simply given an identity card printed with the full individual narrative as we wait on line for the elevators to go up to the main exhibit.[9] And while the museum does exhibit multimedia materials on the persecution of Gypsies, homosexuals, and the handicapped, its documentation on the treatment of the German left by the Nazis turns out to be most critical to complicating its narrative of the Holocaust for the following reason: most conventional 'how did it happen' histories of the Holocaust portray an escalating narrative of obsession with, and restrictions and violence against, Jews that culminates in the Final Solution. By contrast, the museum fills in some of the vacuum surrounding that history by documenting the ruthless suppression (including incarceration and murder) of Socialists and Communists from the start of the Nazi Era (and early on in the exhibit, while museum-goers are still trying to read everything). This inclusion creates a fuller sense of Nazi ideology by offering the additional insight that this violence was constituative of Nazism itself: Nazism, then, both founds itself in violence and escalates its violence in order to perpetuate itself. Including the left in this configuration also challenges the simple binary emplotment of democracy versus fascism.

However, while my readings of the actual museum emphasise sites for constructing multiple meanings and relationships, the fund-raising materials recall the larger ways in which the exhibits are to function. One flyer promises the museum will orchestrate our emotions in the mode of a spectacle designed to command attention, transfix spectators, and narrativise in advance the experience of those who approach it: 'You will watch, horrified' and 'you will weep' over this 'heroic and tragic story'. But there is also an overpowering sense of desire in all these descriptions, a need to create an utterly convincing spectacle that will say it all, stop time and space, prevent denial, and make the suffering known. Of course, no representation can do that even if we hear the 'actual voices of death camp survivors tell of unspeakable horror and pain'. How could the unspeakable of genocide be spoken? How could the interiority of individual suffering on a massive scale be turned inside out into an exterior, if respectful, spectacle? Perhaps this consuming desire for the real in representation, for the convincing spectacular, is inversely proportionate to the process of genocide itself, which includes the production of silence, disappearance, dispersal, and concealment as the underside of its fascistic public spectacles. Perhaps this desire responds to the fear that whatever little is left to mark it afterwards will be forgotten. Or responds to the intense anxiety created by the growing trend Deborah Lipstadt documents in *Denying the Holocaust: The Growing Assault on Truth and Memory*, operating in tandem with the temporal reality that many Holocaust survivors are very old or have died, so that the live, embodied narrative that functions as a bulwark against denial is being extinguished. But the personal artifacts that the letters claim will be collected in one of the museum's rooms – the suitcases, hairbrushes, razors, photographs, diaries, dolls, toys, shoes, eyeglasses, and wedding rings – despite their vivid materiality, are finally only the small detritus of annihilation that point to the inevitable absence of complete representation.

Even the sites of artifacts whose meaning is intended to be self-evident can become spaces, instead of places, changed by the paths visitors themselves create as historical subjects. The museum went to great pains, including revising its architectural plans, to exhibit a fifteen-ton freight car used to deport Jews. Walking through it offers us a physical trace of the frightening darkness and claustrophobic agony of the one hundred people crushed into this and other such cars. But as I moved toward this train-car on the second day of my visit to the museum, I was approached by a married couple, Mrs Sonya Zissman and Mr Harold Zissman, who noticed I was speaking into a tape recorder and came to talk to me. Both had been involved in resistance in rural Poland and were eager to speak about this experience. They also criticised the museum for overemphasising victimisation in its portrayal of the Holocaust, while not including enough material on Jewish acts of resistance in its exhibit. I reproduce part of our conversation at the site of this freight car:

VP: You're survivors?

SZ: I can't look at it [the freight car], I'm sick already. My husband, he was the head of a ghetto uprising . . . it's sickening to look at. You live day and night with that, day and night, as a matter of fact we were in the underground, we [both] escaped to the underground.

VP: Were you in a particular organisation, is that what made you join the underground?

SZ: Organisation? Nah. We were in the ghettos. . . . We were in the Eastern part of Poland and we knew what was going on. . . . Small towns, they had wooded areas, thousands and thousands of miles with wooded areas. We ran to these areas when the killing [of Jews in the ghettos] started and this was how we survived.

HZ: I escaped the ghetto. She ran away after the massacre was taking place in her town while she was in hiding. I escaped before it started in our ghetto – and I have very bad emotions between my family who dared why I should escape [and felt betrayed and who were subsequently killed]. [He weeps.]

SZ: And then the men were forming a fighting squadron . . . and the young ones were fighting.

VP: Did you get to be part of the fighting squad?

SZ: I was. My husband was. Down there in the underground.

VP: What's it like to be in the museum today?

SZ: Horrible. I got a headache already. . . . But *we gave them hell too*, don't worry.

VP: What does that mean?

SZ: Hell. The Germans.

VP: You gave them hell? How?

SZ: We used to mine the trains that were going to the front . . . so the soldiers were going on ten, twenty – that's how long the cars, you know, and they had ammunition going there with the train and [we would] tear them apart [by planting bombs under them]. We had the Russians [helping us], in the later years, '43, I think. They used to send us down sugar and salt and what we needed for [the fighting squadron] to live on. ... My [previous] husband, my two brothers, my mother, got killed in the ghetto. [She weeps.]

VP: How many years were you in the underground?

SZ: For three years, because as soon as the ghetto started we had an underground.

VP: You mean you two were invisible and in hiding for three years?

SZ: Of course. We had to. You had no choice.

The live performance of survivor testimony by the Zissmans, 'unmanaged' as it was by the museum proper, powerfully produced me as an engaged witness to their history, forcing me to negotiate their 'unofficial' story with the 'official' one surrounding it. More particularly, what this conversation marked for me was how the museum's larger project of locating itself within a narrative of US democracy displaced representations of acts of resistance by Jews in order to embed its narrative in the frame of American liberation (and appeal more directly to US consumers of museum information). Mr Harold Zissman put it more trenchantly when I asked him what he thought about the exhibits:

HZ: It's not so much important what I think because we have [lived] through that [history]. ... We've [gone] through the ghetto part [of the museum]. Only very few stories of our part [in this history] is being told. I wrote a scholar of the Holocaust ... because very little is shown about our part [i.e., the Jewish resistance] for reasons beyond my understanding in forty some years. ... My own feeling is too much commercialising became the Holocaust here, the telling about the resistance and the participation of the Jews throughout Europe in resisting the enemy does not bring money, evidently.

VP: Victims do?

HZ: Exactly. Victims do.

Ideologically speaking, then, liberation requires a victim; there don't have to be resisters, and it is American liberators not Jewish resisters that 'sell' the museum to the larger public in this American locale.

[...]

HOLOCAUST MUSEUM AS PERFORMANCE SITE

It is the museum-goers (along with the guards) who constitute the live, performing bodies in museums. They are the focus of a variety of perform-ance strategies deployed by the museum for the sake of 'the production of knowledge taken in and taken home'.[10] Some of these strategies produce the passivity and fascination of 'gawking'; some induce a confirming sense of 'seeing' by covering over what cannot be 'seen' in the very act of offering us valuable information; and some position us to struggle *to see* at the same time we are conscious of our own difficult engagement in 'seeing'.

If the above applies generally to museums, it has special significance for museums that represent the Holocaust. In a museum of the dead, the critical actors are gone, and it is up to us to perform acts of reinterpretation to make meaning and memory. To some degree, then, the usual museum situation (in which we look at objects) is exploited to underscore the absence to be read in the presence of objects that stand for the violent loss of which they are only the remains. To the degree that this historical, material, human loss is allowed to remain a tangible 'presence', a Holocaust museum can constitute a particular metonymic situation: inanimate material objects document and mark the loss instead of simply substituting for them through representation. In this case, the enormity of the absent referent is neither contained nor scaled down through a representation that claims its presence over the terrible absence produced by genocide.

Along with the notion of a moving spectatorship, the idea of performance relates to this museum in the sense that it is so site specific. The museum is also a performance site in the sense that its architect, designers, and management produce representations through objects and so produce a space, a subjectivity for the spectator. In terms of the notion of the museum as performance site, the individual performance strategies are not so much at issue; rather, the museum is a complicated, crowded stage that solicits a certain spectatorial gaze through skilled presentations. Everything one sees in a museum is a production by somebody. A Holocaust museum, in particular, can be a performance environment where we are asked to change from spectator/bystander to witness, where we are asked to make our specific memory into historical memory. In a Holocaust museum, when we are really solicited to change, we are asked to become performers in the event of understanding and remembering the Holocaust. If the self-depiction of the DC museum as '*living* memorial' is to be accurate, it is precisely because of this spectatorial performance.

In order to explore this museum as a performance site, I need to create a working model that intersects reading strategies from cultural and performance studies. Such a model requires adding performance dimensions to de Certeau's notions of 'place' and 'space'. It also implies expanding the concept of performance beyond the prescript of the 'live' in the sense of 'I'm standing up and you're watching me', however important to performance that prescript continues to be. For my purposes, place means a prescripted performance of interpretation, and space produces sites for multiple performances of interpretation that situate/produce the spectator as historical subject.

How is the concept of de Certeauian place related to specific performance sites that produce subjects in particular ways? Place is a site that produces and manages a delimited interpretation. Performance place, then, is narrativised in advance and we are solicited to perform the narrative that is organised for and given to us. [...]

How is the concept of de Certeauian space related to performance in material spaces and not simply to kinds of stories identified as space? De Certeau maintains that we all live in places but should think of them as spaces. Thus the liberating countermove that allows us to understand the experience of everyday life is a move from place to space. When linked to performance, de Certeauian space must be a site for multiple performances, multiple and so not delimited by place. And if space is a site for multiple performances by spectators, it is not just a question of interpreting. Interpretation itself becomes a kind of multiple performance: performance doesn't contain the idea of space until space is connected to multiple performance – which is to say that this kind of performance is predicated on provisional subjectivity. The environment of the museum becomes performative: not only are there multiple performances of interpretation, but the museum design provides multiple scenarios for these performances – scenarios whose relationships to each other are not narrativised in advance.

Throughout the museum, architectural detail creates a performance environment for multiple, overlapping spaces of interpretation. This especially pertains to the Hall of Witness, a huge, skewed, multistoried, glass-topped courtyard at the centre of the museum to which museum-goers have free access (and which contains the museum information desk, some spaces to rest, and so on). In this Hall, repeating architectual detail reverberates associatively: the curved archways in this large sculpted space of brick and metal suggest a train station for deportation; windowlike structures with geometric plates of metal covering them suggest the small spaces of restricted visibility to the outside world left after the ghettos were closed up; metal-barred windows and protruding one-bulb lights suggest the outside of a concentration camp (and structures resembling guard towers surround the glass-topped courtyard ceiling); metal doors shaped like ovens (repeated in the doors to the archive downstairs) along with metal-slatted niches, whose slats open inward, suggest the crematorium itself. These associative details resonate with the literal images documenting these historical events, but provide a greater sense of surprise and discovery, however ominous, for the spectator.

Another provisional and multiple performance of subjectivity at the museum is elicited when spectators cross metal bridges enclosed in glass. These bridges, which we cross from one part of the exhibit to another, span the Hall of Witness (i.e., the large, open courtyard below). The glass walls of the bridges have writing etched into them: on one bridge a listing of the names of predominantly Jewish towns or communities destroyed during the Holocaust, on another a listing of the first names of people killed in the Holocaust, as if to underscore the impossibility of ever listing the massive number of people killed. So, unlike the Vietnam Memorial, which used the names of specific individuals for its powerful effect, this generic death list emphasises the destruction of a culture and a cultural body. Moreover, unlike the Vietnam Memorial, the transparent glass walls allow us to view past the inscriptions to the courtyard below.

The bridges are structured to allow us to see people moving about the courtyard, but because of its height, enclosure, and inscriptions, we cannot communicate with the people below or even be seen by them except in a shadowy way. Thus, the bridges are architecturally structured to resonate with the experience of victims – distanced from, isolated from, and ignored by an everyday world of bystanders. Moreover, the bridges become even more suggestive if we notice a photograph of the Lodz Ghetto included in the Holocaust exhibit. As Berenbaum notes, 'When the Lodz ghetto was established, the trolley car system could not be rerouted around the ghetto. Three bridges were built [so] Jews could walk over the bridges that divided the ghetto.'[11] With '90 per cent of its starving residents working', Lodz Ghetto was akin to a slave-labour camp located in the heart of a city, its labouring Jews undeniably visible. In no way does our walk across the bridges suggest a simpleminded 'you are there' reproduction. But it does put the bystander/ spectator into a process of discovery and potential transformation into witness, even into a chilling resonance with ghetto inhabitants.

My assumption here, then, is that witnessing is an active process of spectatorship rather than a passive consumption of a pre-narrated spectacle. Another possible performance of interpretation at the same site might focus more on the inscriptions than the bridges. Etched on glass, these inscriptions surround spectators, almost hovering in the air. Our perception is coloured by them and the absences they gesture toward, because they are in front of everything we see. Thus names of towns and people destroyed get in the way of seeing the everyday in the courtyard. This also could serve as a larger comment on the experience of the museum itself and the way what it inscribes in individual memory filters how we see the world.

In one sense, we can understand representation in general as about place, while performance is about space. But in another sense, both place and space construct the subject as a performer. If both are performances, the *place* of performance is much more rigid, more likely to be about the spectacular or the quest for the Real. It is the possibility of multiple performances by spectators that might crisscross each other, the possibility of multiple interpretations as historical subjects, that creates a different kind of performance. The critical word is multiple, whatever the particular strategies used to achieve this. But if we think of space in relation to performance, we must think of multiple performances. It is then that the performance interpretation becomes performative.

Walking through the museum can be performative in the sense of discovering it. There has to be a cognitive moment when the spectator realises she is doing it (spectating), when the spectator realises she is *in* a doing. (She can also be in a very fixed kind of doing that is unconscious precisely because it is so fixed and pre-narrativised.) One cognitive moment at the museum hinges on how its designers located some of the video monitors showing archival film footage: they are often located at floor level in such a way that spectator crowding is required even to see what is on the screen. An extreme example occurs on the middle floor, which includes the most elaborate depictions of atrocity: in a kind of raised well are located several monitors (all showing the same thing). Spectators are already clustered tightly around the well, so later spectators must crowd in aggressively to see what the monitors depict. Once there, one views videos of grotesque medical experiments forced by Nazi doctors upon concentration camp inmates. Physical agony and humiliation. And our awareness of pushing to see is foregrounded in the process. What a performance environment like this can do, then, is allow us to experience our subjectivity in unusual ways: when we crowd around the monitors, we are turning ourselves into voyeurs (and not a community of witness). Our curiosity, even our curiosity *to see* itself is thrown back at us. We are challenged, I think, to create a more self-conscious relationship to viewing materials about atrocity and take more responsibility for what we've seen.

Close by this video well, in a glass enclosed space with benches where we hear Auschwitz survivor testimony (no visuals), the museum exploits spatial possibilities differently. Here, in order to make out the words, we must share loose-leaf notebooks containing xeroxed testimony with other museumgoers. The only other thing to look at in this space are the responses of other spectators to the painful material on atrocity. The potential for physical intimacy in the design of this exhibit space creates a site for a community of witness amongst strangers because we are confronted with the presence of other spectators, other bodies, with whom we must cooperate.

Thus, a Holocaust museum becomes a performance space when different activities are performed simultaneously, producing different subjectivities and different goals and aims within the incoherence of that space. It is not analogous to representational theatre because no one perspective can manage it. [...]

HOLOCAUST HISTORY AND 'MANAGEABILITY'

The exhibition was designed, in a number of places, to make you feel confused, disoriented, closed in. The same way that the people who lived during the Holocaust felt. It's narrow in more than one place during the exhibition. You think everything is going all right, you've come into a lot of space, and then all of a sudden it gets narrow again. It creates a mood. The whole exhibition.

(Museum guard at the United States Memorial Holocaust Museum, spoken to the author)

In answer to the problematic question of 'How can we know the Holocaust?' the museum tries to impart knowledge, not only about the history of these events, but about how to remember the Holocaust, how to make memory and experience performatively. Ostensibly, then, the project of the museum is to make the unmanageable history of the Holocaust manageable. This effort to make accessible to us what cannot be absorbed into anything other than itself is both highly ambitious and impossible.

Much of the US Holocaust Memorial Museum presents the history of the Holocaust as an accretion of detail. The irony is that in an effort to make the unmanageable manageable through this accretion of detail (place), the museum produces a sense of unmanageability (space). The use of artifacts and dense documentation to produce knowledge and historical presence, and to shape memory, also convey the incommeasurability of the loss by making this density unmanageable for the viewer. What is critical about the museum, then, in its use of small bits of everything – shoes, documents, photographs, artifacts – is the sheer, unbearable magnitude of detail. An example of the way we are made to enact this unmanageability of detail occurs at what I refer to as the tower of pictures. During the exhibit, we must cross via walkways through a tower of pictures that is taller than the exhibit's three stories. The enlarged photographs, taken between 1890 and 1941, convey the quality of Jewish life and culture that was extinguished in the Polish town of Ejszyszki where almost no one Jewish survived. One virtue of these pictures is that they represent how these people wanted to be seen, rather than how the Nazis made them look or how they looked when the liberators found them. But while the photographs' arrangement in the structure of a tower keeps directing us to look up, the top photos are so high they recede into invisibility. So we rehearse with our bodies not only the immeasurability of the loss, but the imperfect structure of memory itself. This is one of many spaces in the museum that call for physical activity in combination with our hermeneutic and emotional activity.

Insofar as history also is an accretion of human detail, of lists, of too much, the museum offers the unmanageability of history itself. Moreover, these details represent only fragments of the people and the genocidal event that killed them. Thus the museum conveys the unmanageability of this particular genocidal history, and the unmanageability of the detail of that history. Accretion of detail, then, makes the Holocaust not just a fearful absence, but totally unmanageable in a cognitive sense. In doing so it points to the terrifying abyss, the horrific rupture, that is the history of the Holocaust. The shoes are a case in point.

The museum's choice to include a roomful of nothing but piles of shoes is effective, in part because shoes are malleable enough to retain the shape of their individual owners and, even, here and there, an impractical bow or a tassel. So each shoe provides a small, intimate remnant of survival in the loss; collected in piles, the shoes convey the magnitude of that loss without becoming abstracted or aestheticised. The piles of shoes metonymically represent the huge body of shoes collected by the Nazis, which, in turn, metonymically represent the murdered people who wore them, and in so doing convey the unmanageability of the history to which they point. In their very materiality the shoes represent at once absence and presence. Moreover, despite constantly blowing fans, the shoes smell (from their own disintegration) and thus involve our bodies in making memory. The smell of the shoes is organic, like a live body, and in that way they become performers, standing in for the live bodies that are absent. Thus the shoes, as objects made to perform an absent subjectivity, are performative. Their accumulated detail buttresses the specificity of who has been lost, while we performatively enact the trajectory of memory in relation to them. To borrow Peggy Phelan's words in *Unmarked*, the shoes, as objects made to perform, do 'not reproduce' what is lost, but 'rather help us to restage and restate the effort to remember what is lost'. The performativity of the shoes 'rehearses and repeats the disappearance of the subject who longs always to be remembered'.[12]

In fact, the museum seems to acknowledge in its very architecture that such a modernist project of accretion is only a rearguard effort to produce manageability. The sense of this history as absence and as loss echoes through the great empty Halls that alternate with the densely detailed exhibits. These large spaces of absence become part of the performance space: the horrific notion of absence, which is all one can really experience of the slaughter, is built into the museum architecture itself. Edifice produces edification. Inviting us into emptiness allows us an awareness of the unseeable of genocide. And, by creating subtle links among objects, repeating structures and movement elicited from spectators, the museum provides resonances that are not limited to one narrative performance but position spectators to perform in spaces that are, ultimately, unmanageable.

Even the seeming obviousness of the ideological envelope of democracy and liberation that encases the museum is overlapped with a subtler narrative that could render the ideological narrative unmanageable. There are repeating metal gates throughout the inside and surrounding the outside of the museum (including the loading dock). They look, at first glance, like prison doors and so seem to fit in with the resonating architectural details

I mentioned earlier. But, unobtrusively located among other exhibits is the artifact that inspired this repeating design: the double gates of a Jewish cemetery, brought here, to North America. They signify the desecrated realm of the Jewish dead. But the echoes of the cemetery gates encircling the museum also suggest another enveloping structure for the museum itself: we move in the topography of the desecrated dead of Jewish genocide whenever we enter this museum. The gates of the cemetery and the gates of the museum make it clear that the whole museum is a graveyard. Notably, even the presidential inscriptions on the outside of the museum that confirm the 'Americanness' of this project also look like inscriptions on giant tombstones, so that not even the most obvious ideological narrative is wholly manageable. The gates, in relation to the cemetery, lend the museum a sense of unreality; it bursts out of the boxes, the containment, of the usual museum exhibit.

[The chapter originally ended with a discussion of the Beit Hashoah Museum of Tolerance.]

8

Hearing Anita Hill and Clarence Thomas

Peggy Phelan

Sexual injury illuminates a broad problem in the performance of legal justice. Some of the most culturally troubling legal cases of the past decade in the United States have involved sexual injury, a concept recently redefined by feminist legal scholars and activists. I am interested here in how a psychoanalytic concept of sexual injury, usually called sexual trauma (which encompasses incest, child abuse, eroticised beatings) informs and distorts the legal notion of sexual injury (which encompasses rape, sexual assault, incest, and sometimes sexual harassment). The Anita Hill–Clarence Thomas hearings provide an interesting case through which to consider legal and psychoanalytic understandings of sexual injuries because the hearings were conducted between these two discursive systems. Precisely because they were not conducted in a court of law nor on a psychoanalytic couch, the hearings can illuminate how each system of understanding has both perils and possibilities for redressing sexual injury.

The logic of law and the logic of sexual injury have an uneasy, often hostile, relationship. The logic of law seeks to draw a line between the truth of the empirical and the fiction of the lie; the force of sexual injury often makes it impossible to make this distinction. Insisting that it is possible and necessary to separate 'objective' evidence from subjective testimony when assessing damages, the law prefers firm test results as against medical speculation or claimants' descriptions of pain. The law, in other words, believes that while people may lie, the body generally tells the truth, providing the test and diagnosis are clear enough. Medicine, for law, functions to guarantee body-truth. But when the injury is sexual, it is virtually impossible to separate the empirically verifiable from the phantasm of the trauma. Sexual trauma tears the fabric of knowledge itself: it is a wound in the system of meaning through which the subject knows the world, knows him or herself. Sexual trauma can perhaps never be fully interpreted, but the tear it creates may be mended as it is rehearsed, rewritten, revised.[1]

Part of the social function of law is to assure the populace that the law can redress injury. If the claimant suffers an unfair or avoidable harm at the hands of a defendant, the law promises the claimant an opportunity to receive moral solace and/or financial compensation. In terms of injuries to property or names, claims are evaluated according to a rigid notion of 'proof' – in which the claimant is asked to produce visible and/or material evidence that the injury occurred and that the defendant had an obligation to avoid causing injury to the claimant. In cases related to sexual injuries, however, the law is asked to interpret and adjudicate 'evidence' that is informed by the complexity of the unconscious. It is with a great deal of uneasiness that law 'submits' to the rules of the unconscious, rules most fully articulated by psychoanalysis. This uneasiness surfaced in the long battle over criminal procedure statutes that required corroboration of sexual injury – for example, physical evidence of penetration in addition to a claimant's account of rape or sodomy. At the heart of such a battle lies the question of whether or not any sexual injury ever happened. ('She asked for it.' 'She consented.' 'She is hallucinating.')

Law attempts to make clear rulings, to establish guilt (innocence is assumed, not established), and to name winners and losers.[2] Legal hearings often involve two competing versions of narrative sequences that proceed according to the logic of cause and effect. The unconscious eschews the logic of cause and effect and achieves coherent mental associations and sequences through the logic of repression.

The Anita Hill–Clarence Thomas hearings occurred at the threshold between the opposing discursive practices of psychoanalysis and the law. What was deeply unsettling about the hearings was the exposure of their acute inadequacy to interpret satisfactorily what had and had not occurred between Hill and Thomas. Moreover, the hearings raised several profoundly important questions for those interested in rethinking the contemporary purpose of the 'talking cure'. Can law redress sexual injury? How must the terms of sexual injury be translated into a language that law can decipher? How can law find a logic supple enough to follow the repressions and distortions that psychoanalysis tells us always accompany sexual trauma? And how can these distortions be separated from legal definitions of 'temporary insanity'?[3] I cannot answer all of these questions here but I hope that this chapter will map the chasm between the logic of law and the logic of sexual trauma that was so dramatically revealed in the Hill–Thomas hearings.

The Senate Judiciary Committee hearings in October 1991 investigated Professor Anita Hill's allegations of sexual harassment against President George Bush's nominee for the Supreme Court, Judge Clarence Thomas. But the hearings uncovered and concealed much more than anyone had intended. Part of the fascination of the hearings derived from their form, their mutating genre. National and international 'from gavel to gavel' television and radio coverage, unprecedented numbers of viewers, and the nature of the accusations themselves, quickly transformed the hearings into a riveting public display of the nation's sexual and racial wounds. The hearings seemed, at times, to turn into a criminal trial – although everyone, except for Thomas, denied that that was happening. Hill continually emphasised that she was not making a criminal charge of sexual harassment and Joseph Biden, chair of the confirmation process, repeatedly said the hearings were not 'a court of law'. At other times the hearings turned into a kind of public psychotherapy session in which terms like 'erotomaniac', 'proclivities' and 'fantasy world' were bandied about as 'explanations' for Hill's motives.[4] Poised midway between criminal trial and public psychotherapy, the televised hearings generated a furious momentum that displayed the searing limitations of both criminal trials and public psychotherapy as truth-finders. These limitations were in turn amplified by the disjuncture between the media's boasts of complete coverage and the content of the hearings which made repeated references to secret conversations, badly summarised FBI reports, inaccurately dated phone logs and secret 'leaks' to the press. All of these gaps underlined the fact that the televised mediated hearings were a mere surgical cut, a small incision, in the larger political struggle for control of the Supreme Court, that supreme judicial body whose main political function is now often understood as legislating sexual reproduction and abortion.[5]

The chasm between the formal claim to see-all and to show-all and the constant references to a past that could not be agreed upon drove the search for the truth of the authentic body – a body – any body that could not, would not, lie. Thus the racist fascination with the size of Thomas' penis, quickly gave way to a fascination with the interior spaces of Hill's body – particularly, her stomach.[6] Psychoanalysis elaborates the impossibility of ever mastering the truth of the body; law insists that the truth can be the uncovered. In the liminal zone between law and psychoanalysis where the Hill–Thomas hearings occurred, disturbances in the corporeal were interpreted as truth-meters. While Hill argued that her stomach pain was the result of stress on the job, and Thomas argued that his weight loss was attributable to the stress he felt from the hearings, his somatic response was read as normal and hers was seen as pathological. Thomas' character witnesses argued that it was more than Hill's 'stomach' that was upset; Hill herself was unstable and motivated by unrequited love, they argued. Eventually many senators concluded that her claims 'came out of nowhere', and that they had 'no substance'.

Confirming Thomas, however, required that the senators adopt the structural logic of the criminal trial where guilt must be established beyond a reasonable doubt. Many senators said they voted to confirm Thomas because they believed that they owed him, as they would an alleged criminal, the presumption of innocence, even though Thomas was not charged with a crime. The question of whether or not Thomas was qualified to be a Supreme Court Justice was repressed in the frantic attempt to establish Thomas' 'innocence'. Thomas understood that this was impossible; I suspect his explicit reminder of that impossibility led some senators to vote to confirm him as a form of compensation.

It is useful to tell the story of the hearings again, and again differently, for repetition contains within it the possibility of reversal.

President Bush's decision to nominate Thomas to replace Thurgood Marshall was immediately seen by many as a desire to fill the 'black man's seat' with a conservative, 'white man's Negro'.[7] Attempting to dispel this interpretation, the Republican administration insisted that Thomas' race had no relevance in his nomination. Bush put it with typical inelegance at the initial press conference announcing Thomas' nomination: '[W]hat I did is look for the best man. The fact that he is black and a minority had nothing to do with this in the sense that he is the best qualified at this time. . . . I don't feel he's a quota.'[8] The very terms of Bush's 'defence' are themselves offensive, and Thomas, perhaps cynically, perhaps naïvely, decided to take Bush at his word. In the first round of the confirmation hearings, Thomas simply performed the part of a man with a worrisome amnesia but who was nonetheless the 'best qualified'. Wagering that the Senate did not have to like him, or agree with him, Thomas was content to be confirmed. But in declaring himself a victim of a hightech lynching in the second round of the hearings, Thomas accented his identity as a black man. This move helped set up the curious parallel he drew between himself and Martin Luther King. Thomas' lynching comparison, coupled with his 'you don't have to like me' stance, echoed Martin Luther King's famous statement during his trial in Alabama, 'The law may not be able to make a man love me, but at least it can keep him from lynching me'.[9]

By invoking lynching, Thomas insisted he was a black man who was being unfairly judged by white America. For the white senators, Thomas' masculinity was never an issue; but his relation to race was. As a successful conservative married to a white woman, a man who said that 'the civil rights groups had done "nothing right" and that all civil rights leaders do is "bitch, bitch, bitch, moan, and whine"', Thomas posed several dilemmas for the white male senators even before round two.[10] Throughout round one of the confirmation process (what Thomas called 'my real confirmation hearings' as against the 'Kafkaesque' drama of the second round), Thomas simply said that he could not recall discussing any controversial legal cases. His strategy was that if he did not admit to having any controversial opinions he would be confirmed, if only because many white senators feared being labelled 'racist' for voting against a black man. But by employing the lynching analogy in round two, Thomas fundamentally recast the form and the substance of the hearings. He placed himself firmly in a historical plot in which he was the victim. In this script, if Thomas cast himself as the falsely accused black man hanged in the town square, he cast Hill as the white woman who lusted after a black man and who, when he spurned her or when she found herself caught out, falsely denounced him as a rapist. In his drama, Hill perforce played the part of the white woman and, as Kimberle Crenshaw put it, was thereby 'de-raced'.[11] Once positioned as a white woman, Anita Hill became susceptible to the historical strategy that emerged in the nineteenth century and continues to greet white women who protest men's sexual appetites: she became pathologised.

Thomas' lynching strategy was clever because it allowed him to play the part of the dead man; he had already 'died a thousand deaths' before he appeared before the cameras. The blood was dry in him, but it was still flowing in Anita Hill. As a dead man, his relation to sex was arrested and buried in the past. His sexual behaviour was merely a matter of his imperfect recollection; moreover, it was trenched in on all sides by a newly awakened fidelity to privacy. Ironically, Thomas' new language echoed the language of Justice William Brennan when, in *Eisenstadt* v. *Baird* he laid the groundwork for *Roe* v. *Wade* which was decided one year later: 'If the right of privacy means anything it is the right of the individual, married or single, to be free from unwarranted government intrusion into matters so fundamentally affecting a person as the decision whether or not to bear or beget a child' (*Eisenstadt* v. *Baird*, 405 U.S. 438, 453 [1972]). This is precisely the logic that Thomas took up to defend himself from 'unwarranted government intrusion' when he told the senators: 'I am not going to engage in discussions nor will I submit to roving questions of what goes on in the most intimate parts of my private life, or the sanctity of my bedroom. These are the most intimate parts of my privacy, and they remain just that: private.' This is a statement that can go unchallenged when uttered by a heterosexual man of a certain class. We still live in a culture where economically secure heterosexual men can either brag about sexual conquests or claim 'privacy', while gay men, women of all sexual preferences, and those who seek financial assistance from the state, must endlessly 'confess' their sexual histories.

During the Hill–Thomas hearings, a strange link between gay men and women was evoked. While the language of 'privacy' has been most resonant in legal decisions involving women's reproductive choices, it has also played a decisive part in case law involving gay male sexuality.[12] In 1986, in a very controversial opinion, the Supreme Court held (five to four) that the right to sexual privacy does not extend to male homosexuals. In *Bowers* v. *Hardwick*, the court ruled that 'the presumed belief of a majority of the electorate in Georgia that homosexual sodomy is immoral and unacceptable' is sufficient to justify the prohibition of sodomy between homosexuals.[13] Given that this presumed belief is also presumed rational, the statute only needs to pass the requirements of 'minimum scrutiny' for the statute to be upheld. Under the requirements of minimum scrutiny, the state need only demonstrate some 'rational basis' for the discriminatory law, rather than demonstrate that the law serves the state's 'compelling interest'. Thomas' claim that he was going to protect the 'sanctity of [his] bedroom' was a right he enjoyed because of his heterosexuality: a similar claim could not be legally made by a homosexual man in Georgia.

In addition then to staging a conflict about race and gender, the Hill–Thomas hearings, I am suggesting, also staged a conflict over heterosexuality and homosexuality. This is a crucial, if often unmarked, aspect of the hearings. The hearings created a crisis about *diagnosing* the nature of the accusations themselves. This doubt led to troubling questions about the nature of Hill's sexuality.

In contrast to Thomas' 'private' (hetero)sexuality, the story of Hill's sexuality, in Alan Simpson's insidious description, was coming in 'over the transom. ... I've got letters hanging out my pocket, I've got faxes ... saying "Watch out for this woman." ... And I'm talking about the stuff I'm getting from women in America ... and especially women in Oklahoma.' After bemoaning the fact that the Senate could not spend 104 days investigating Hill's 'proclivities', Simpson neatly found a different reason to elicit the word 'faggot' from Thomas. He asked Thomas why he had fired Angela Wright, another African-American woman who had told the FBI that Thomas had made inappropriate advances toward her while she was working at the Equal Employment Opportunity Commission (EEOC).

> Simpson: Did you fire her, and if you did, what for?
> Thomas : I indicated, Senator, I summarily dismissed her. ... I felt her performance was ineffective. ... And the straw that broke the camel's back was a report to me from one of my staff that she referred to another male member of my staff as a faggot.
> Simpson: As a faggot.
> Thomas : And that's inappropriate conduct and that's a slur, and I was not going to have it.
> Simpson: That was enough for you?
> Thomas : That was more than enough for me.

Simpson wanted to demonstrate that Thomas would not tolerate homophobic and offensive remarks in his office. Framing the discussion of 'homophobia' within an interrogation that begins with the assertion that Hill is a woman of unknown, or unnamable, proclivities, Simpson continues to weave the theme of 'a love that dare not speak its name' into the public hearing. Furthermore, this exchange has the effect of dismissing Angela

Wright's accusations against Thomas. Had Wright been asked to testify and could corroborate Hill's story, it may well have been considerably more difficult, if not impossible, for the senators to have confirmed Thomas' appointment to the Supreme Court.

If Thomas had made 'inappropriate remarks' to Wright as she stated in her sworn testimony to the FBI, and she had rebuffed him, he may well have wanted to 'summarily dismiss' her – both at the EEOC and from the hearings. But if the account of Timothy Phelps and Helen Winternitz in *Capitol Games* is accurate, Thomas' and Simpson's version of Wright's dismissal is almost impossible to believe; she claimed that Thomas left a note on her chair saying she was fired.[14] When she asked him why, he said she had not fired enough people in the agency during a time of budgetary cutbacks. But even if we grant that the story Thomas tells in the hearings is absolutely true, it raises a different, but equally difficult, problem. Thomas is boasting of dismissing an employee because of an unnamed staff member's report of Wright's inappropriate and sexually offensive remark. Hill started out as an unnamed staff member who was accusing Thomas himself of inappropriate and offensive sexual remarks. While it is enough for him to fire a member of his staff based on such a report, he is outraged at the possibility that his confirmation might be in jeopardy because of Hill's allegation of his own sexually offensive language. Thomas objects that Hill's 'unsubstantiated rumours' are being used to 'lynch' him even while he boasts of acting on less cause when he fired Wright. I will return to the role of rumours in these hearings later, but for now I want to point out that the hearings circulated rumours that led to dismissals of women and the confirmation of men.

[…]

The political-legal body is rife with 'foreign bodies' whose phantasmatic force must be contained, even incarcerated. The black male body is the 'representative' criminal body in the contemporary United States, and the criminal justice system is charged by the political-legal body with managing the 'dirt' that that criminally-black body carries. As Thomas himself put it, 'This is a case in which … dirt was searched for by staffers, … and was then leaked to the media, and this … body validated it and displayed it at prime time over our entire nation.' So traumatised by the 'filth and dirt' generated by the hearings, Thomas' own body wasted away. He complained that he had lost 15 pounds in two weeks. The hearings were 'eating his insides out'.

While Thomas said he spent two weeks 'eating his insides out', Hill's 'insides' had been eaten out, she testified, by the alleged events which gave rise to the hearings. Hill told the senators that she had been hospitalised for 'five days on an emergency basis for acute stomach pain, which [she] attributed to stress on the job'. The psychic trauma she believed she had to endure from her boss manifested itself in physical symptoms. But these symptoms were interpreted in the hearings according to the distorted logic of sexual difference.

The psychological interpretation of the structure of the socio-political relation between Hill and Thomas went unexamined. During the time of the alleged harassment, Thomas was Hill's boss. Thus they had an asymmetrical social relationship: he was her superior. Psychoanalysis helps us see that such structural asymmetries can produce psychological violence – before a word is spoken. These consequences can be heightened by the particular performative (speech) acts of those in power; these acts can also be made 'more' violent by the ways in which individual subjects interpret these acts. (These interpretive processes are established by earlier schooling in asymmetrical social relations; classical psychoanalysis examined the pedagogy of asymmetry undertaken in and by the family.) Parents and children, teachers and students, and employers and employees, are engaged in social relations which, because they are also always already asymmetrical relations of power, produce psychic violence.

The energy of this repressed violence enables the return of the repressed. The Hill–Thomas hearings staged the return of the repressed in relation to two different narratives of the past. The 'truth' of the past is located in both unconscious and conscious memories. Thomas and Hill have a past social relation that can never be re-presented entirely accurately. Each of their narratives about it will be partially phantasmatic, partially real. Hill's testimony indicates that she truly believes herself to be the victim of Thomas' sexually harassing speech. In this sense her testimony is at once a performative and transformative speech act in which her public account of that private sexual *victimisation* attempts to repudiate – in the very public and politicised form of its telling – her position as 'victim'. (It is precisely the transformation accomplished by the voiced speech act that makes the psychoanalytic talking cure possible.) But if Hill's speech act is taken to be 'the truth' (if her accusation is believed), then that very success makes possible the truth of the other, the other truth articulated by Thomas. Thomas' testimony is organised around his belief that Hill's public speech act victimises him; her accusation transforms him into a victim. His protest against this positioning was evident in his counter-charge that he is a *victim* of 'a high-tech lynching'. In order for the narrative truth of the asymmetrical social relation to be maintained, which is one of the functions of 'confirmation' hearings – a performance of gathering evidence to *confirm* the legal order, the order of (white juridical) discrimination – the hierarchy of the criminal/victim relation must itself be confirmed. Thomas' lynching analogy underlines what exactly is in need of confirmation even while he fights to hang the noose around Hill's neck rather than his own: the discriminating order of justice. This order of justice is itself more sympathetic to men-as-victims than to women. Hill's performative speech act makes it possible for her to evacuate the position of victim, but it also leaves the position of victim open. Thomas claimed that vacated position. In his performative speech act, Thomas confirmed the power given to men by the asymmetry of the social relation we call sexual difference.

In failing to address the structural asymmetry of the political-social relation between Hill and Thomas (both when she worked for him and when she appeared in Congress), the hearings reproduced the violence of that asymmetry. But perhaps they also made it more difficult to keep such violence repressed. It may well be that the most salutary result of the Hill–Thomas hearings is the conscious attention they called to the unspoken violence of the routine performance of discriminating justice. The return of this repressed may help to transform the narratives through which individuals (and cultures) interpret asymmetrical social relations, especially those we attribute to sexual difference.

One could go on in this way for a very long time and there have been many excellent analyses of the subtexts of the hearings.[15] But I firmly believe the 'truth' of the relations between Hill–Thomas is not recoverable. What matters now is the way in which the public exposure of the uncertainty of their relations makes a wedge into political history itself. The question that is still open, I believe, is how retrospective critical interpretations of the hearings will analyse the psychical trauma they inflicted on the contemporary cultural unconscious. Anita Hill's allegations helped expose the fact that official political history is the smooth story of solid non-leaking bodies, bodies who learn not to bleed in order to assure their political immortality. The dramaturgy of the hearings made clear that real political power lies in the interpretation of the always bleeding line between public and private bodies. Moreover, these interpretations must be seen to repeat historical patterns – what law calls precedents and psychoanalysis calls reminiscences – whose symbolic force is great and whose details are vague. Thomas' invocation of the lynching script provided an interpretative model that the befuddled senators were all too happy to seize upon. Given a choice between being immortalised in history books as racist or sexist, the majority of the senators decided they would rather have the blood of a 'de-raced' black woman on their hands than the blood of a black man who denounced them as a lynch mob. Hill accused Thomas, but Thomas accused them. Thus, in order to defend themselves and prove him wrong, given the perverse logic of psychic trauma, they had to confirm him. The crudity of the perception that that was the choice makes it likely that the injury will be repeated until we see it differently and change the usual outcome.

The Hill–Thomas hearings dramatised a crisis about law's inability to heal a sexual wound. Traumas that involve the sexualised body and the 'neutral' corpus of law contain within them reminiscences of events – imagined or real

– that repeat other traumas. Our best hope is that the exposure of these repetitions may bring about a critical reversal of the trauma. By trauma I mean a hole in the symbolic network that cries out to be mended, rehearsed, revised. Perhaps a performative psychoanalysis of this public trauma might begin to inscribe a different political history, a history written with and through the bodies of women as they appear and disappear in the discursive narratives of both law and psychoanalysis. By performative psychoanalysis, I mean a calculated public rehearsal of the psychoanalytic 'reminiscence' undertaken within the contemporary event. I am not suggesting that the reminiscence consciously informs that event; but I am suggesting that, by using the psychoanalytic reminiscence as a way to interpret the contemporary event, a way to temper (if not quite reverse) its effects may emerge. One of the central assertions of theatrical performance is that the affective experience of the body can be authentically conveyed regardless of whether or not such experience is the consequence of a 'real' event or a well-rehearsed repetition of an imagined one. Thus psychoanalysis and performance are congenial enterprises and, when strategically marshalled, can help us to reassess what bodily truths signify.

Hill testified that while she was working for Thomas she was hospitalised for 'five days on an emergency basis for acute stomach pain, which [she] attributed to stress on the job'. No further testimony about this injury was heard. Few emergency rooms would allow a patient to stay for five days. Or perhaps she meant that she went to the emergency room five different times during her tenure under Thomas. Hill probably meant that she was admitted to an emergency room and then transferred to a regular hospital room for four additional days. If this is what she meant, it is likely that she was treated for a bleeding ulcer, the most common cause of acute stomach pain due to stress. I am interested in what such a bleeding inner cavity in the body of a woman might set off in the unconscious of the male senators. For the hearings staged an accusation against more than Thomas. The senators well knew that they themselves were on trial, and like medical doctors (and lawyers), the men were terrified of being accused of malpractice. Their terror of course only guaranteed their inept performance.
[...]
   Acutely conscious that the Hill–Thomas hearings were not revealing 'the whole story', auditors began to invest belief in other systems of explanation. Rumours about the hearings were almost as riveting, in some ways perhaps more riveting, than the formal hearings. One of the most persistent rumours was that a deal had been made before the hearings. One version of the rumour goes like this: Thomas' side agreed not to mention that Hill once had a lesbian affair, if Hill's side agreed not to produce receipts from Thomas' x-rated video rentals (including the *Long Dong Silver* flick).[16] In

the second version of the rumour, Thomas' side agreed not to mention that Hill was a lesbian if Hill's side agreed not to mention that one of the grounds for divorce from his first wife had been that he beat her.[17] These rumours help explain detailed and otherwise inexplicable references in the hearings – Thomas' allusion to news reporters' trying to get hold of his divorce papers by searching his garage and his suddenly razor-sharp memory of Hill's basketball playing roommate and her sweat pants. Asked if he had ever met Hill's roommate, Thomas replied, 'Yes. ... She was, as I remember, a basketball player. I think she was in a basketball league. And occasionally she would walk by in her sweats, or be there in her sweats.' In testimony filled with large overdetermined gaps in memory about significant legal cases, Thomas' detailed memory about Hill's roommate's sartorial habits seems strategically rehearsed.

Rumours function to sustain the belief that the 'real truth' is, ultimately, recoverable. But even as they declare themselves 'rumours', they disable the recovery of truth. By virtue of their status as rumour they displace what they seek to restore. Multiplying and mutating as they go – from one lesbian relationship to the ontic status 'lesbian' – from porn-flick watcher to wife-beater – rumours underline the incoherence of the story they seek to verify and explain. In the face of the painful gap between the structure of legal inquiry and the psychic trauma and doubt the story unleashed, rumours worked to link what many experienced as a chasm between the empirically verifiable and the phantasmatic.

The legal category of sexual offence, which includes crimes of rape, sexual assault, sexual harassment, incest, and sodomy, continues to bedevil the law because it lends itself so promiscuously to the phantasmatic. The law currently provides a sorry forum for the redress of sexual injury. At best, it can make transfers of injury between the victim and the criminal, but it can do little to heal the psychic injury of sexual trauma. Psychoanalysis must re-theorise the distinction between genuine sexual abuse and seduction fantasies before it can effectively instruct law on rules of evidence. Until this happens, we will continue to live with what resembles a gossip network between the two modes of thought: the crudity of the law's understanding of sexual injury, for example, is itself arrived at from an analysis that is, essentially, psychological (as against psychoanalytic) gossip.[18] The inadequacy of the join between law and psychoanalysis makes it almost impossible, under current arrangements, for the law to redress sexual trauma. This near impossibility fuels the circulation of rumours which restage the desire for a cure, for a full explanation, for a way to know. In that restaging the phantasmatic is 'explained'; but that explanation can satisfy only at the level of rumour. Once the phantasmatic is interrogated according to the strictures of legal 'proof' it becomes incoherent.

Recognising the bias and flaws in the discursive framework of the law, feminist scholars and lawyers have worked hard to introduce a new legal standard for sexual injury cases. Instead of having to prove that remarks or behaviour would be offensive to 'a reasonable man', the traditional legal measure for over 150 years, judges in several federal courts have begun to acknowledge that men and women might, reasonably, interpret the same event quite differently. In a sexual harassment case in Jacksonville, Florida, the judge allowed testimony that reported a poll in which 75 per cent of the men said they would be 'flattered' by sexual advances in the work place and 75 per cent of the women said they would be 'offended' by such advances.[19] The judge then went on to rule in favour of a woman who alleged that pornographic pinups in the work place and 'a boys' club atmosphere' violated Title VII of the 1964 Civil Rights Act. Some feminist legal scholars are betting that the 'reasonable woman' standard will make it easier for law to redress sexual injury. While it is still too early to know if this bet is sound, it is significant that the law is beginning to recognise the ways in which the so-called 'neutral' language of rationality may be gendered male. As the Ninth US Circuit Court of Appeals in San Francisco argued, 'we adopt the perspective of a reasonable woman primarily because we believe that a sex-blind reasonable person standard tends to be male biased and tends to systematically ignore the experiences of women.'[20]

But these apparently progressive movements forward must be tempered by the brute facts of the Hill–Thomas hearings.[21] During the hearings, the majority (approximately 58 per cent) of people polled said they believed Clarence Thomas, while only 24 per cent said they believed Hill. There was 'little difference in response between men and women, or between blacks and whites. But Republicans were more inclined to believe Judge Thomas than were Democrats.'[22] Several months after the hearing, when the legal apparatus had disappeared and people evaluated what had happened, the majority of people said they now believed Hill. It is hard to 'explain' the shift since no new evidence emerged,[23] but it may have something to do with the fact that political and legal hearings – in their physical and psychic settings – underline the associations between power, rationality, truth and masculinity – before a word is said. Women, on the other hand, and perhaps especially black women, may seem simply not to belong in such a setting and therefore are judged to be wrong.

[...]

The intertexts of the hearings – innuendoes about homosexuality and circulating rumours, serve to illustrate the ways in which the hearings failed to provide the truth of what or may not have happened between Hill and Thomas. But they did offer insights into the different ways in which law and psychoanalysis treat sexual injuries and traumas. Asymmetrical social relationships (in the classroom, the church, the office, the family, the state) produce and reflect sexual violence. If we are ever to imagine a way to redress sexual injury and trauma, the law must learn to address the psychic consequences of the asymmetries that constitute the law of the sexual relation itself.

9

The Street is the Stage

Richard Schechner

I mean our thing's for TV. We don't want to get on Meet the Press.
What's that shit? We want Ed Sullivan, [the] Johnny Carson show, we
want the shit where people are lookin' at it and diggin' it.

(Abbie Hoffman)[1]

[A constitutional republic] cannot forever withstand continual carnival on
the streets of its cities and the campuses of the nation. Unless sage debate
replaces the belligerent strutting now used so extensively, reason will be
consumed and the death of logic will surely follow.

(Vice-President Spiro Agnew, May 1969)[2]

...old authority and truth pretend to be absolute, to have an extratem-
poral importance. Therefore, their representatives ... are gloomily serious.
They cannot and do not wish to laugh; they strut majestically, consider
their foes the enemies of eternal truth, and threaten them with eternal
punishment. They do not see themselves in the mirror of time, do not
perceive their own origin, limitations, and end; they do not recognize their
own ridiculous faces or the comic nature of their pretensions to eternity
and immutability. And thus these personages come to the end of their role
still serious, although their spectators have been laughing for a long time.
... Time has transformed old truth and authority into a Mardi Gras
dummy, a comic monster that the laughing crowd rends to pieces in the
marketplace.

(Mikhail Bakhtin)[3]

The role of the revolutionary is to create theatre which creates a revolutionary frame of reference. The power to define is the power to control. ...
The goal of theatre is to get as many people as possible to overcome fear
by taking action. We create reality wherever we go by living our fantasies.

(Jerry Rubin)[4]

What is the relation between 'the authorities' and 'the people' when the
people occupy public streets, squares, plazas, and buildings? Do carnivals
encourage giddy, drunken, sexy feelings and behaviour – or does the very

110

action of taking spaces, of 'liberating' them, make people giddy? Is it accidental that official displays consist of neat rectangles, countable cohorts, marching past and under the fixed gaze of the reviewing stand, while unofficial mass gatherings are vortexed, whirling, full of shifting ups and downs, multifocused events generating tension between large-scale actions and many local dramas? And why is it that unofficial gatherings elicit, permit, or celebrate the erotic, while official displays are so often associated with the military?

[...]

Festivals and carnivals – almost but not quite the same – are comic theatrical events: comic in desire, even if sometimes tragic in outcome. When people go into the streets *en masse*, they are celebrating life's fertile possibilities. They eat, drink, make theatre, make love, and enjoy each other's company. They put on masks and costumes, erect and wave banners, and construct effigies not merely to disguise or embellish their ordinary selves, or to flaunt the outrageous, but also to act out the multiplicity each human life is. Acting out forbidden themes is risky so people don masks and costumes. They protest, often by means of farce and parody, against what is oppressive, ridiculous, and outrageous. For one to join the many as a part(ner), is not just a sexy act, it is also a socially and politically generative activity. Festive actions playfully, blasphemously, and obscenely expose to the general eye for approval and/or ridicule the basic (and therefore bodily) facts of human life and death. Such playing challenges official culture's claims to authority, stability, sobriety, immutability, and immortality.

Sometimes street actions bring about change – as in Eastern Europe in 1989. But mostly such scenes, both celebratory and violent, end with the old order restored. Frequently, the old order sponsors a temporary relief from itself. Obeying strict calendars, and confined to designated neighbourhoods, the authorities can keep track of these carnivals and prepare the police. But despite such preparations, rebellions swell to almost musical climaxes around sacralised dates – anniversaries of the deaths or funerals of heroes and martyrs or of earlier popular uprisings (as in China) or the Christmas season and the approach of the New Year (as in Eastern Europe). To allow people to assemble in the streets is always to flirt with the possibility of improvisation – that the unexpected might happen.

Revolutions in their incipient period are carnivalesque. Written on a Sorbonne wall in 1968, 'The more I make love, the more I want to make revolution – the more I make revolution, the more I want to make love'.[5] This is because both revolution and carnival propose a free space to satisfy desires, especially sexual and drunken desires, a new time to enact social relations more freely. People mask and costume or act in ways that are 'not me'. These behaviours are almost always excessive relative to ordinary life. Sometimes people drink, fuck, loot, burn, riot, and murder: or practise rough justice on those they feel have wronged them. But sooner or later, either at a defined moment – when the church bells ring in Ash Wednesday, when school begins again after Spring Break, when a new government is firmly in power – the liminal period ends and individuals are inserted or reinserted into their (sometimes new, sometimes old but always defined) places in society. 'Festivity, ceremonial form, and the transgression of social boundaries are animated with the strongest possible feeling of solidarity and community affiliation.'[6]

All well and good, but what about violence, dissidence, and the playing out of irreconcilable differences? René Girard argues that 'the fundamental purpose of the festival is to set the stage for a sacrificial act that marks at once the climax and the termination of the festivities'.[7] Michael Bristol explains:

> A substitute victim is murdered in order to ward off a more terrifying, indiscriminate violence among the members of the same community. This sacrificial murder [events such as public executions or representations such as Greek tragedy] is the partly hidden meaning of all religion and thus of all social life.[8]

Festive sacrifice is necessary to innoculate society against 'falling into interminable violence'.[9] Roger Caillois goes further:

> In its pure form, the festival must be defined as the paroxysm of society, purifying and renewing it simultaneously. The paroxysm is not only its climax from a religious but also from an economic point of view. It is the occasion for the circulation of wealth, of the most important trading, of prestige gained through the distribution of accumulated reserves. It seems to be a summation, manifesting the glory of the collectivity, which imbues its very being.[10]

The potlatches of native Americans on the Pacific coast in the late nineteenth century are clear examples of what Caillois was talking about. The public destruction of goods was both a display of wealth and an act of violent dissipation. After a great potlatch there was nothing left but to get back to amassing the resources needed to stage another. Unlike the Roman Saturnalia where a scapegoat slave was sacrificed, or the Athenian theatre of Dionysus where actors pretended to suffer and die, potlatchers gave up the real thing: the material substance of their wealth.

Caillois regarded modern European carnivals 'as a sort of moribund echo of ancient festivals . . . a kind of atavism, a heritage of the times in which it was felt vitally necessary to reverse everything or commit excesses at the time of the new year'.[11] As Bristol points out, in modern times state apparatus takes over from festivity the function of guaranteeing social solidarity. Rectangular and linear parades replace the more vortexed and chaotic choreography of carnivals. The state fears unregulated traffic. Over time in Europe and Europeanised America, festivals were cut to size, hemmed in by regulations, transformed into Chamber of Commerce boosterism, coopted by capitalism's appetite for profit, relatively desexualised (Miss America at least has to pretend to 'innocence'), and served up as models of social order and conformity. With rare exceptions, today's festivals and carnivals are not inversions of the social order but mirrors of it. 'Lords of Misrule' in the Mardi Gras or Gasparilla are rarely drawn from the lower or oppressed classes or enabled to rule (even for a day). For example, New York's Halloween parade, originating in the 1960s as a display of (mostly gay) cross-dressers, maskers, and costume buffs, meandering its noisy way through Greenwich Village's small streets, has been regularised over time, tamed and contained by police watchfulness, and rerouted on to wide main streets where it is more a parade and less an infiltration.

But unofficial culture worms or bullies its way back into public outdoor spaces. If there is a tradition (and not only in the West) of constructing grand monuments specifically to present performances – arenas, stadiums, and theatres – so there is as well a long history of unofficial performances 'taking place' in (seizing as well as using) locales not architecturally imagined as theatres.[12] A big part of the celebration is experiencing the transformation of work space, or traffic space, or some kind of official space into a playfield. Over the past thirty years, performance experimenters, an art branch of unofficial culture, have used outdoor spaces – courtyards, streets, walls, beaches, lakes, rooftops, plazas, and mountainsides – for a number of overlapping purposes – aesthetic, personal, ritual, and political. And while Western dramatists from Ibsen, Strindberg, and Chekhov to Miller, Pinter, Shepard, and Mamet abandoned the public squares of Renaissance theatre for the living room, kitchen, bedroom, motel, and office, the emerging festival theatre – liminoid rather than liminal – repositioned itself in places where public life and social ritual have traditionally been acted out.[13] Doubtless, there has been a mutually fruitful exchange between art performances and symbolic public actions. By the 1960s, these actions constituted a distinct liminoid–celebratory–political–theatrical–ritual genre with its own dramaturgy, *mise-en-scène*, role enactments, audience participation, and reception. This theatre is ritual because it is efficacious, intending to produce real effects by means of symbolic causes. It is most theatrical at the cusp where the street show meets the media, where events are staged for the camera.

Many examples could be given. One I witnessed took place in Shanghai in May 1989 when millions of workers, students, and spectators flowed into Nanjing Road, Shanghai's main street and then on to the Bund, the city's riverfront avenue.[14] Looking down from an overpass all I could see, forward or back, were marchers proceeding between rows of cheering spectators lined ten or more deep on both sides of the road. Above were office workers leaning-out of windows waving handkerchiefs; construction gangs in hard hats thirty stories up unfinished skyscrapers clanging their hammers against the steel girders (in some wild simulation of the cymbals of Chinese opera) as they unfurled 50-foot banners calling for the resignation of Premier Li Peng and the retirement of Deng Xiaoping. People rushed from roadside restaurants with wet towels, cool tea, and snacks to refresh the marchers. Streets were festive, people moving hand in hand, raising their fists in exhilarated defiance or forming the 'V for victory' sign with their fingers. In a drunken delirium of desire, they shouted words that even one month before could hardly be whispered: 'China's present government are bums!' 'Give me liberty or give me death!' 'Democracy now!'

On the way back from the Bund, students from the Shanghai Theatre Academy turned off the main path of the march and approached the gates of Shanghai's TV station. One demonstrator was bound in chains, another wore a skeletal death mask, several were drenched in stage blood; all writhed in melodramatic agony: a grisly tableau of how they experienced China – a spectacle not unlike similar kinds of American guerrilla street theatre. Around the students thousands of demonstrators congealed into a mass pressing so fiercely against the TV station's walls and gate that I had the breath squashed out of me. A number of Canons, Nikons, and humbler equipment condensed from the crowd, but the students were angry and dissatisfied. They demanded a camera crew videotape them for broadcast to the nation. A man in a white shirt and pressed slacks emerged from the building. Engaging him in a hot colloquy, the students threatened – with the crowd's support – to crash the gate. The man trotted inside. A very few minutes later, to resounding cheers, out came a camera crew to begin taping the students who acted up a storm, writhing and screaming bloody murder. Now, they felt, the event was real. Shanghai and maybe all China and the whole world would see. Being seen and reported on was a morsel of the 'transparency' and free press the democracy movement was so vehemently demanding.

But the Shanghai march was just a sideshow down the coast from the main arena, Beijing's Tiananmen Square.

Tiananmen Square is no European Piazza. More than 100 acres in size, and capable of holding hundreds of thousands of people, it is the centre of a city of ten million people, which is the capital of the People's Republic of China, Beijing. It is the symbol of China and Chinese government in the same way that Red Square and the Kremlin symbolise the USSR, and Washington with its white monuments the USA. ... [In] Tiananmen

Square is situated the huge Monument to the People's Heroes and the Mausoleum of Mao Zedong. On the west side of the Square is the Great Hall of the People, the meeting place for government bodies. ... On the east side of the Square is the Museum of Chinese History, which is attached to the Museum of the Revolution. At the north end of the Square is the reviewing stand which stands over the entrance to the Forbidden City, now the Palace Museum. To the west of the Forbidden City is the Zhongnanhai compound for senior government and party personnel. ... Running east-west ... through the north end of the Square is [Beijing's] major thoroughfare, Changan Avenue.[15]

But until 1949 this version of Tiananmen Square did not exist. Earlier photos show a smallish open space in front of the Gate of Heavenly Peace, the southern entrance to the Forbidden City.

Until China's last dynasty fell in 1912, it was through this gate that the main axis of the Emperor's power was believed to run, as he sat in his throne hall, facing south, the force of his presence radiating out across the courtyards and ornamental rivers of the palace compound, passing through the gate, and so to the great reaches of the countryside beyond.[16]

After the communist triumph,

the crowded alleys in front of the gate were levelled, and a massive parade ground was created; in the centre of the vast space rose the simple monument to the martyrs of the revolution. ... During the Cultural Revolution of 1966 [to 1976] the gate, dominated now by an immense coloured portrait of Chairman Mao Zedong, became a reviewing stand in front of which marched the Red Guards, a million or more strong.[17]

Clearly, the creation of Tiananmen Square was intended to refocus cere-monial – that is, theatrical – power from behind the Forbidden City's walls to the big open space, a more fitting symbol of what the new order promised. Mao, the new emperor, no longer sat on a throne behind the Gate, but was mounted in front, gazing out over the Square and from there to all of China. Power was no longer to radiate from secret forbidden places but be displayed for all people to see and share. The nation itself was renamed The People's Republic of China. And what the students who came to Tiananmen Square in 1978, 1986, and 1989 demanded, more than anything, was what they called 'transparency' – defined as an openness in government operations corresponding to the open square that symbolised the new China. In occu-pying Tiananmen Square the students were challenging the government, actualising the students' belief that the government was not living up to its promises. There were precedents for such actions in the dramatic May 4th Movement of 1919 and the more recent democracy movements in 1978 and 1986 – all of which focused on Tiananmen Square. Joseph Esherick and Jeffrey Wasserstrom argue strongly that the 1989 democracy movement was political theatre.

> First of all it was street theatre: untitled, improvisational, with constantly changing casts. Though fluid in form, it nevertheless followed what Charles Tilly[18] calls a historically established 'repertoire' of collective action. This means that, even when improvising, protesters worked from familiar 'scripts' which gave a common sense of how to behave during a given action, where and when to march, how to express their demands, and so forth. Some of these scripts originated in the distant past, emerging out of traditions of remonstrance and petition stretching back for millennia. More were derived (consciously or unconsciously) from the steady stream of student-led mass movements that have taken place [in China] since 1919.[19]

The struggle in China, before it became violent, was over controlling the means and style of information. As Esherick and Wasserstrom note, state rituals, the funerals of leaders (in 1989 that of Hu Yaobang, a former General Secretary of the Communist Party who the students highly regarded), and anniversaries of earlier demonstrations or uprisings are of great importance. In 1989 the question became: would official culture or the student-led democracy movement write the script? The theatrical stakes were even higher in May because fortune laid ceremony atop ceremony. Hu Yaobang died on 15 April, close to the anniversary of the May 4th Movement; Soviet President Mikhail Gorbachev was set to arrive in Beijing on 15 May, possibly healing decades of bad relations between China and the USSR. Clearly, the leadership wanted to impress Gorbachev. The students also wanted to impress him, but with a different show. They admired the Soviet President's policies of *glasnost* and *perestroika*. If Chinese officials wanted Gorbachev to see an orderly China under their control, the students wanted him to see a powerful and seething people's movement akin to those in Eastern Europe and his own country. On 15 May about 800,000 people gathered in Tiananmen Square even as Chinese officials steered Gorbachev around Beijing pretending that this vast spectacle at the very core of power was not occurring. Instead of greeting Gorbachev in the Square, official public ceremonies were held at the Beijing airport, a non-place historically.

Within the overall dramaturgy of the 1989 demonstrations were particular molecules of theatre related to what I saw in Shanghai. Esherick and Wasserstrom describe as 'one of the best acts' that put on by Wuer Kaixi in the May 18th dialogue with Li Peng. The costuming was important: he appeared in his hospital pajamas [on hunger strike]. So, too, was the timing: he upstaged the Premier by interrupting him at the very start. And props: later in the session, he dramatically pulled out a tube inserted into his nose (for oxygen?) in order to make a point. Especially for the young people in the nationwide television audience, it was an extraordinarily powerful performance.[20]

Then there was the dramatic meeting the next day, 19 May, between hunger-striking students and Communist Party Secretary Zhao Ziyang. This encounter had the quality of a tragic *perepeteia* (reversal) and *anagnorisis* (recognition). Speaking through tears, Zhao said 'I came too late, I came too late ... [but] the problems you raised will eventually be solved.' And, of course, on 30 May the 'Goddess of Democracy and Freedom' – a multivocal figure resembling the Statue of Liberty, a Bread & Puppet Theatre effigy, a 'traditional Bodhisattva, ... [and] the giant statues of Mao that were carried through the Square during some National Day parades of the sixties'.[21] The Goddess was a big hit. Before her appearance the crowds had been sagging, but she brought many back to the Square. Earlier, on 25 May in Shanghai, a more exact replica of the Statue of Liberty had come onto the streets – thus ideas for effigies and banners, staging, all kinds of information were circulating through the movement's various parts. Students freely adapted costumes and slogans from non-Chinese sources, including 'We shall overcome'. Across China the democracy movement was 'connected', a single organism. Serious in their demands and aspirations, the Chinese students still found plenty of time to celebrate, to dance, to enjoy the freedom of the streets. At the same time, the government was getting its forces together, bringing in troops and key leaders from the far reaches of the country.

Esherick and Wasserstrom theorise that the struggle in Tiananmen Square was between official ritual and student theatre:

> there is always the chance that people will turn a ritual performance into an act of political theatre. Central to the notion of ritual is the idea that only careful adherence to a traditionally prescribed format will ensure the efficacy of a performance. With any departure from a traditional script, a ritual ceases to be ritual. ... Theatre, by nature, is more liberated from the rigid constraints of tradition, and provides autonomous space for the creativity of playwrights, directors, and actors. This gives theatre a critical power never possessed by ritual. ... Educated [Chinese] youths have repeatedly managed to transform May 4th rituals into May 4th theatre.[22]

Such a distinction between theatre and ritual is too rigid (in fact, Esherick and Wasserstrom do not always stick to it). As Victor Turner has emphasised, and as I have pointed out, the relation between ritual and theatre is dialect-ical and braided; there is plenty of entertainment and social critique in many rituals.[23] Conversely, theatre in its very processes of training, preparation, display, and reception is ritualised. The struggle in Tiananmen Square before the entrance of the tanks was not between rigid ritual and rebellious theatre, but between two groups of authors (or authorities) each of whom desired to compose the script of China's future and each of whom drew on both theatre and ritual. The students improvised in public, while the officials, as always, rehearsed their options behind closed doors. The students took Tiananmen Square, the centre stage and ritual focus of Chinese history. Official culture was literally upstaged. When Deng Xiaoping, Li Peng, and the generals of the People's Liberation Army felt their authority slipping, they radically shifted the basis of the confrontation from theatre and ritual to military force. But even after the slaughter of 3–4 June, there were moments of high theatre such as when an unarmed man, his fate since unknown, stood his ground in front of a column of tanks.

For their stage the students claimed not just any old spot, but the symbolic and operational focus of Chinese political power. And despite the orderli-ness of their demonstrations and the seriousness of their intentions, the students acted up a carnival. Their mood of fun, comradeship, irony, and subversion enraged and frightened China's officialdom. Students camped out willy-nilly all over the place in patterns as different as can be imagined from the rigid rectangles and precise lines of official gatherings. The students sang and danced, they spoke from impromptu 'soap boxes', and granted interviews to the world press. They unfurled sarcastic, disrespectful banners including one depicting hated Premier Li Peng as a pig-snouted Nazi officer. 'Flying tigers' – students on motorbikes – carried news to and from various parts of Beijing, linking the Square to the city and the rest of China. Even the hunger strike, in which thousands participated, had the feel of melodrama rather than the sanctity of one of Gandhi's laydowns (though certainly the Mahatma knew his political theatre – and how sanctity would play in India and Britain).

Events in Beijing from the perspective of Shanghai underline the import-ance of theatricalising media. From mid-May until 8 June I was in Shanghai directing a new Chinese play about the aftermath of the cultural revolution at the People's Art Theatre. What was happening in Beijing was of great importance to me and those I was working with. During the days immedi-ately preceding the Tiananmen Square massacre of 3–4 June, official media – TV, radio, and newspapers – kept changing tune according to whether hardliners or people sympathetic to the students were calling the shots. Once the tanks rolled in the media toed the line, but in an eerie way. The main headline of the 5 June *China Daily* (the official English language newspaper) reported the death of Ayatollah Khomeini. A lesser headline, bereft of capital letters, said, 'Martial law troops are ordered to firmly "restore order".' For several days on TV only the reporters' voices were heard, no images. Unofficial media worked very differently. At the person-to-person level, students went back and forth from Shanghai to Beijing bringing news by word of mouth. Once martial law was declared at the end of May, it was rare to meet someone who 'was there'. People listened to the Voice of America and BBC; newspapers and magazines in Chinese and English came in from Hong Kong (for sale at the big tourist hotels or smuggled by individuals). After the massacre in Tiananmen Square, a friend rented a room at the satellite-equipped Shanghai Hilton. Even as Chinese official media were claiming that only thirty-six students had been killed in the Square, and that the students had been the aggressors, a crowd of Chinese and foreigners in the hotel room watched with terror and excitement as CNN broadcast direct shots from Beijing, routed back to Atlanta and relayed by satellite to the world. The satellite link was still up, as were phone lines and faxes, when I was evacuated from Shanghai on 8 June. On 4 and 5 June rumours of civil war were brought to rehearsals. Peering at handdrawn maps, we saw the progress of an army marching toward Beijing to overthrow Deng and Li, while 20,000 troops from Nanjing were massing just outside Shanghai in support of Deng and Li. The celebratory exaltation of May changed to fear. Access to unofficial media was sharply curtailed, especially in the countryside where most of China's 1.1 billion live. When it was certain that the government had used major force against the students, some of whom were the children of the elite, people hunkered down. Rice hoarding began; I changed my residence from the Shanghai Theatre Academy to a hotel to be out of the way of the army should it decide to move against the Academy, a focus of radicalism.

This radicalism the Chinese government called *luan*, or chaos, a word which in certain of its uses implies dissipation and drunkenness. Because of the 'tigers' – and world media (more about which I shall say later) – the Chinese leadership feared the virus of luan would spread from Tiananmen Square to the rest of Beijing and China. After all, it was from the Square that official power radiated. Had the students turned inward, not attempting Chinawide and worldwide communication, the government might have waited them out. But Tiananmen Square is not an inwardly focused place: it is a consciously designed, very bright stage, visible all over China. From the government's point of view, luan acted out in Tiananmen Square could not be ignored any more than the Nixon administration could, nineteen years earlier, ignore the ever more carnivalesque anti-Vietnam War demonstrations invading Washington. Meaningful theatrical luan is a potent weapon.

[. . .]

The system of communist domination of Eastern Europe and the USSR, and the cold war between that system and the north Atlantic alliance, was symbolised by the Berlin Wall. Existing for only twenty-eight years (1961–89), the 103-mile-long Wall lacked architectural grace or ornament. Like the Bastille, it not only symbolised a hated regime and physically helped preserve it, but was demolished as soon as that regime fell. While it was there, more than 5000 people went over, under, or through it – climbing, leaping, ballooning, gliding, tunnelling, and ramming. At least another 5000 were captured and 191 were killed trying to escape.[24] Ugly and mean, the Wall disgusted and attracted people, including Presidents John F. Kennedy and Ronald Reagan, who exploited it as a theatrical backdrop for communist-bashing speeches. Still others considered it a tourist 'must'.

The events leading to the destruction of the Wall – and the collapse of communism throughout Eastern Europe – are complex.[25] The system was imposed from without, sustained by military force, and failed to deliver the material goods people desired. There were many revolts and several major uprisings crushed by Soviet armies or the clear threat of Soviet intervention. When in the mid-1980s Gorbachev began restructuring the USSR, Eastern Europeans saw an opportunity, but the actual licence for radical change was not issued until Gorbachev's declaration on 25 October 1989 that the USSR had no right to interfere in the internal affairs of its Eastern European neighbours. He may have been driven to this position by events. The social drama began in the summer of 1989 – shortly after the brutal crushing of the democracy movement in China – when Hungary opened its border to East Germans. Many thousands got out of the GDR at rates unequalled since the building of the Wall.

Throughout September and October, the East German government – led by one of those who authored the Wall, 77-year-old Erich Honecker – shilly-shallied regarding the exodus. Meanwhile, the festival that always accompanies a 'revolution from below' began.

> A carnival atmosphere greeted the first large convoy of jubilant East Germans to arrive today in this city [Passau, West Germany] on the Danube in south-eastern Bavaria. Hundreds of onlookers watched and cheered as five buses unloaded an estimated 700 East Germans who were welcomed with speeches, free balloons, bananas, beer and soft pretzels. . . . A similar welcome was given to East Germans arriving at five tent cities set up by the West German Red Cross in nearby towns.[26]

Following a Bakhtinian script, headlines in the *New York Times* proclaimed: 'Exodus galls East Berlin/Nation's sovereignty seems to be mocked'.[27] But the climax was not yet reached – the streets of Berlin were relatively quiet and empty.

Then, as in China earlier in 1989, an important date sparked street protests. Friday 6 October was the GDR's fortieth anniversary. Ordinarily one could expect a rectangular parade of military muscle in front of and below rigidly saluting generals and commissars mounted on a viewing stand. As in China that May, globe-hopping Gorbachev was scheduled to make an appearance and, as in China, the official celebration turned sour. 'Honecker faces the birthday party...humiliated, derided, and threatened.'[28] Gorbachev was seized on by both sides, soon becoming a contradictory sign. Addressing 'an elite congregation gathered in the glittering Palace of the Republic...[he] assailed demands that Moscow dismantle the Berlin wall', while earlier many Berliners hailed him with shouts of 'Gorby! Gorby!' a known code for the reforms they were demanding from Honecker's government.[29] On 9 October more than 50,000 demonstrated in Leipzig. On 18 October Honecker was replaced by his protégé, 52-year-old Egon Krenz – a man who had just paid a praising visit to Li Peng and Deng Xiaoping.

The East German people replied with more demonstrations. People were openly disrespectful of Krenz.

A retired factory hand, speaking in the pungent accent and mocking vocabulary of the Berlin working class, nearly exploded with derisive laughter. ... 'From him?' he asked with a snort. 'After he went to China to congratulate them for the blood they spilled? After he rigged our last election? After being the boss of State Security? The sparrows on the roof wouldn't believe him.'[30]

Ferment was spreading. On 23 October 300,000 marched in Leipzig demanding change, including the legalisation of opposition parties and an independent labour movement. Smaller demonstrations took place in Berlin, Dresden, Halle, Schwerin, and Magdeburg. People grew bolder. Political debates erupted in the streets of East Berlin. Meanwhile big demonstrations were starting in Prague. Not only were East Germans challenging their leadership, the once docile press and TV were giving open coverage to the emergent debates. The demonstrations got more and more festive. On 30 October, Leipzig's 'old city centre was virtually taken over for three hours by people of every age and from every walk of life. ... The centre [was filled] with cheers, jeers, and chants from all sides'.[31] On 2 November the East German government dropped its ban on travel and thousands crossed into Czechoslovakia heading west. On 7 November the East German cabinet resigned, but the Politburo – the core of official power – held fast. By 8 November more than 50,000 East Germans a day were streaming from Czechoslovakia into West Germany where, according to law, they instantly became citizens.

On 9 November, the GDR government opened its borders. Once the announcement was made, a tentative trickle of East Germans testing the new regulations quickly turned into a jubilant horde, which joined at the border crossings with crowds of flag-waving, cheering West Germans. Thousands of Berliners clambered across the wall at the Brandenburg Gate, passing through the historic arch that for so long had been inaccessible to Berliners of either side.[32]

The Brandenburg Gate, like Beijing's Tiananmen Square, is heavily symbolic. Erected in 1888–9 at the western end of the Unter den Linden, and soon dubbed Germany's Arc de Triomphe, the Gate celebrates the military prowess of Prussia and the unity of Germany. On 9 November, in a flash, the Berlin Wall's symbolic value was reversed. What had been avoided or surpassed became the chosen place of celebration. Because it had been such a terrifying barrier it was now where people wanted to act out how totally things had changed. People couldn't wait to climb it, sit on it, pop champagne and dance on it, and chip away souvenir chunks of it.[33] Formerly murderous East German border guards went out of their way to be friendly. The show on the Wall was a media bonanza. Dominating the front page of the 10 November *New York Times* was a four-column photograph of 'East Berliners dancing atop the Berlin Wall near the Brandenburg Gate'. The same picture, or others very like it, appeared on front pages around the world. Again and again, TV showed people clambering on to and over the wall.

The Wall was not 'interesting' everywhere along its 103-mile route. The focus was on the segment in front of the Brandenburg Gate or bifurcating Potsdamer Platz which, before the Wall, was the centre of Berlin, among the busiest intersections in Europe. Just as Tiananmen Square was the necessary stage for China's democracy movement, so the Wall at these places was where Berliners focused the 'unparalleled celebration that swirled through Berlin day and night'.[34] Cheers, sparkling wine, flowers and applause greeted the new arrivals. ... At the Brandenburg Gate ... hundreds of people chanted, "Gate open! Gate open!" ' A middle-aged East German woman broke through a police cordon to give flowers and a 'vigorous kiss' to a young West German cop as 'the crowd roared'. 'A festival air seized the entire city. West Berliners lined entry points to great East Berliners with champagne, cheers, and hugs. Many restaurants offered the visitors free food. A television station urged West Berliners to call in with offers of theatre tickets, beds, dinners, or just guided tours.' The popular Hertha soccer team gave away 10,000 free tickets for its Saturday game. That giddy weekend the West German government gave every visitor from the East 100 marks of 'greeting money' for spending in West Berlin's glittering shops. 'In an unprecedented step for a place with the most rigid business hours in Western Europe, West Berlin banks will be open on both Saturday and Sunday for East Germans wishing to pick up cash.' It was only a matter of time before the East German state collapsed into the arms of the West.

It could have ended otherwise. Craig R. Whitney reports that 'there was a written order from Honecker for a Chinese solution' (1989: A27).[35] But the Politburo overrode its ageing boss. Once events are in the saddle, the speed of the reversals is breathtaking. A faltering regime in China suddenly re-asserts itself; a seemingly invincible state in East Germany crumbles like dust. Hindsight discloses the 'inevitability' of events. But 'what if' haunts all such talk. What if the Chinese leadership had not sent in the army? What if the East Germans had? At what point does a regime lose control of its military? There are too many variables for anyone to answer these questions. What can be known is that when oppressed or angry people sense official power weakening, they take to the streets. Their carnival can last only so long – every Mardi Gras meets its Ash Wednesday. Whether or not that Wednesday will see a new order or the return of the old cannot be known in advance.

10

Culture and Performance in the Circum-Atlantic World

Joseph Roach

The white man who made the pencil also made the eraser.

(Yoruba Proverb)

'The real magic happens', says Anna Deavere Smith, 'when the word hits your breath.'[1] Those who have seen her performances will understand the validity of this statement as a description of her work. In this essay, I want to explore its resonant implications for professors of the discipline that might still be called English: in the study of language and culture, literature is not enough. My theme today is the interdependence of performance and collective memory. It emerges from a project that would recast the category of literature, as a repository of texts, in relation to what my colleague Ngugi wa Thiong'o calls 'orature', the range of cultural forms invested in speech, gesture, song, dance, storytelling, proverbs, customs, rites, and rituals. Ngugi defined orature indirectly when he said of the singer: 'He is a sweet singer when everybody joins in. The sweet songs last longer, too.' As Kwame Anthony Appiah notes, 'there are many devices for supporting the transmission of a complex and nuanced body of practice and belief without writing'.[2] This continuing dialogue between literature and orature, however, does not accept a schematised opposition between literacy and orality as transcendent categories; rather, it rests upon the conviction that these modes of communication have produced one another interactively over time, and that their historic operations may be usefully examined under the rubric of performance.

The concept of performance engages 'The Politics of Theatre' through its implicit critique of the culturally coded meaning of the word *theatre*. Derived from the Greek word for seeing and sight, *theatre*, like *theory*, is a limiting term for a certain kind of spectatorial participation in a certain kind of event. *Performance*, by contrast, though it frequently makes reference to theatricality as the most fecund metaphor for the social dimensions of cultural production, embraces a much wider range of human behaviours. Such behaviours may include what Michel de Certeau calls 'the practice of

everyday life', in which the role of spectator expands into that of participant.[3] De Certeau's 'practice' has itself enlarged into an open-ended
category marked 'performative'. As the Editor's Note to a recent issue of
PMLA ('Special Topic: Performance') observes: 'What once was an event
has become a critical category, now applied to everything from a play to a
war to a meal. The performative ... is a cultural act, a critical perspective, a
political intervention.'[4]

From the perspective of the interdiscipline – or the postdiscipline – of
performance studies, poised on the cusp of the arts and human sciences,
moving between anthropology and theatre, the term *performance* may be
more precisely delineated as what Richard Schechner calls the 'restoration of
behaviour'. 'Restored behaviour' or 'twice-behaved behaviour' is that which
can be repeated, rehearsed, and above all *recreated*.[5] But therein lies an
anomaly that evokes Anna Deavere Smith's 'magic'. The paradox of the
restoration of behaviour resides in the phenomenon of repetition itself: no
action or sequence of actions may be performed exactly the same way twice;
they must be reinvented or recreated at each appearance. In this improvisa-
tory behavioural space, memory reveals itself as imagination.

Variations on the theme of 'repetition with a difference' may be discerned,
of course, in a range of poststructuralist positions. Most pertinent to my
concerns today, the African-American tradition of 'signifyin(g)', as explained
by Henry Louis Gates, Jr, with reference to Jelly Roll Morton's stomp
variation on Scott Joplin's rag, and applied as 'repetition with revision' to
Yoruba ritual by Margaret Thompson Drewal,[6] illuminates the theoretical
possibilities of restored behaviour, not merely as the recapitulation, but as the
transformation of experience through the renewal of its cultural forms. In this
sense, performance offers itself as a governing concept for literature and
orature alike.

Thus understood, performance highlights a distinction between social
memory and history as different forms of cultural transmission across
time: memory requires collective participation, whether at theatrical events,
shamanic rituals, or Olympic opening ceremonies; history entails the critical
(and apparently solitary) interpretation of written records. Both also function as forms of forgetting: cultures select what they transmit through
memory and history. The persistence of collective memory through restored
behaviour, however, represents an alternative and potentially contestatory
form of knowledge – bodily knowledge, habit, custom. The academic pre-
occupation with textual knowledge – whereby a culture continually refers
itself to its archives – tends to discredit memory in the name of history.[7] In
fact, both forms of cultural transmission have their distinctive efficacies:
textual knowledge, for instance, though it travels apparently intact through
space and time, obviously lacks the vitality of kinesthetic awareness that
characterises the participatory enactments of memory. Knowledge of such

memories comes more readily to the observer-participant, who has danced the dance or joined the procession, than it does to the reader. At the same time, the diachronous relations of such performance can quite readily disappear from critical consciousness, transforming memory into the most volatile forms of nostalgia.

Both history and memory participate in the production of restored behaviour, circulating in performance genres as diverse as street carnivals, intelligence testing (which measures 'performance'), post-operative therapies for breast prostheses, slave auctions, and operas. The study of restored behaviours in their diachronous dimension, however, is a relatively new field of research, organising itself around what I call 'genealogies of performance'. Genealogies of performance 'document the historical transmission and dissemination of cultural practices through collective representations'.[8] For this formulation, I am indebted to Jonathan Arac's definition, revising Nietzsche and Foucault, of a 'critical genealogy', which 'aims to excavate the past that is necessary to account for how we got here and the past that is useful for conceiving alternatives to our present condition'.[9] Genealogies of performance approach literature as a repository of the restored behaviours of the past. They excavate the lineage of restored behaviours still at least partially visible in contemporary culture, in effect 'writing the history of the present'.[10] But they intensify when they treat performances of cultural self-declaration in the face of encounter and exchange – the performance of culture in the moment of its most acute reflexivity, when it attempts to explain and to justify itself to others. For this reason, my argument, as my title indicates, is geographically located in broad hemispheric vortices as well as local sites, and this location itself requires some explanation.

I began with the Yoruban proverb, itself a powerfully compact mnemonic conveyance, to emphasise the indispensability of African diasporic and Native American memories to my account of culture and performance. I insist on the term *circum*-Atlantic, as opposed to *trans*-Atlantic, to underscore the compelling truth of Paul Gilroy's observation: 'A new structure of cultural exchange has been built up across the imperial networks which once played host to the triangular trade of sugar, slaves and capital.'[11] The creation of those imperial networks, which was one of the most vastly consequential undertakings of the early modern period in Europe or of any other time in human history, required modernisation of the European economy predicated on the genocidal exploitation of West African and American peoples. What compels me in restating this fact of history is a claim I want to make about the creation of the triangle of exchange between Northern Europe, Africa, and the Americas: the vast scale of the project – and the scope of the contact between cultures it required – limited the degree to which it could be eradicated from the memory of those who had the deepest motivation and the surest means to forget it; but it also fostered complex and ingenious schemes to displace, refashion, and transfer those persistent memories into representations more amenable to those who most frequently wielded the pencil and the eraser. In that sense, the creation of the circum-Atlantic world is a monumental study in the pleasures and torments of incomplete forgetting.

Historians have attended to the shift of decisive trade and power rivalries from the Mediterranean world to the Atlantic, which occurred in the late seventeenth and early eighteenth centuries, especially in the years leading up to and immediately following the Treaty of Utrecht in 1713.[12] The rivalry between Britain and France, particularly their struggle to dominate the slave economies in the West Indies and North America, shaped the cultural formations I am addressing here and the performances by which they are memorialised. The cultural politics of the odyssey from Mediterranean to Atlantic made it an epic story, living on the tips of many tongues.[13] As Homer and the tragic dramatists recorded and celebrated what they saw as the enormous, epochal shift of cultural and political gravity from the Asiatic world to the Mycenaean, as Virgil immortalised the similar movement out from the Aegean into the larger world of *mare nostrum*, so the poets, dramatists, and storytellers of the early modern period could once again poetically witness a transfer of the imperial vortex from its historic locus.

Africa plays a hinge-role in turning the Mediterranean-centred consciousness of European memory into an Atlantic-centred one, and not only because African labour produced the addictive substances (sugar, coffee, tobacco, and – most insidiously – sugar and chocolate in combination) that revolutionised the world economy.[14] The scope of that role largely disappears from history until fairly recent times: Africa leaves its historic traces amid the incomplete erasures, beneath the superscriptions, and within the layered palimpsests of more-or-less systematic cultural misrecognition. But diasporic Africa also leaves much more than historic traces; it regenerates the living enactments of memory through orature – and more recently through literature, which now links the perimeter of the circum-Atlantic world (American, Caribbean, African) with lyrics, narratives, and dramas of world-historical prominence.

I will focus here on a particular kind of performance – the funeral, as it is both represented in literature and enacted through orature. On the one hand, customs of death and burial, changing slowly over time, serve as grist for the mill of the *annalistes*: historical practices so conservative that even over the *longue durée* they look like structures. On the other hand, funerals can easily and often do become sites for the enunciation and contestation of topical issues. They are also characterised by the conditions of specificity that, according to ethnographer Barbara Kirshenblatt-Gimblett, attract investigators to such sites: 'performance-oriented approaches to culture place a premium on the particularities of human action, on language as spoken and ritual as performed.'[15]

In establishing the genealogy of circum-Atlantic performance genres, multimedia events prove the most promising, perhaps because their varied sensory modalities provide different kinds of memories. The funeral frequently combines music, poetry, dramatic action, and spectacle in a form that resembles opera, a coincidence that Wagner was neither the first nor last composer to exploit. The operatic mode of performance unites literature and orature, especially in the baroque *opera seria*, which delegated many of its vocal effects to the singers' improvisations. The most celebrated passage in early English opera, for instance, is the final aria sung by Dido, Queen of Carthage, in Henry Purcell's *Dido and Aeneas*, which is followed by a chorus that describes the obsequies performed to commemorate her death. This enactment of Mediterranean encounter, rupture, and dynastic establishment premiered in an amateur performance at a girls' school in 1689, the same year that James II involuntarily turned his interest in the Royal Africa Company, founded by brother Charles in 1672, over to its ambitious investors and sailed away.[16] There has been informed speculation about the local political allegory of *Dido and Aeneas* relating to the royal succession and Williamite policy,[17] but my genealogical reading is circum-Atlantic in scope.

The libretto of *Dido* is by Nahum Tate, better remembered for his improvements to *King Lear*. In fact, a number of Tate's works for the stage derive directly or indirectly from the materials in Geoffrey of Monmouth's *Historia Regum Britanniae*, a narrative from which he grafted some details onto the fourth book of Virgil's *Aeneid* to produce the *Dido* libretto. In the 1670s, Tate had begun a play on the Dido and Aeneas story, but he decided to adapt the plot to fit the epic voyages of the legendary Trojan Brutus, Aeneas's grandson (or great-grandson in some versions). In this play, called *Brutus of Alba; or, the Enchanted Lovers* (1678), the hero loves and leaves the Queen of Syracuse as Aeneas abandons the Queen of Carthage: the grandfather sails away to found Rome; the grandson, according to Tate's dramatisation of Geoffrey of Monmouth's account of the oral tradition, sails away to found Britain.

Moving from the Mediterranean world to the Atlantic, this mythic reiteration of origins, an evocation of collective memory, hinges on the narrative of abandonment, a public performance of forgetting. In the score's most stunning moment of musical declamation, which prepares for the death of the forsaken queen and the observances performed over her body, Tate gave Purcell a deceptively simple line to set. As Aeneas sets sail for Rome and empire, Dido's last words seem to speak for the victims of transoceanic ambitions:

Remember me, but ah! forget my fate.[18]

Dido pleads that she may be remembered as a woman, even as the most pertinent events of her story are erased, a sentiment that more appositely expresses the agenda of the departing Trojans. Dryden's translation of Virgil catches the drama of this decisive moment:

Dire auguries from hence the Trojans draw;
Till neither fires nor shining shores they saw.
Now seas and skies their prospect only bound;
An empty space above, a floating field around.[19]

As Aeneas casts a parting look back to the rising pillar of smoke, his ambivalence fuses memory and forgetting into one gesture. In that gesture, he enacts the historic tendency of Europeans, when reminded, to recall only emotions of deep love for the peoples whose cultures they have left in flames, emotions predicated on the sublime vanity that their early departure would not have been celebrated locally as deliverance.

The key to the genealogy of performance derived from this moment of a Restoration opera, however, rests on the musical setting for the text. The ground bass accompaniment for the vocal line of Dido's lament is a chaconne. This form became widely popular in Europe at the beginning of the seventeenth century, first in Spain, as a dance in triple metre with erotic connotations, then in France, as a more stately court dance, associated especially with weddings. Purcell came to know it from the French. The only agreement about the origin of what the Spanish call the *chacona* and the Italians *ciaccona*, however, is that it was not European, and that it drove women crazy. Spaniards attributed it to the Indians of Peru or perhaps the West Indies, where it gave its name to a mythical island, a utopia also called Cucuña (or in English 'Cockaigne'). Beauchamps, the French dancing master, confidently traced the chaconne to Africa.[20]

Whatever the precise history of the chaconne across four continents, the very confusions about its points of origin suggest its emergence out of an early version of what James Clifford describes as the 'creolised "inter-culture"' of the Caribbean.[21] Its assimilation into the musical life of a finishing school for daughters of English merchants suggests the invisible domestication and consumption of the Atlantic triangle's vast cultural produce, which, like sugar, its textures effaced, metamorphosed from brown syrup into white powder, until only the sweetness remained. That Dido's final lament, stately threnody that it is, derives its cadences and musical style from a forgotten Native American or African form, lends an eerily doubled meaning to the queen's invocation of memory as her lover sails boldly away from the coast of Africa, bound for amnesia.

The cultural appropriation that plays itself out along the routes of the circum-Atlantic triangle – conjoining and resegregating Europeans, Africans, and Native Americans – appears most emphatically where the genealogy of performance encompasses what I call surrogation, the theatrical principle of substitution of one persona for another. The triangular relationship of white, red, and black peoples seems both to threaten and accelerate the process of surrogation, which requires the elimination or the abjection of the third party.

The impetus of circum-Atlantic contact to performative self-definition through cultural surrogation produced diverse effects at various sites along the oceanic rim. In a recent study of the role of theatricality in the early cultural history of the United States, for instance, *Declaring Independence: Jefferson, Natural Language, and the Culture of Performance*, Jay Fliegelman begins with the significant but neglected fact that the Declaration of Independence was just that – a document written to be spoken aloud as oratory. He goes on to document generally the elocutionary dimension of Anglo-American self-invention, which emerged in relationship to Native Americans, on one hand, and Africans, on the other. Thomas Jefferson identified the supposedly transparent Anglo-Americans with the 'natural eloquence' of Indian orators. When he was accused of inventing the words of the Shawnee chief Logan's great speech in *Notes on the State of Virginia*, Jefferson replied that its authorship was immaterial because, in any case, 'it would still have been American'.[22] This same desideratum disqualified Africans from political expression, however, because the supposed uniformity and fixity of their colour allegedly rendered them inscrutable behind what Thomas Jefferson called 'that immovable veil of black which covers all the emotions'.[23]

Like theatrical doubling, surrogation operates in two modes. In the first mode, one actor stands in for another (as in the film trade's 'stunt double' or 'body double') so that, in effect, two actors share one mask. In the second mode of doubling, one actor plays more than one role – two (or more) masks appear on one actor. In the doubling of Logan, Jefferson casts himself as stand-in for the Shawnee chief: two actors wear the one mask coded 'American'. By contrast, in the doubling accomplished by blackfaced minstrelsy, one actor wears two distinct masks – the mask of blackness on the surface and the mask of whiteness underneath, which the printed programme for minstrel shows ostentatiously feature in portraits of the performers out of makeup, acting white.[24] In the first case, the surrogated original, the Native American, disappears into white speech. In the second, the doubled African American remains ventriloquised. In both cases, Anglo-American self-definition occurs in performances that feature the obligatory disappearance or captive presence of circum-Atlantic cohabitants.

Performances of encounter, however, do not belong to Europeans by right of manifest destiny. Circum-Atlantic contact and cultural exchange between Native Americans and Africans have produced performance traditions in the Caribbean and, on its northernmost rim, in Louisiana, that flourish today, though their rich meanings depend on relationships forged in colonial times. My work on performance genealogies began when I first learned about the Mardi Gras Indian 'tribes' of New Orleans, African Americans who parade as Native Americans (in gorgeous, fantastical, hand-sewn costumes) and therefore re-enact at carnival time the historical sense of the shared experience of peoples from two continents.[25]

The persistent power of surrogation in the performance of such cultural and ethnic difference resides, I believe, in the social liminality of the designated performers. According to Victor Turner, the temporary liminality of the performer in 'social dramas' (such as rites of passage) creates conditions of reflexivity, of cultural self-consciousness, or in Turner's own words, 'a limited area of transparency in the otherwise opaque surface of regular, uneventful social life'.[26] At the limit of the boundaries of a culture, performers are paradoxically 'at once the distillation and typification of its corporate identity'.[27]

From this perspective, the funerals of actors provide particularly promising sites for performance genealogies, because they involve a figure whose performance of both liminality and surrogation was all in a day's work. In any funeral, the liminal body of the deceased literally performs the limits of the community called into being by the need to mark its passing. United around a corpse that is no longer inside but not yet outside its boundaries, the community reflects upon the constructedness, the permeability, and not infrequently the violence of its borders.[28]

Liminality helps to explain why transvestism, for instance, seems historically constitutive of performance, a prior urgency to which the theatre provides an epiphenomenal elaboration or publicity. Marjorie Garber's insightful account of the funeral of Laurence Olivier ('a transvestite Olivier') as the surrogated burial of Shakespeare in Westminster Abbey ('only this time, much more satisfyingly, *with* a body') focuses on the uses of liminality in the creation of memory: 'That impossible event in literary history, a state funeral for the poet-playwright who defines Western culture, doing him appropriate homage – an event long-thwarted by the galling absence of certainty about his identity and whereabouts – had now at last taken place.'[29] While I warmly embrace this analysis of the meaning of the event, I argue that it was hardly the first of such rituals, but rather one repetition among many in a genealogy of performance that dates from at least 1710. In such obsequies, the dead actor stood in for the Bard, who stood in for the imagined community, summoned into illusory fullness of being by the performance of what it thought it was not. Unlike the anxious atmosphere of homophobia and misogyny that produced the transvestite liminality necessary to Olivier's apotheosis as a surrogated double, however, the sacred monsters of earlier times were produced by 'playing off' the circum-Atlantic world's obsession with race.

In a sombre, even haunting *Tatler* number (4 May 1710), Richard Steele recounts his evening walk to the cloisters of Westminster Abbey, there to attend the interment of the remains of Thomas Betterton, the most celebrated actor of that age. As Steele stands in the lengthening shadows of the burial place of English kings, awaiting the corpse of a stage player, he reflects on the kindred significance of two kinds of performance: first, the public rites and obsequies accorded to the venerated dead; second, the expressive power and the didactic gravity of the stage. 'There is no Human Invention,' he concludes, 'so aptly calculated for the forming a Free-born people as that of a Theatre.'[30] In the civic-minded, Augustan language of liberal moral instruction, Steele's eulogy sets forth the principal argument that I am trying to make about the stimulus of restored behaviour to the production of cultural memory in the crucible of human difference along the circum-Atlantic rim.

Betterton's funeral in 1710 marked the end of a fifty-year career (some have called it a 'reign') on the London stage. In that time, he played over 183 roles in every genre, 131 of which he created.[31] Contemporaries took pride in Betterton's link to Shakespeare through bodily memory across the gulf of the Interregnum: the actor learned the physical business and intonations of some roles from Davenant, who claimed to have learned them from Taylor, whom Shakespeare supposedly coached in person. In an age that had a low opinion of actors and actresses on principle, Betterton's burial in Westminster Abbey was momentous. When Steele surveyed the entirety of the English Roscius's career, however, he chose one special role from the 183 to demonstrate the defining power of theatrical performance in 'the forming of a Free-born people':

I have hardly a Notion that any Performer of Antiquity could surpass the Action of Mr. *Betterton* on any of the Occasions in which he has appeared on our Stage. The wonderful Agony which he appeared in, when he examined the Circumstances of the Handkerchief in *Othello*; the Mixture of Love that intruded upon his Mind upon the innocent Answers *Desdemona* makes, betrayed in his Gesture such a Variety and Vicissitude of Passions, as would admonish a Man to be afraid of his own Heart, and perfectly convince him, that it is to stab it, to admit that worst of Daggers, Jealousy. Whoever reads in his Closet this admirable Scene, will find that he cannot, except he has as warm an Imagination as *Shakespeare* himself, find any but dry, incoherent, and broken Sentences: but a Reader that has seen *Betterton* act it, observes there could not be a Word added; that longer Speech had been unnatural, nay impossible, in *Othello's* Circumstances. The charming Passage in the same Tragedy, where he tells the Manner of winning the Affection of his Mistress, was urged with so moving and graceful and Energy, that while I walked in the Cloysters [of Westminster Abbey], I thought of him with the same Concern as if I waited for the Remains of a Person who had in real Life done all that I had seen him represent.[32]

Betterton, paragon of Anglo orature, vessel of its collective memory, thus doubles Shakespeare in Steele's vision of 'forming a Free-born people', but he does so wearing blackface, just as Thomas Jefferson did it in war paint, and Lord Olivier more recently played it in drag.

In circum-Atlantic terms, canon formation in European culture parallels the spiritual principle to which bell hooks, in her essay on 'Black Indians', attributes the deep affinity of African and Native American peoples: 'that the dead stay among us so that we will not forget'.[33] This principle animates the deeply moving account by Kwame Anthony Appiah of the funeral of his father, in whose house, we are made to understand, were many mansions: 'Only something so particular as a single life – as my father's life, encapsulated in the complex pattern of social and personal relations around his coffin – could capture the multiplicity of our lives in the postcolonial world.'[34] Around the Atlantic rim today, this principle of memory and identity still provokes intercultural struggles over the possession of the dead by the living. These struggles take many forms, of which the most remarkable are those in which the participatory techniques of orature – people speaking in one another's voices – predominate.

Last year in New Orleans, Joe August, the rhythm and blues pioneer known as 'Mr. Google Eyes', was buried 'with music'. To be buried with music in New Orleans means that the ordinary service will be followed by what the death notices call a 'traditional Jazz Funeral'. Jazz funerals represent festive occasions in the community – no disrespect for the dead intended. As Willie Pajaud, trumpeter for the Eureka Brass Band, put it: 'I'd rather play a funeral than eat a turkey dinner.'[35] Well-known and esteemed local musicians, black or white, will likely receive such a send off, and Joe August, who recorded 'Poppa Stoppa's Be-Bop Blues' for Coleman Records, and 'No Wine, No Women' and 'Rough and Rocky Road' for Columbia, who also wrote one of Johnny Ace's biggest hits, 'Please Forgive Me', and who founded the activist agency Blacks That Give a Damn, qualified on both counts.[36] Before the Olympia Brass Band led the way to the cemetery, Malcolm Rebennack, better known as Dr John, the white jazz celebrity, eulogised Joe August thus: 'it is with great pride that we carry the message of the blues that you instilled in us as children.'[37]

The festive procession of the Jazz Funeral then followed, and Joe August's remains were escorted towards the cemetery by a crowd of mourners, following the elegant grand marshal (or 'Nelson') and the band, in a restoration of behaviour that participants trace to West Africa, a recreated diasporic memory.[38] Gwendolyn Midlo Hall, in her magisterial *Africans in*

Colonial Louisiana, documents the discrete pattern whereby the French imported slaves from one area of West Africa. Following the Treaty of Utrecht in 1713, the French slavers evaded the British domination of the West Indian slave trade (and eschewed the British practice of mixing together African peoples from different language groups and cultures) by concentrating on Mandekan-speaking peoples from Senegambia. One consequence of this French policy was a cohesion and continuity in Louisiana slave society that enabled it to retain performance-rich African traditions relatively intact, including celebrations of death founded on religious belief in the participation of ancestral spirits in the world of the present. After the suppression of the great slave revolt of 1795, for instance, 'festivals of the dead', held in defiance of the authorities, honoured the executed freedom fighters.[39]

In opposition to the official voice of history, which, like Aeneas looking back on the pillar of smoke, has tended to emphasise the cultural annihilations of the diaspora, the voice of collective memory, which derives from performance, speaks of the stubborn reinventiveness of restored behaviour. Funerals offer an occasion for the playing out of what James C. Scott, in *Domination and the Arts of Resistance*, calls 'hidden transcripts'.[40] Translating Scott's terms to the history of Afrocentric funeral rites in Louisiana, 'festivals of the dead' became a vehicle for the covert expression of officially discouraged solidarity masked by publicly permissible expressions of mourning. The fact of broad participation itself, then, may silently resist the dominant public transcript by affirming the rites of collective memory. When the French naturalist Claude C. Robin visited New Orleans at the time of the sale of Louisiana to the United States, he remarked: 'I have noticed especially in the city that the funerals of white people are only attended by a few, those of coloured people are attended by a crowd, and mulattoes, quadroons married to white people, do not disdain attending the funeral of a black.'[41] Such a performance event opens up, with its formal repetitions, a space for play. Its genius for participation resides in the very expandability of the procession: marchers with very different connections to the deceased (or perhaps no connections at all) join together on the occasion to make connections with one another. In 1962, Richard Allen, an observer of the revellers in the most joyous part of a Jazz Funeral (after the body is 'cut loose' and sent on its way), noted: 'At least two boys and two women dancing with partners of opposite sex and colour.'[42] In the midst of this extraordinary Afrocentric ritual, however, in the very space it has created for memory as improvisation, the process of circum-Atlantic surrogation unfolds. Dr John, who eulogised Joe August, is a white man who takes his stage name from the formidable, nineteenth-century New Orleans Voodoo, alias Bayou John, who intimidated slaves and slaveholders alike. Malcolm Rebennack spoke the eulogy under his own name as a carrier of the 'message of blues', instilled in him by Joe August, but he records and performs under the assumed name of Dr John, who claimed that he was a Senegalese Prince, whose face was scarified in the African manner, and whose voice, it was said, could be heard from two miles away.[43] Perhaps it can be heard across surprising expanses of time as well.

In 1960, Joe August, who got his stage name for the way he once looked at a waitress, was arrested and charged under Louisiana's antimiscegenation law. Although the charges were eventually dropped, his career, as his obituary put it, 'slowed'. The state of liminality, like the State of Louisiana, both of which ethnographers find so rich in cultural expressiveness, can be very hard on the people who are actually trying to live there. In relation to southern protocols of ocular circumspection between the races, the adoption of 'Mr. Google Eyes' as a stage name proved a tactless choice. Joe August cut his last record in 1963, nearly thirty years before his death.[44]

Like the fate of the chaconne in the seventeenth century, the contributions of other cultures to Western forms tend to become disembodied as 'influences', distancing them from their original contexts (and from the likelihood of a contract for their initiators). This form of reversed ventriloquism permeates circum-Atlantic performance, of which American popular culture is now the most ubiquitous and fungible nectar. The voice of African-American rhythm and blues carries awesomely over time and distance, through its cadences, its intonations, its accompaniment, and even its gestures. Elvis Presley, like Dr John, inverted the doubling pattern of minstrelsy – black music pours from a white face – and this surrogation has begotten others. It seems to me that the degree to which this voice haunts American memory, the degree to which it promotes obsessive attempts at simulation and impersonation, derives from its ghostly power to insinuate memory between the lines, in spaces between the words, in the intonation and placements by which they are shaped, in the silences by which they are deepened or contradicted. By such means, the dead remain among the living. This is the purview of orature, where poetry travels on the tips of tongues and memory flourishes as the opportunity to participate.

Yet, as I hope I have demonstrated, such memories haunt literature – the libretto of *Dido and Aeneas*, a *Tatler* paper – as pervasively, if not as overtly, as they inhabit orature. At the outset, I identified performance as the transformation of experience through the renewal of its cultural forms. I want to conclude with the possibility that the study of performance might assist in the ongoing renovation of the discipline of English – not simply as an additive to the coverage model of specialties in period and genre, but as a transformative force, revising the place of literature in relation to other cultural forms. In my own work I have tried to recognise that poems, essays, and plays are not simply texts – a recognition that is particularly difficult to achieve when virtually all phenomena, from cityscapes to Madonna videos, are read as texts. Rather, literary texts participate in a world system, the relationship of whose parts are obscured by the conditions of their local production and often ignored by a discipline that devalues any form of production except the textual – with the bizarre exception of conference papers.

Although theories of colonial and postcolonial discourse have done a great deal to liberate the field from the confines of its academic insularity, the relation of a text to its colonial or postcolonial context is most frequently presented as a process in which the insular text is constituted by its opposition to a racial or cultural Other. But that formulation reduces the Other to a role of simple instrumentality in a process that is effective only to the extent that it erases its instrument. Genealogies of performance, however, resist such erasures by taking into account the give and take of transmissions, posted in the past, arriving in the present, delivered by living messengers, speaking in tongues not entirely their own. Orature is an art of listening as well as speaking; improvisation is an art of collective memory as well as invention; repetition is an art of recreation as well as restoration. Texts may obscure what performance tends to reveal: memory challenges history in the construction of circum-Atlantic cultures, and it revises the yet unwritten epic of their fabulous cocreation.

11

'Jewels Brought from Bondage': Black Music and the Politics of Authenticity

Paul Gilroy

My nationality is reality.
>   (Kool G Rap)

Since the mid-nineteenth century a country's music has become a political ideology by stressing national characteristics, appearing as a representative of the nation, and everywhere confirming the national principle...Yet music, more than any other artistic medium, expresses the national principle's antinomics as well.

>   (T. W. Adorno)

O black and unknown bards of long ago,
How came your lips to touch the sacred fire?
How in your darkness, did you come to know
The power and beauty of the minstrel's lyre?
Who first from midst his bonds lifted his eyes?
Who first from out the still watch, lone and long,
Feeling the ancient faith of prophets rise
Within his dark-kept soul burst into song?
Heart of what slave poured out such melody

As 'Steal away to Jesus'? On its strains
His spirit must have nightly floated free,
Though still about his hands he felt his chains.
Who heard great 'Jordan Roll'? Whose starward eye
Saw chariot 'swing low'? And who was he
That breathed that comforting melodic sigh,
'Nobody knows de trouble I see'?

>   (James Weldon Johnson)

The contemporary debates over modernity and its possible eclipse have largely ignored music. This is odd given that the modern differentiation of the true, the good, and the beautiful was conveyed directly in the transformation of public use of culture in general and the increased public importance of all kinds of music.[1] I have suggested that the critiques of modernity articulated by successive generations of black intellectuals had their rhizomorphic systems of propagation anchored in a continued proximity to the unspeakable terrors of the slave experience. I argued that this critique was nurtured by a deep sense of the complicity of racial terror with reason. The resulting ambivalence towards modernity has constituted some of the most distinctive forces shaping black Atlantic political culture. What follows will develop this argument in a slightly different direction by exploring some of the ways in which closeness to the ineffable terrors of slavery was kept alive – carefully cultivated – in ritualised, social forms.

The question of racial terror always remains in view when these modernisms are discussed because imaginative proximity to terror is their inaugural experience. This focus is refined somewhat in the progression from slave society into the era of imperialism. Though they were unspeakable, these terrors were not inexpressible, and my main aim here is to explore how residual traces of their necessarily painful expression still contribute to historical memories inscribed and incorporated into the volatile core of Afro-Atlantic cultural creation. Thinking about the primary object of this chapter – black musics – requires this reorientation towards the phatic and the ineffable.

Through a discussion of music and its attendant social relations, I want to clarify some of the distinctive attributes of black cultural forms which are both modern and modernist. They are modern because they have been marked by their hybrid, creole origins in the West, because they have struggled to escape their status as commodities and the position within the cultural industries it specifies, and because they are produced by artists whose understanding of their own position relative to the racial group and of the role of art in mediating individual creativity with social dynamics is shaped by a sense of artistic practice as an autonomous domain either reluctantly or happily divorced from the everyday lifeworld.

These expressive cultural forms are thus western and modern, but this is not all they are. I want to suggest that their special power derives from a doubleness, their unsteady location simultaneously inside and outside the conventions, assumptions, and aesthetic rules which distinguish and periodise modernity. These musical forms and the intercultural conversations to which they contribute are a dynamic refutation of the Hegelian suggestions that thought and reflection have outstripped art and that art is opposed to philosophy as the lowest, merely conscious form of reconciliation between nature and finite reality.[2] The stubborn modernity of these black musical forms would require a reordering of Hegel's modern hierarchy of cultural achievements. This might claim, for example, that music should enjoy higher status because of its capacity to express a direct image of the slaves' will.

The anti-modernity of these forms, like their anteriority, appears in the (dis)guise of a premodernity that is both actively reimagined in the present and transmitted intermittently in eloquent pulses from the past. It seeks not simply to change the relationship of these cultural forms to newly autonomous philosophy and science but to refuse the categories on which the relative evaluation of these separate domains is based and thereby to transform the relationship between the production and use of art, the everyday world, and the project of racial emancipation.

The topos of unsayability produced from the slaves' experiences of racial terror and figured repeatedly in nineteenth-century evaluations of slave music has other important implications. It can be used to challenge the privileged conceptions of both language and writing as pre-eminent expressions of human consciousness. The power and significance of music within the black Atlantic have grown in inverse proportion to the limited expressive power of language. It is important to remember that the slaves' access to literacy was often denied on pain of death and only a few cultural opportunities were offered as a surrogate for the other forms of individual autonomy denied by life on the plantations and in the barracoons. Music becomes vital at the point at which linguistic and semantic indeterminacy/polyphony arise amidst the protracted battle between masters, mistresses, and slaves. This decidedly modern conflict was the product of circumstances where language lost something of its referentiality and its privileged relationship to concepts.[3] In his narrative, Frederick Douglass raised this point when discussing Gore, the overseer who illustrates the relationship between the rationalism of the slave system and its terror and barbarity:

Mr Gore was a grave man, and, though a young man, he indulged in no jokes, said no funny words, seldom smiled. His words were in perfect keeping with his looks, and his looks were in perfect keeping with his words. Overseers will sometimes indulge in a witty word, even with the slaves; not so with Mr Gore. He spoke but to command, and commanded but to be obeyed; he dealt sparingly with words, and bountifully with his whip, never using the former where the latter would answer as well... His savage barbarity was equalled only by the consummate coolness with which he committed the grossest and most savage deeds upon the slaves under his charge.[4]

Examining the place of music in the black Atlantic world means surveying the self-understanding articulated by the musicians who have made it, the symbolic use to which their music is put by other black artists and writers, and the social relations which have produced and reproduced the unique expres-

sive culture in which music comprises a central and even foundational element. I want to propose that the possible commonality of post-slave, black
cultural forms be approached via several related problems which converge in
the analysis of black musics and their supporting social relations. One particularly valuable pathway into this is provided by the distinctive patterns of
language use that characterise the contrasting populations of the modern,
western, African diaspora.[5] The oral character of the cultural settings in
which diaspora musics have developed presupposes a distinctive relationship
to the body – an idea expressed with exactly the right amount of impatience by
Glissant: 'It is nothing new to declare that for us music, gesture, dance are
forms of communication, just as important as the gift of speech. This is how
we first managed to emerge from the plantation: aesthetic form in our cultures
must be shaped from these oral structures.'[6]

The distinctive kinesics of the post-slave populations was the product of
these brutal historical conditions. Though more usually raised by analysis of
sports, athletics, and dance it ought to contribute directly to the understanding
of the traditions of performance which continue to characterise the production
and reception of diaspora musics. This orientation to the specific dynamics of
performance has a wider significance in the analysis of black cultural forms
than has so far been supposed. Its strengths are evident when it is contrasted
with approaches to black culture that have been premised exclusively on
textuality and narrative rather than dramaturgy, enunciation, and gesture –
the pre- and anti-discursive constituents of black metacommunication.

Each of these areas merits detailed treatment in its own right.[7] All of them
are configured by their compound and multiple origins in the mix of African
and other cultural forms sometimes referred to as creolisation. However, my
main concern in this chapter is less with the formal attributes of these
syncretic expressive cultures than with the problem of how critical, evalu-
ative, axiological, (anti)aesthetic judgements on them can be made and with
the place of ethnicity and authenticity within these judgements. What special
analytical problems arise if a style, genre, or particular performance of music
is identified as being expressive of the absolute essence of the group that
produced it? What contradictions appear in the transmission and adaptation
of this cultural expression by other diaspora populations, and how will they
be resolved? How does the hemispheric displacement and global dissemination of black music get reflected in localised traditions of critical writing,
and, once the music is perceived as a world phenomenon, what value is
placed upon its origins, particularly if they come into opposition against
further mutations produced during its contingent loops and fractal trajec-
tories? Where music is thought to be emblematic and constitutive of racial
difference rather than just associated with it, how is music used to specify
general issues pertaining to the problem of racial authenticity and the
consequent self-identity of the ethnic group? Thinking about music – a

non-representational, non-conceptual form – raises aspects of embodied subjectivity that are not reducible to the cognitive and the ethical. These questions are also useful in trying to pin-point the distinctive aesthetic components in black communication.

The invented traditions of musical expression which are my object here are equally important in the study of diaspora blacks and modernity because they have supported the formation of a distinct, often priestly caste of organic intellectuals[8] whose experiences enable us to focus upon the crisis of modernity and modern values with special clarity. These people have often been intellectuals in the Gramscian sense, operating without the benefits that flow either from a relationship to the modern state or from secure institutional locations within the cultural industries. They have often pursued roles that escape categorisation as the practice of either legislators or interpreters and have advanced instead as temporary custodians of a distinct and embattled cultural sensibility which has also operated as a political and philosophical resource. The irrepressible rhythms of the once forbidden drum are often still audible in their work. Its characteristic syncopations still animate the basic desires – to be free and to be oneself – that are revealed in this counterculture's unique conjunction of body and music. Music, the grudging gift that supposedly compensated slaves not only for their exile from the ambiguous legacies of practical reason but for their complete exclusion from modern political society, has been refined and developed so that it provides an enhanced mode of communication beyond the petty power of words – spoken or written.

Paradoxically, in the light of their origins in the most modern of social relations at the end of the eighteenth century, modernity's ethnocentric aesthetic assumptions have consigned these musical creations to a notion of the primitive that was intrinsic to the consolidation of scientific racism. The creators of this musically infused subculture and counter-power are perhaps more accurately described as midwives, an appropriate designation following Julia Kristeva's provocative pointers towards the 'feminisation' of the ethical bases from which dissident political action is possible.[9] They stand their ground at the social pivot of atavistic nature and rational culture. I want to endorse the suggestion that these subversive music makers and users represent a different kind of intellectual not least because their self-identity and their practice of cultural politics remain outside the dialectic of pity and guilt which, especially among oppressed people, has so often governed the relationship between the writing elite and the masses of people who exist outside literacy. I also want to ask whether for black cultural theory to embrace or even accept this mediated, tactical relationship to the unrepresentable, the pre-rational, and the sublime would be to sip from a poisoned chalice. These questions have become politically decisive since these cultural forms have colonised the interstices of the cultural industry on behalf not just of black Atlantic peoples but of the poor, exploited, and downpressed everywhere.

The current debate over modernity centres either on the problematic relationships between politics and aesthetics or on the question of science and its association with the practice of domination.[10] Few of these debates operate at the interface of science and aesthetics which is the required starting point of contemporary black cultural expression and the digital technology of its social dissemination and reproduction. These debates over modernity conventionally define the political instance of the modern social totality through a loose invocation of the achievements of bourgeois democracy. The discrete notion of the aesthetic, in relation to which this self-sustaining political domain is then evaluated, is constructed by the idea and the ideology of the text and of textuality as a mode of communicative practice which provides a model for all other forms of cognitive exchange and social interaction. Urged on by the poststructuralist critiques of the metaphysics of presence, contemporary debates have moved beyond citing language as the fundamental analogy for comprehending all signifying practices to a position where textuality (especially when wrenched open through the concept of difference) expands and merges with totality. Paying careful attention to the structures of feeling which underpin black expressive cultures can show how this critique is incomplete. It gets blocked by this invocation of all-encompassing textuality. Textuality becomes a means to evacuate the problem of human agency, a means to specify the death (by fragmentation) of the subject and, in the same manoeuvre, to enthrone the literary critic as mistress or master of the domain of creative human communication.

At the risk of appearing rather esoteric, I want to suggest that the history and practice of black music point to other possibilities and generate other plausible models. This neglected history is worth reconstructing, whether or not it supplies pointers to other more general cultural processes. However, I want to suggest that bourgeois democracy in the genteel metropolitan guise in which it appeared at the dawn of the public sphere should not serve as an ideal type for all modern political processes. Secondly, I want to shift concern with the problems of beauty, taste and artistic judgement, so that discussion is not circumscribed by the idea of rampant, invasive textuality. Foregrounding the history of black music making encourages both of these propositions. It also requires a different register of analytic concepts. This demand is amplified by the need to make sense of musical performances in which identity is fleetingly experienced in the most intensive ways and sometimes socially reproduced by means of neglected modes of signifying practice like mimesis, gesture, kinesis, and costume. Antiphony (call and response) is the principal formal feature of these musical traditions. It has come to be seen as a bridge from music into other modes of cultural

expression, supplying, along with improvisation, montage, and dramaturgy, the hermeneutic keys to the full medley of black artistic practices.
[...]

The intense and often bitter dialogues which make the black arts movement move offer a small reminder that there is a democratic, communitarian moment enshrined in the practice of antiphony which symbolises and anticipates (but does not guarantee) new, non-dominating social relationships. Lines between self and other are blurred and special forms of pleasure are created as a result of the meetings and conversations that are established between one fractured, incomplete, and unfinished racial self and others. Antiphony is the structure that hosts these essential encounters. Ralph Ellison's famous observation on the inner dynamics of jazz production uses visual art as its central analogy but it can be readily extended beyond the specific context it was written to illuminate:

> There is in this a cruel contradiction implicit in the art form itself. For true jazz is an art of individual assertion within and against the group. Each true jazz moment ... springs from a contest in which the artist challenges all the rest; each solo flight, or improvisation, represents (like the canvasses of a painter) a definition of his [*sic*] identity: as individual, as member of the collectivity and as a link in the chain of tradition. Thus because jazz finds its very life in improvisation upon traditional materials, the jazz man must lose his identity even as he finds it ... [11]

This quote offers a reminder that apart from the music and the musicians themselves, we must also take account of the work of those within the expressive culture of the black Atlantic who have tried to use its music as an aesthetic, political, or philosophical marker in the production of what might loosely be called their critical social theories. Here it is necessary to consider the work of a whole host of exemplary figures: ex-slaves, preachers, self-educated scholars and writers, as well as a small number of professionals and the tiny minority who managed to acquire some sort of academic position in essentially segregated educational systems or took advantage of opportunities in Liberia, Haiti, and other independent states. This company spreads out in discontinuous, transverse lines of descent that stretch outwards across the Atlantic from Phyllis Wheatley onwards. Its best feature is an anti-hierarchical tradition of thought that probably culminates in C. L. R. James's idea that ordinary people do not need an intellectual vanguard to help them to speak or to tell them what to say. [12] Repeatedly, within this expressive culture it is musicians who are presented as living symbols of the value of self-activity. [13] This is often nothing more or less than a question of style.

The basic labours of archaeological reconstruction and periodisation aside, working on the contemporary forms of black expressive culture involves struggling with one problem in particular. It is the puzzle of what analytic status should be given to the variation within black communities and between black cultures which their musical habits reveal. The tensions produced by attempts to compare or evaluate differing black cultural formations can be summed up in the following question: How are we to think critically about artistic products and aesthetic codes which, though they may be traceable back to one distinct location, have been changed either by the passage of time or by their displacement, relocation, or dissemination through networks of communication and cultural exchange? This question serves as a receptacle for several even more awkward issues. They include the unity and differentiation of the creative black self, the vexed matter of black particularity, and the role of cultural expression in its formation and reproduction. These problems are especially acute because black thinkers have been unable to appeal to the authoritative narratives of psychoanalysis as a means to ground the cross-cultural aspirations of their theories. With a few noble exceptions, critical accounts of the dynamics of black subordination and resistance have been doggedly monocultural, national, and ethnocentric. This impoverishes modern black cultural history because the transnational structures which brought the black Atlantic world into being have themselves developed and now articulate its myriad forms into a system of global communications constituted by flows. This fundamental dislocation of black culture is especially important in the recent history of black musics which, produced out of the racial slavery which made modern western civilisation possible, now dominate its popular cultures.

In the face of the conspicuous differentiation and proliferation of black cultural styles and genres, a new analytic orthodoxy has begun to grow. In the name of anti-essentialism and theoretical rigour it suggests that since black particularity is socially and historically constructed, and plurality has become inescapable, the pursuit of any unifying dynamic or underlying structure of feeling in contemporary black cultures is utterly misplaced. The attempt to locate the cultural practices, motifs, or political agendas that might connect the dispersed and divided blacks of the new world and of Europe with each other and even with Africa is dismissed as essentialism or idealism or both.[14]

The alternative position sketched out in the rest of this chapter offers a tentative rebuke to that orthodoxy which I regard as premature in its dismissal of the problem of theorising black identity. I suggest that weighing the similarities and differences between black cultures remains an urgent concern. This response relies crucially on the concept of diaspora.[15] For present purposes I want to state that diaspora is still indispensable in focusing on the political and ethical dynamics of the unfinished history of blacks in the modern world. The dangers of idealism and pastoralisation associated with this concept ought, by now, to be obvious, but the very least that it offers is an heuristic means to focus on the relationship of identity and non-identity in black political culture. It can also be employed to project the plural richness of black cultures in different parts of the world in counterpoint to their common sensibilities – both those residually inherited from Africa and those generated from the special bitterness of new world racial slavery. This is not an easy matter. The proposition that the post-slave cultures of the Atlantic world are in some significant way related to one another and to the African cultures from which they partly derive has long been a matter of great controversy capable of arousing intense feeling which goes far beyond dispassionate scholastic contemplation. The situation is rendered even more complex by the fact that the fragile psychological, emotional, and cultural correspondences which connect diaspora populations in spite of their manifest differences are often apprehended only fleetingly and in ways that persistently confound the protocols of academic orthodoxy. There is, however, a great body of work which justifies the proposition that some cultural, religious, and linguistic affiliations can be identified even if their contemporary political significance remains disputed. There are also valuable though underutilised leads to be found in the work of the feminist political thinkers, cultural critics, and philosophers who have formulated stimulating conceptions of the relationship between identity and difference in the context of advancing the political projects of female emancipation.[16]

UK BLAK

The issue of the identity and non-identity of black cultures has acquired a special historical and political significance in Britain. Black settlement in that country goes back many centuries, and affirming its continuity has become an important part of the politics that strive to answer contemporary British racism. However, the bulk of today's black communities are of relatively recent origin, dating only from the post-World War II period. If these populations are unified at all, it is more by the experience of migration than by the memory of slavery and the residues of plantation society. Until recently, this very newness and conspicuous lack of rootedness in the 'indigenous' cultures of Britain's inner cities conditioned the formation of racial subcultures which drew heavily from a range of 'raw materials' supplied by the Caribbean and black America. This was true even where these subcultures also contributed to the unsteady equilibrium of antagonistic class relationships into which Britain's black settlers found themselves inserted as racially subordinated migrant labourers but also as working-class black settlers.

The musics of the black Atlantic world were the primary expressions of cultural distinctiveness which this population seized upon and adapted to its new circumstances. It used the separate but converging musical traditions of the black Atlantic world, if not to create itself anew as a conglomeration of black communities, then as a means to gauge the social progress of spontaneous self-creation which was sedimented together by the endless pressures of economic exploitation, political racism, displacement, and exile. This musical heritage gradually became an important factor in facilitating the transition of diverse settlers to a distinct mode of lived blackness. It was instrumental in producing a constellation of subject positions that was openly indebted for its conditions of possibility to the Caribbean, the United States, and even Africa. It was also indelibly marked by the British conditions in which it grew and matured.

It is essential to appreciate that this type of process has not been confined to settlers of Afro-Caribbean descent. In reinventing their own ethnicity, some of Britain's Asian settlers have also borrowed the sound system culture of the Caribbean and the soul and hip hop styles of black America, as well as techniques like mixing, scratching, and sampling as part of their invention of a new mode of cultural production with an identity to match.[17] The popularity of Apache Indian[18] and Bally Sagoo's[19] attempts to fuse Punjabi music and language with reggae music and raggamuffin style raised debates about the authenticity of these hybrid cultural forms to an unprecedented pitch. The experience of Caribbean migrants to Britain provides further examples of complex cultural exchange and of the ways in which a self-consciously synthetic culture can support some equally novel political identities. The cultural and political histories of Guyana, Jamaica, Barbados, Grenada, Trinidad, and St Lucia, like the economic forces at work in generating their respective migrations to Europe, are widely dissimilar. Even if it were possible, let alone desirable, their synthesis into a single black British culture could never have been guaranteed by the effects of racism alone. Thus the role of external meanings around blackness, drawn in particular from black America, became important in the elaboration of a connective culture which drew these different 'national' groups together into a new pattern that was not ethnically marked in the way that their Caribbean cultural inheritances had been. Reggae, a supposedly stable and authentic category, provides a useful example here. Once its own hybrid origins in rhythm and blues were effectively concealed,[20] it ceased, in Britain, to signify an exclusively ethnic, Jamaican style and derived a different kind of cultural legitimacy both from a new global status and from its expression of what might be termed a pan-Caribbean culture.

The style, rhetoric, and moral authority of the civil rights movement and of Black Power suffered similar fates. They too were detached from their original ethnic markers and historical origins, exported and adapted, with evident respect but little sentimentality, to local needs and political climates. Appearing in Britain through a circulatory system that gave a central place to the musics which had both informed and recorded black struggles in other places, they were rearticulated in distinctively European conditions. How the appropriation of these forms, styles, and histories of struggle was possible at such great physical and social distance is in itself an interesting question for cultural historians. It was facilitated by a common fund of urban experiences, by the effect of similar but by no means identical forms of racial segregation, as well as by the memory of slavery, a legacy of Africanisms, and a stock of religious experiences defined by them both. Dislocated from their original conditions of existence, the sound tracks of this African-American cultural broadcast fed a new metaphysics of blackness elaborated and enacted in Europe and elsewhere within the underground, alternative, public spaces constituted around an expressive culture that was dominated by music.

The inescapably political language of citizenship, racial justice, and equality was one of several discourses which contributed to this transfer of cultural and political forms and structures of feeling. A commentary on the relationship of work to leisure and the respective forms of freedom with which these opposing worlds become identified provided a second linking principle. A folk historicism animating a special fascination with history and the significance of its recovery by those who have been expelled from the official dramas of civilisation was a third component here. The representation of sexuality and gender identity, in particular the ritual public projection of the antagonistic relationship between black women and men in ways that invited forms of identification strong enough to operate across the line of colour, was the fourth element within this vernacular cultural and philosophical formation dispersed through the musics of the black Atlantic world.

The conflictual representation of sexuality has vied with the discourse of racial emancipation to constitute the inner core of black expressive cultures. Common rhetorical strategies developed through the same repertory of enunciative procedures have helped these discourses to become interlinked. Their association was pivotal, for example, in the massive secularisation that produced soul out of rhythm and blues, and it persists today. It can be easily observed in the bitter conflict over the misogynist tone and masculinist direction of hip hop. Hip hop culture has recently provided the raw material for a bitter contest between black vernacular expression and repressive censorship of artistic work. This has thrown some black commentators into a quandary which they have resolved by invoking the rhetoric of cultural insiderism and drawing the comforting cloak of absolute ethnicity even more tightly around their anxious shoulders. The most significant recent illustration of this is provided by the complex issues stemming from the obscenity trial of 2 Live Crew, a Florida-based rap act led by Luther Cambell, a commercially minded black American of Jamaican descent. This episode is not notable because the forms of misogyny that attracted the attention of the police and the district attorneys were new.[21] Its importance lay in the fact that it was the occasion for an important public intervention by black America's best known academic and cultural critic, Henry Louis Gates, Jr.[22] Gates went beyond simply affirming the artistic status of this particular hip hop product, arguing in full effect that the Crew's material was a manifestation of distinctively black cultural traditions which operated by particular satirical codes where one man's misogyny turns out to be another man's parodic play. Rakim, the most gifted rap poet of the eighties, had a very different perspective on the authenticity of 2 Live Crew's output.

> That [the 2 Live Crew situation] ain't my problem. Some people might think it's our problem because rap is one big happy family. When I make my bed, I lay on it. I don't say nothin' I can't stand up for, 'cause I seen one interview, where they asked him [Luther Cambell] a question and he started talkin' all this about black culture. That made everybody on the rap tip look kinda dense. He was sayin' 'Yo this is my culture.' That's not culture at all.[23]

It is striking that apologists for the woman-hating antics of 2 Live Crew and other similar performers have been so far unconcerned that the vernacular tradition they rightly desire to legitimise and protect has its own record of reflection on the specific ethical obligations and political responsibilities which constitute the unique burden of the black artist. Leaving the question of misogyny aside for a moment, to collude in the belief that black vernacular is *nothing* other than a playful, parodic cavalcade of Rabelaisian subversion decisively weakens the positions of the artist, the critical commentator, and the community as a whole. What is more significant is surely the failure of either academic or journalistic commentary on black popular music in America to develop a reflexive political aesthetics capable of distinguishing 2 Live Crew and their ilk from their equally authentic but possibly more compelling and certainly more constructive peers.

I am not suggesting that the self-conscious racial pedagogy of recognisably political artists like KRS1, the Poor Righteous Teachers, Lakim Shabazz, or the X Clan should be straightforwardly counterposed against the carefully calculated affirmative nihilism of Ice Cube, Tim Dog, the Ghetto Boys, Above the Law, and Compton's Most Wanted. The different styles and political perspectives expressed within the music are linked both by the bonds of a stylised but aggressively masculinist discourse and by formal borrowings from the linguistic innovations of Jamaica's distinct modes of 'kinetic orality'.[24] This debt to Caribbean forms, which can only undermine the definition of hip hop as an exclusively American product, is more openly acknowledged in the ludic Africentrisms of the Jungle Brothers, De La Soul, and A Tribe Called Quest, which may represent a third alternative – both in its respectful and egalitarian representation of women and in its more ambivalent relationship to America and Americanism. The stimulating and innovative work of this last group of artists operates a rather different, eccentric conception of black authenticity that effectively contrasts the local (black nationalism) with the global (black internationalism) and measures Americanism against the appeal of Ethiopianism and pan-Africanism. It is important to emphasise that all three strands within hip hop – pedagogy, affirmation, and play – contribute to a folk-cultural constellation where neither the political compass of weary leftism nor the shiny navigational instruments of premature black postmodernism[25] in aesthetics have so far offered very much that is useful.

In dealing with the relationship of race to class it has been commonplace to recall Stuart Hall's suggestive remark that the former is the modality in which the latter is lived. The tale of 2 Live Crew and the central place of sexuality in the contemporary discourses of racial particularity point to an analogous formulation that may prove equally wieldy: gender is the modality in which race is lived. An amplified and exaggerated masculinity has become the boastful centrepiece of a culture of compensation that self-consciously salves the misery of the disempowered and subordinated. This masculinity and its relational feminine counterpart become special symbols of the difference that race makes. They are lived and naturalised in the distinct patterns of family life on which the reproduction of the racial identities supposedly relies. These gender identities come to exemplify the immutable cultural differences that apparently arise from absolute ethnic difference. To question them and their constitution of racial subjectivity is at once to be ungendered and to place oneself outside of the racial kin group. This makes these positions hard to answer, let alone criticise. Experiencing racial sameness through particular definitions of gender and sexuality has also proved to be eminently exportable. The forms of connectedness and identification it makes possible across space and time cannot be confined within the borders of the nation state and correspond closely to lived experience. They may even create new conceptions of nationality in the conflictual interaction between the women who quietly and privately reproduce the black national community and the men who aspire to be its public soldier citizens.

These links show no sign of fading, but the dependence of blacks in Britain on black cultures produced in the new world has recently begun to change. The current popularity of Jazzie B and Soul II Soul, Maxi Priest, Caron Wheeler, Monie Love, the Young Disciples, and others in the United States confirms that during the eighties black British cultures ceased to simply mimic or reproduce wholesale forms, styles, and genres which had been lovingly borrowed, respectfully stolen, or brazenly highjacked from blacks elsewhere. Critical space/time cartography of the diaspora needs therefore to be readjusted so that the dynamics of dispersal and local autonomy can be shown alongside the unforeseen detours and circuits which mark the new journeys and new arrivals that, in turn, release new political and cultural possibilities.[26]

At certain points during the recent past, British racism has generated turbulent economic, ideological, and political forces that have seemed to act upon the people they oppressed by concentrating their cultural identities into a single powerful configuration. Whether these people were of African, Caribbean, or Asian descent, their commonality was often defined by its reference to the central, irreducible sign of their common racial subordination – the colour black. More recently, though, this fragile unity in action has fragmented and their self-conception has separated into its various constituent elements. The unifying notion of an open blackness has been largely rejected and replaced by more particularistic conceptions of cultural difference. This retreat from a politically constructed notion of racial solidarity has initiated a compensatory recovery of narrowly ethnic culture and identity. Indeed, the aura of authentic ethnicity supplies a special form of comfort in a situation where the very historicity of black experience is constantly undermined.

These political and historical shifts are registered in the cultural realm. The growth of religious fundamentalism among some Asian-descended populations is an obvious sign of their significance, and there may be similar processes at work in the experience of the peoples of Caribbean descent for whom an equivalent retreat into pure ethnicity has acquired pronounced generational features. Their desire to anchor themselves in racial particularity is not dominated by the longing to return to the Victorian certainties and virtues of Caribbean cultural life. However, in conjunction with the pressures of economic recession and populist racism, this yearning has driven many older settlers to return to the lands in which they were born. Among their descendants, the same desire to withdraw has achieved a very different form of expression. It has moved towards an overarching Africentrism which can be read as inventing its own totalising conception of black culture. This new ethnicity is all the more powerful because it corresponds to no actually existing black communities. Its radical utopianism, often anchored in the ethical bedrock provided by the history of the Nile Valley civilisations, transcends the parochialism of Caribbean memories in favour of a heavily mythologised Africanity that is itself stamped by its origins not in Africa but in a variety of pan-African ideology produced most recently by black America. The problems of contemporary Africa are almost completely absent from its concerns. This complex and sometimes radical sensibility has been recently fostered by the more pedagogic and self-consciously politicised elements within hip hop. The 'college-boy rap' of the more edutainment minded groups represents one pole in the field that reproduced it, while the assertive stance of hip hop's narrow nationalists represents the other. This political change can be registered in the deepening splits within hip hop over the language and symbols appropriate for black self-designation and over the relative importance of opposing racism on the one hand, and of elaborating the symbolic forms of black identity on the other. These necessary tasks are not synonymous or even co-extensive though they can be rendered compatible. What is more significant for present purposes is that in the Africentric discourse on which both sides of opinion draw, the idea of a diaspora composed of communities that are both similar *and* different tends to disappear somewhere between the invocations of an African motherland and the powerful critical commentaries on the immediate, local conditions in which a particular performance of a piece of music originates. These complexities aside, hip hop culture is best understood as the latest export from black America to have found favour in black Britain. It is especially interesting then that its success has been built on transnational structures of circulation and intercultural exchange established long ago. [...]

12

Critically Queer

Judith Butler

Discourse is not life; its time is not yours.
> (Michel Foucault, *Politics and the Study of Discourse*)

How is it that a term that signalled degradation has been turned – 'refunctioned' in the Brechtian sense – to signify a new and affirmative set of meanings? Is this a simple reversal of valuations such that 'queer' means either a past degradation or a present or future affirmation? Is this a reversal that retains and reiterates the abjected history of the term? When the term has been used as a paralysing slur, as the mundane interpellation of pathologised sexuality, it has produced the user of the term as the emblem and vehicle of normalisation; the occasion of its utterance, as the discursive regulation of the boundaries of sexual legitimacy. Much of the straight world has always needed the queers it has sought to repudiate through the performative force of the term. If the term is now subject to a reappropriation, what are the conditions and limits of that significant reversal? Does the reversal reiterate the logic of repudiation by which it was spawned? Can the term overcome its constitutive history of injury? Does it present the discursive occasion for a powerful and compelling fantasy of historical reparation? When and how does a term like 'queer' become subject to an affirmative resignification for some when a term like 'nigger', despite some recent efforts at reclamation, appears capable of only reinscribing its pain? How and where does discourse reiterate injury such that the various efforts to recontextualise and resignify a given term meet their limit in this other, more brutal, and relentless form of repetition?[1]

In *On the Genealogy of Morals*, Nietzsche introduces the notion of the 'sign-chain' in which one might read a utopian investment in discourse, one that re-emerges within Foucault's conception of discursive power. Nietzsche writes, 'the entire history of a "thing", an organ, a custom can be a continuous sign-chain of ever new interpretations and adaptations whose causes do not even have to be related to one another but, on the contrary, in some cases succeed and alternate with one another in a purely chance fashion.'[2] The 'ever new' possibilities of resignification are derived from the postulated historical discontinuity of the term. But is this postulation itself suspect? Can

152

resignifiability be derived from a pure historicity of 'signs'? Or must there be a way to think about the constraints on and in resignification that takes account of its propensity to return to the 'ever old' in relations of social power? And can Foucault help us here or does he, rather, reiterate Nietzchean hopefulness within the discourse of power? Investing power with a kind of vitalism, Foucault echoes Nietzsche as he refers to power as 'ceaseless struggles and confrontations ... produced from one moment to the next, at every point, or rather in every relation from one point to another'.[3]

Neither power nor discourse are rendered anew at every moment; they are not as weightless as the utopics of radical resignification might imply. And yet how are we to understand their convergent force as an accumulated effect of usage that both constrains and enables their reworking? How is it that the apparently injurious effects of discourse become the painful resources by which a resignifying practice is wrought? Here it is not only a question of how discourse injures bodies, but how certain injuries establish certain bodies at the limits of available ontologies, available schemes of intelligibility. And further, how is it that the abjected come to make their claim through and against the discourses that have sought their repudiation?

PERFORMATIVE POWER

Eve Sedgwick's recent reflections on queer performativity ask us not only to consider how a certain theory of speech acts applies to queer practices, but how it is that 'queering' persists as a defining moment of performativity.[4] The centrality of the marriage ceremony in J. L. Austin's examples of performativity suggests that the heterosexualisation of the social bond is the paradigmatic form for those speech acts which bring about what they name. 'I pronounce you ...' puts into effect the relation that it names. But from where and when does such a performative draw its force, and what happens to the performative when its purpose is precisely to undo the presumptive force of the heterosexual ceremonial?

Performative acts are forms of authoritative speech: most performatives, for instance, are statements that, in the uttering, also perform a certain action and exercise a binding power.[5] Implicated in a network of authorisation and punishment, performatives tend to include legal sentences, baptisms, inaugurations, declarations of ownership, statements which not only perform an action, but confer a binding power on the action performed. If the power of discourse to produce that which it names is linked with the question of performativity, then the performative is one domain in which power acts *as* discourse.

Importantly, however, there is no power, construed as a subject, that acts, but only, to repeat an earlier phrase, a reiterated acting that *is* power in its persistence and instability. This is less an 'act', singular and deliberate, than a nexus of power and discourse that repeats or mimes the discursive gestures of power. Hence, the judge who authorises and installs the situation he names invariably *cites* the law that he applies, and it is the power of this citation that gives the performative its binding or conferring power. And though it may appear that the binding power of his words is derived from the force of his will or from a prior authority, the opposite is more true: it is *through* the citation of the law that the figure of the judge's 'will' is produced and that the 'priority' of textual authority is established.[6] Indeed, it is through the invocation of convention that the speech act of the judge derives its binding power; that binding power is to be found neither in the subject of the judge nor in his will, but in the citational legacy by which a contemporary 'act' emerges in the context of a chain of binding conventions.

Where there is an 'I' who utters or speaks and thereby produces an effect in discourse, there is first a discourse which precedes and enables that 'I' and forms in language the constraining trajectory of its will. Thus there is no 'I' who stands *behind* discourse and executes its volition or will *through* discourse. On the contrary, the 'I' only comes into being through being called, named, interpellated, to use the Althusserian term, and this discursive constitution takes place prior to the 'I'; it is the transitive invocation of the 'I'. Indeed, I can only say 'I' to the extent that I have first been addressed, and that address has mobilised my place in speech; paradoxically, the discursive condition of social recognition *precedes and conditions* the formation of the subject: recognition is not conferred on a subject, but forms that subject. Further, the impossibility of a full recognition, that is, of ever fully inhabiting the name by which one's social identity is inaugurated and mobilised, implies the instability and incompleteness of subject-formation. The 'I' is thus a citation of the place of the 'I' in speech, where that place has a certain priority and anonymity with respect to the life it animates: it is the historically revisable possibility of a name that precedes and exceeds me, but without which I cannot speak.

QUEER TROUBLE

The term 'queer' emerges as an interpellation that raises the question of the status of force and opposition, of stability and variability, *within* performativity. The term 'queer' has operated as one linguistic practice whose purpose has been the shaming of the subject it names or, rather, the producing of a subject *through* that shaming interpellation. 'Queer' derives its force precisely through the repeated invocation by which it has become linked to accusation, pathologisation, insult. This is an invocation by which a social bond among homophobic communities is formed through time. The interpellation echoes past interpellations, and binds the speakers, as if they spoke in unison across time. In this sense, it is always an imaginary chorus that taunts 'queer!' To what extent, then, has the performative 'queer' operated alongside, as a deformation of, the 'I pronounce you...' of the marriage ceremony? If the performative operates as the sanction that performs the heterosexualisation of the social bond, perhaps it also comes into play precisely as the shaming taboo which 'queers' those who resist or oppose that social form as well as those who occupy it without hegemonic social sanction.

On that note, let us remember that reiterations are never simply replicas of the same. And the 'act' by which a name authorises or deauthorises a set of social or sexual relations is, of necessity, *a repetition*. 'Could a performative succeed,' asks Derrida, 'if its formulation did not repeat a "coded" or iterable utterance... if it were not identifiable in some way as a "citation"?'[7] If a performative provisionally succeeds (and I will suggest that 'success' is always and only provisional), then it is not because an intention successfully governs the action of speech, but only because that action echoes prior actions, and *accumulates the force of authority through the repetition or citation of a prior, authoritative set of practices*. What this means, then, is that a performative 'works' to the extent that *it draws on and covers over* the constitutive conventions by which it is mobilised. In this sense, no term or statement can function performatively without the accumulating and dissimulating historicity of force.

This view of performativity implies that discourse has a history[8] that not only precedes but conditions its contemporary usages, and that this history effectively decentres the presentist view of the subject as the exclusive origin or owner of what is said.[9] What it also means is that the terms to which we do, nevertheless, lay claim, the terms through which we insist on politicising identity and desire, often demand a turn *against* this constitutive historicity. Those of us who have questioned the presentist assumptions in contemporary identity categories are, therefore, sometimes charged with depoliticising theory. And yet, if the genealogical critique of the subject is the interrogation of those constitutive and exclusionary relations of power through which contemporary discursive resources are formed, then it follows that the critique of the queer subject is crucial to the continuing *democratisation* of queer politics. As much as identity terms must be used, as much as 'outness' is to be affirmed, these same notions must become subject to a critique of the exclusionary operations of their own production: For whom is outness a historically available and affordable option? Is there an unmarked class character to the demand for universal 'outness'? Who is represented by *which* use of the term, and who is excluded? For whom does the term present an impossible conflict between racial, ethnic, or religious affiliation and sexual politics? What kinds of policies are enabled by what kinds of usages,

d which are backgrounded or erased from view? In this sense, the genealogical critique of the queer subject will be central to queer politics to the
extent that it constitutes a self-critical dimension within activism, a persistent
reminder to take the time to consider the exclusionary force of one of
activism's most treasured contemporary premises.

[...]

GENDER PERFORMATIVITY AND DRAG

How, if at all, is the notion of discursive resignification linked to the notion
of gender parody or impersonation? First, what is meant by understanding
gender as an impersonation? Does this mean that one puts on a mask or
persona, that there is a 'one' who precedes that 'putting on', who is something other than its gender from the start? Or does this miming, this imper-
sonating precede and form the 'one', operating as its formative precondition
rather than its dispensable artifice?

The construal of gender-as-drag according to the first model appears to be
the effect of a number of circumstances. One of them I brought on myself by
citing drag as an example of performativity, a move that was taken then, by
some, to be *exemplary* of performativity. If drag is performative, that does
not mean that all performativity is to be understood as drag. The publication
of *Gender Trouble* coincided with a number of publications that did assert
that 'clothes make the woman', but I never did think that gender was like
clothes, or that clothes make the woman. Added to these, however, are the
political needs of an emergent queer movement in which the publicisation of
theatrical agency has become quite central.[10]

The practice by which gendering occurs, the embodying of norms, is a
compulsory practice, a forcible production, but not for that reason fully
determining. To the extent that gender is an assignment, it is an assignment
which is never quite carried out according to expectation, whose addressee
never quite inhabits the ideal s/he is compelled to approximate. Moreover,
this embodying is a repeated process. And one might construe repetition as
precisely that which *undermines* the conceit of voluntarist mastery designated by the subject in language.

As *Paris Is Burning* made clear, drag is not unproblematically subversive.
It serves a subversive function to the extent that it reflects the mundane
impersonations by which heterosexually ideal genders are performed and
naturalised and undermines their power by virtue of effecting that exposure.
But there is no guarantee that exposing the naturalised status of heterosexuality will lead to its subversion. Heterosexuality can augment its hegemony
through its denaturalisation, as when we see denaturalising parodies that
reidealise heterosexual norms *without* calling them into question.

On other occasions, though, the transferability of a gender ideal or gender norm calls into question the abjecting power that it sustains. For an occupation or reterritorialisation of a term that has been used to abject a population can become the site of resistance, the possibility of an enabling social and political resignification. And this has happened to a certain extent with the notion of 'queer'. The contemporary redeployment enacts a prohibition and a degradation against itself, spawning a different order of values, a political affirmation from and through the very term which in a prior usage had as its final aim the eradication of precisely such an affirmation.

It may seem, however, that there is a difference between the embodying or performing of gender norms and the performative use of discourse. Are these two different senses of 'performativity', or do they converge as modes of citationality in which the compulsory character of certain social imperatives becomes subject to a more promising deregulation?/Gender norms operate by requiring the embodiment of certain ideals of femininity and masculinity, ones that are almost always related to the idealisation of the heterosexual bond. In this sense, the initiatory performative, 'It's a girl!' anticipates the eventual arrival of the sanction, 'I pronounce you man and wife'. Hence, also, the peculiar pleasure of the cartoon strip in which the infant is first interpellated into discourse with 'It's a lesbian!' Far from an essentialist joke, the queer appropriation of the performative mimes and exposes both the binding power of the heterosexualising law *and its expropriability*.

To the extent that the naming of the 'girl' is transitive, that is, initiates the process by which a certain 'girling' is compelled, the term or, rather, its symbolic power, governs the formation of a corporeally enacted femininity that never fully approximates the norm. This is a 'girl', however, who is compelled to 'cite' the norm in order to qualify and remain a viable subject. Femininity is thus not the product of a choice, but the forcible citation of a norm, one whose complex historicity is indissociable from relations of discipline, regulation, punishment. Indeed, there is no 'one' who takes on a gender norm. On the contrary, this citation of the gender norm is necessary in order to qualify as a 'one', to become viable as a 'one', where subject-formation is dependent on the prior operation of legitimating gender norms.

It is in terms of a norm that compels a certain 'citation' in order for a viable subject to be produced that the notion of gender performativity calls to be rethought. And [it is] precisely in relation to such a compulsory citationality that the theatricality of gender is also to be explained. Theatricality need not be conflated with self-display or self-creation. Within queer politics, indeed, within the very signification that is 'queer', we read a resignifying practice in which the desanctioning power of the name 'queer' is reversed to sanction a contestation of the terms of sexual legitimacy. Paradoxically, but also with great promise, the subject who is 'queered' into public discourse through homophobic interpellations of various kinds *takes up* or *cites* that very term as the discursive basis for an opposition. This kind of citation will emerge as *theatrical* to the extent that it *mines and renders hyperbolic* the discursive convention that it also *reverses*. The hyperbolic gesture is crucial to the exposure of the homophobic 'law' that can no longer control the terms of its own abjecting strategies.

To oppose the theatrical to the political within contemporary queer politics is, I would argue, an impossibility: the hyperbolic 'performance' of death in the practice of 'die-ins' and the theatrical 'outness' by which queer activism has disrupted the closeting distinction between public and private space have proliferated sites of politicisation and AIDS awareness throughout the public realm. Indeed, an important set of histories might be told in which the increasing politicisation *of* theatricality for queers is at stake (more productive, I think, than an insistence on the two as polar opposites within queerness). Such a history might include traditions of cross-dressing, drag balls, street walking, butch-femme spectacles, the sliding between the 'march' (New York City) and the parade (San Francisco); die-ins by ACT UP, kiss-ins by Queer Nation; drag performance benefits for AIDS (by which I would include both Lypsinka's and Liza Minelli's in which she, finally, does Judy[11]); the convergence of theatrical work with theatrical activism;[12] performing excessive lesbian sexuality and iconography that effectively counters the desexualisation of the lesbian; tactical interruptions of public forums by lesbian and gay activists in favour of drawing public attention and outrage to the failure of government funding of AIDS research and outreach.

The increasing theatricalisation of political rage in response to the killing inattention of public policy-makers on the issue of AIDS is allegorised in the recontextualisation of 'queer' from its place within a homophobic strategy of abjection and annihilation to an insistent and public severing of that interpellation from the effect of shame. To the extent that shame is produced as the stigma not only of AIDS, but also of queerness, where the latter is understood through homophobic causalities as the 'cause' and 'manifestation' of the illness, theatrical rage is part of the public resistance to that interpellation of shame. Mobilised by the injuries of homophobia, theatrical rage reiterates those injuries precisely through an 'acting out', one that does not merely repeat or recite those injuries, but that also deploys a hyperbolic display of death and injury to overwhelm the epistemic resistance to AIDS and to the graphics of suffering, or a hyperbolic display of kissing to shatter the epistemic blindness to an increasingly graphic and public homosexuality.

MELANCHOLIA AND THE LIMITS OF PERFORMANCE

The critical potential of 'drag' centrally concerns a critique of a prevailing truth-regime of 'sex', one that I take to be pervasively heterosexist: the distinction between the 'inside' truth of femininity, considered as psychic disposition or ego-core, and the 'outside' truth, considered as appearance or presentation, produces a contradictory formation of gender in which no fixed 'truth' can be established. Gender is neither a purely psychic truth, conceived as 'internal' and 'hidden', nor is it reducible to a surface appearance; on the contrary, its undecidability is to be traced as the play *between* psyche and appearance (where the latter domain includes what appears *in words*). Further, this will be a 'play' regulated by heterosexist constraints though not, for that reason, fully reducible to them.

In no sense can it be concluded that the part of gender that is performed is therefore the 'truth' of gender; performance as bounded 'act' is distinguished from performativity insofar as the latter consists in a reiteration of norms which precede, constrain, and exceed the performer and in that sense cannot be taken as the fabrication of the performer's 'will' or 'choice'; further, what is 'performed' works to conceal, if not to disavow, what remains opaque, unconscious, unperformable. The reduction of performativity to performance would be a mistake.

The rejection of an expressive model of drag which holds that some interior truth is exteriorised in performance needs, however, to be referred to a psychoanalytic consideration on the relationship between how gender *appears* and what gender *signifies*. Psychoanalysis insists that the opacity of the unconscious sets limits to the exteriorisation of the psyche. It also argues, rightly I think, that what is exteriorised or performed can only be understood through reference to what is barred from the signifier and from the domain of corporeal legibility.

How precisely do repudiated identifications, identifications that do not 'show', circumscribe and materialise the identifications that do? Here it seems useful to rethink the notion of gender-as-drag in terms of the analysis of gender melancholia.[13] Given the iconographic figure of the melancholic drag queen, one might consider whether and how these terms work together. Here, one might ask also after the disavowal that occasions performance and that performance might be said to enact, where performance engages 'acting out' in the psychoanalytic sense.[14] If melancholia in Freud's sense is the effect of an ungrieved loss (a sustaining of the lost object/Other as a psychic figure with the consequence of heightened identification with that Other, self-beratement, and the acting out of unresolved anger and love),[15] it may be that performance, understood as 'acting out', is significantly related to the problem of unacknowledged loss. Where there is an ungrieved loss in drag performance (and I am sure that such a generalisation cannot be universalised), perhaps it is a loss that is refused and incorporated in the performed identification, one that reiterates a gendered idealisation and its radical uninhabitability. This is neither a territorialisation of the feminine by the masculine nor an 'envy' of the masculine by the feminine, nor a sign of the

essential plasticity of gender. What it does suggest is that gender performance allegorises a loss it cannot grieve, allegorises the incorporative fantasy
of melancholia whereby an object is phantasmatically taken in or on as a
way of refusing to let it go.

The analysis above is a risky one because it suggests that for a 'man'
performing femininity or for a 'woman' performing masculinity (the latter is
always, in effect, to perform a little less, given that femininity is often cast as
the spectacular gender) there is an attachment to and a loss and refusal of the
figure of femininity by the man, or the figure of masculinity by the woman.
Thus, it is important to underscore that drag is an effort to negotiate cross-
gendered identification, but that cross-gendered identification is not the
exemplary paradigm for thinking about homosexuality, although it may be
one. In this sense, drag allegorises some set of melancholic incorporative
fantasies that stabilise *gender*. Not only are a vast number of drag performers straight, but it would be a mistake to think that homosexuality is best
explained through the performativity that is drag. What does seem useful in
this analysis, however, is that drag exposes or allegorises the mundane
psychic and performative practices by which heterosexualised genders form
themselves through the renunciation of the *possibility* of homosexuality, a
foreclosure that produces a field of heterosexual objects at the same time
that it produces a domain of those whom it would be impossible to love.
Drag thus allegorises *heterosexual melancholy*, the melancholy by which a
masculine gender is formed from the refusal to grieve the masculine as a
possibility of love; a feminine gender is formed (taken on, assumed) through
the incorporative fantasy by which the feminine is excluded as a possible
object of love, an exclusion never grieved, but 'preserved' through the
heightening of feminine identification itself. In this sense, the 'truest' lesbian
melancholic is the strictly straight woman, and the 'truest' gay male melancholic is the strictly straight man.

What drag exposes, however, is the 'normal' constitution of gender presentation in which the gender performed is in many ways constituted by a set
of disavowed attachments or identifications that constitute a different
domain of the 'unperformable'. Indeed, it may well be that what constitutes
the *sexually* unperformable is performed instead as *gender identification*.[16]
To the extent that homosexual attachments remain unacknowledged within
normative heterosexuality, they are not merely constituted as desires that
emerge and subsequently become prohibited. Rather, these are desires
that are proscribed from the start. And when they do emerge on the far
side of the censor, they may well carry that mark of impossibility with them,
performing as it were, as the impossible within the possible. As such, they
will not be attachments that can be openly grieved. This is, then, less *the
refusal* to grieve (a formulation that accents the choice involved) than a pre-
emption of grief performed by the absence of cultural conventions for

avowing the loss of homosexual love. And it is this absence that produces a culture of heterosexual melancholy, one that can be read in the hyperbolic identifications by which mundane heterosexual masculinity and femininity confirm themselves. The straight man *becomes* (mimes, cites, appropriates, assumes the status of) the man he 'never' loved and 'never' grieved; the straight woman *becomes* the woman she 'never' loved and 'never' grieved. It is in this sense, then, that what is most apparently performed as gender is the sign and symptom of a pervasive disavowal.

Moreover, it is precisely to counter this pervasive cultural risk of gay melancholia (what the newspapers generalise as 'depression') that there has been an insistent publicisation and politicisation of grief over those who have died from AIDS; the NAMES Project Quilt is exemplary, ritualising and repeating the name itself as a way of publically avowing the limitless loss.[17]

Insofar as grief remains unspeakable, the rage over the loss can redouble by virtue of remaining unavowed. And if that very rage over loss is publicly proscribed, the melancholic effects of such a proscription can achieve suicidal proportions. The emergence of collective institutions for grieving are thus crucial to survival, to the reassembling of community, the reworking of kinship, the reweaving of sustaining relations. And insofar as they involve the publicisation and dramatisation of death, they call to be read as life-affirming rejoinders to the dire psychic consequences of a grieving process culturally thwarted and proscribed.

GENDERED AND SEXUAL PERFORMATIVITY

How then does one link the trope by which discourse is described as 'performing' and that theatrical sense of performance in which the hyperbolic status of gender norms seems central? What is 'performed' in drag is, of course, *the sign* of gender, a sign that is not the same as the body that it figures, but that cannot be read without it. The sign, understood as a gender imperative – 'girl!' – reads less as an assignment than as a command and, as such, produces its own insubordinations. The hyperbolic conformity to the command can reveal the hyperbolic status of the norm itself, indeed, can become the cultural sign by which that cultural imperative might become legible. Insofar as heterosexual gender norms produce inapproximable ideals, heterosexuality can be said to operate through the regulated production of hyperbolic versions of 'man' and 'woman'. These are for the most part compulsory performances, ones which none of us choose, but which each of us is forced to negotiate. I write 'forced to negotiate' because the compulsory character of these norms does not always make them efficacious. Such norms are continually haunted by their own inefficacy; hence, the anxiously repeated effort to install and augment their jurisdiction.

The resignification of norms is thus a function of their *inefficacy*, and so the question of subversion, of *working the weakness in the norm*, becomes a matter of inhabiting the practices of its rearticulation. The critical promise of drag does not have to do with the proliferation of genders, as if a sheer increase in numbers would do the job, but rather with the exposure or the failure of heterosexual regimes ever fully to legislate or contain their own ideals. Hence, it is not that drag *opposes* heterosexuality, or that the proliferation of drag will bring down heterosexuality; on the contrary, drag tends to be the allegorisation of heterosexuality and its constitutive melancholia. As an allegory that works through the hyperbolic, drag brings into relief what is, after all, determined only in relation to the hyperbolic: the understated, taken-for-granted quality of heterosexual performativity. At its best, then, drag can be read for the way in which hyperbolic norms are dissimulated as the heterosexual mundane. At the same time these same norms, taken not as commands to be obeyed, but as imperatives to be 'cited', twisted, queered, brought into relief as heterosexual imperatives, are not, for that reason, necessarily subverted in the process.

It is important to emphasise that although heterosexuality operates in part through the stabilisation of gender norms, gender designates a dense site of significations that contain and exceed the heterosexual matrix. Although forms of sexuality do not unilaterally determine gender, a non-causal and non-reductive connection between sexuality and gender is nevertheless crucial to maintain. Precisely because homophobia often operates through the attribution of a damaged, failed, or otherwise abject gender to homosexuals, that is, calling gay men 'feminine' or calling lesbians 'masculine', and because the homophobic terror over performing homosexual acts, where it exists, is often also a terror over losing proper gender ('no longer being a real or proper man' or 'no longer being a real and proper woman'), it seems crucial to retain a theoretical apparatus that will account for how sexuality is regulated through the policing and the shaming of gender.
[. . .]

In psychoanalytic terms, the relation between gender and sexuality is in part negotiated through the question of the relationship between identification and desire. And here it becomes clear why refusing to draw lines of causal implication between these two domains is as important as keeping open an investigation of their complex interimplication. For, if to identify as a woman is not necessarily to desire a man, and if to desire a woman does not necessarily signal the constituting presence of a masculine identification, whatever that is, then the heterosexual matrix proves to be an *imaginary* logic that insistently issues forth its own unmanageability. The heterosexual logic that requires that identification and desire be mutually exclusive is one of the most reductive of heterosexism's psychological instruments: if one identifies *as* a given gender, one must desire a different gender. On the one hand, there is no one femininity with which to identify, which is to say that femininity might itself offer an array of identificatory sites, as the proliferation of lesbian femme possibilities attests. On the other hand, it is hardly descriptive of the complex dynamic exchanges of lesbian and gay relationships to presume that homosexual identifications 'mirror' or replicate one another. The vocabulary for describing the difficult play, crossing, and destabilisation of masculine and feminine identifications within homosexuality has only begun to emerge within theoretical language: the non-academic language historically embedded in gay communities is here much more instructive. The thought of sexual difference *within* homosexuality has yet to be theorised in its complexity.

For one deciding issue will be whether social strategies of regulation, abjection, and normalisation will not continue to relink gender and sexuality such that the oppositional analysis will continue to be under pressure to theorise their interrelations. This will not be the same as reducing gender to prevailing forms of sexual relations such that one 'is' the effect of the sexual position one is said to occupy. Resisting such a reduction, it ought to be possible to assert a set of non-causal and non-reductive relations between gender and sexuality, not only to link feminism and queer theory, as one might link two separate enterprises, but to establish their constitutive interrelationship. Similarly, the inquiry into both homosexuality and gender will need to cede the priority of *both* terms in the service of a more complex mapping of power that interrogates the formation of each in specified racial regimes and geopolitical spatialisations. And the task, of course, does not stop here, for no one term can serve as foundational, and the success of any given analysis that centres on any one term may well be the marking of its own limitations as an exclusive point of departure.

The goal of this analysis, then, cannot be pure subversion, as if an undermining were enough to establish and direct political struggle. Rather than denaturalisation or proliferation, it seems that the question for thinking discourse and power in terms of the future has several paths to follow: how to think power as resignification together with power as the convergence or interarticulation of relations of regulation, domination, constitution? How to know what might qualify as an affirmative resignification – with all the weight and difficulty of that labour – and how to run the risk of reinstalling the abject at the site of its opposition? But how, also, to rethink the terms that establish and sustain bodies that matter?

The film *Paris Is Burning* has been interesting to read less for the ways in which it deploys denaturalising strategies to reidealise whiteness and heterosexual gender norms than for the less stabilising rearticulations of kinship it occasioned. The drag balls themselves at times produce high femininity as a function of whiteness and deflect homosexuality through a transgendering that *reidealises* certain bourgeois forms of heterosexual exchange. And yet, if those performances are not immediately or obviously subversive, it may be that it is rather in the *reformulation of kinship*, in particular, the redefining of the 'house' and its forms of collectivity, mothering, mopping, reading, and becoming legendary, that the appropriation and redeployment of the categories of dominant culture enable the formation of kinship relations that function quite supportively as oppositional discourse. In this sense, it would be interesting to read *Paris Is Burning* against, say, Nancy Chodorow's *The Reproduction of Mothering* and ask what happens to psychoanalysis and kinship as a result. In the former, the categories like 'house' and 'mother' are derived from that family scene, but also deployed to form alternative households and community. This *resignification* marks the workings of an agency that is (a) not the same as voluntarism, and that (b) though *implicated* in the very relations of power it seeks to rival, is not, as a consequence, reducible to those dominant forms.

Performativity describes this relation of being implicated in that which one opposes, this turning of power against itself to produce alternative modalities of power, to establish a kind of political contestation that is not a 'pure' opposition, a 'transcendence' of contemporary relations of power, but a difficult labour of forging a future from resources inevitably impure.

How will we know the difference between the power we promote and the power we oppose? Is it, one might rejoin, a matter of 'knowing?' For one is, as it were, in power even as one opposes it, formed by it as one reworks it, and it is this simultaneity that is at once the condition of our partiality, the measure of our political unknowingness, and also the condition of action itself. The incalculable effects of action are as much a part of their subversive promise as those that we plan in advance.

The effects of performatives, understood as discursive productions, do not conclude at the terminus of a given statement or utterance, the passing of legislation, the announcement of a birth. The reach of their signifiability cannot be controlled by the one who utters or writes, since such productions are not owned by the one who utters them. They continue to signify in spite of their authors, and sometimes against their authors' most precious intentions.

It is one of the ambivalent implications of the decentring of the subject to have one's writing be the site of a necessary and inevitable expropriation. But this yielding of ownership over what one writes has an important set of political corollaries, for the taking up, reforming, deforming of one's words does open up a difficult future terrain of community, one in which the hope of ever fully recognising oneself in the terms by which one signifies is sure to be disappointed. This not owning of one's words is there from the start, however, since speaking is always in some ways the speaking of a stranger through and as oneself, the melancholic reiteration of a language that one never chose, that one does not find as an instrument to be used, but that one is, as it were, used by, expropriated in, as the unstable and continuing condition of the 'one' and the 'we', the ambivalent condition of the power that binds.

13

Choreographies of Gender

Susan Leigh Foster

In 1989 and again in 1990, Teresa de Lauretis argued that the charge of essentialism as ascribed to certain feminist theory or theorists promulgated a divisive factionalism within the feminist movement that would serve the patriarchal status quo far better than any antifeminist agendas. She urged a reconsideration of the term *essentialism*, one that would re-envision it not as a biologically based fixity but rather as a political and conceptual stance that encompassed the knowledges, practices, and discourses within which a given author or text is immersed. Essential differences would therefore not derive from natural or biological differences, but from the historically specific conditions that imparted to theories or theorists their values and assumptions, methodological and conceptual approaches, and forms of address and of critical reflection.[1] Although de Lauretis's redefinition of essentialism sublates the oppositionality between gynocentric and poststructuralist feminisms, or between analytical approaches informed by identity politics or deconstruction, her proposal has gone largely unheeded, especially in the ensuing focus on gender as performance.

The project of conceptualising gender as performance, pervasive within cultural studies, has been widely debated in gender studies and feminist theory for the past five years. Such a project, consonant with feminism's dedication to the extrication of gendered behaviour from the biological body, foregrounds the opportunity to analyse and observe gender's ostensible features, its appearance and activities, promising a more critical diagnosis of gender's influence and effects, while at the same time holding out the possibility for social change. If, the argument goes, gender is 'only' a performance, albeit deeply routinised and ingrained, then the theoretical space exists wherein such behaviour could be resisted, altered, and refashioned so as to alleviate the prescriptions for gendered behaviour that are experienced as oppressive by so many.

The separation between actor and performance implied by this approach to the analysis of gender supports a theorisation of personhood as fluid and protean cultural construction, capable not only of change but also of inhabiting, perhaps even representing, multiple, distinctive cultural arenas. Such a conception of identity radically challenges the essentialist notion of

166

an organic and inviolable connection between the biological determinants of sex, race, or sexual orientation and their cultural elaboration. This organicist conception of the link between body and identity, a founding argument in so many forms of racial, gender, and sexual discrimination, has been deconstructed by poststructuralist critiques that focus attention on the very mechanisms of knowledge production through which the connection between biological destiny and cultural possibility is made and maintained. Yet, the tension between essential and deconstructed models of experience endures, trenchantly and eloquently summarised here with regard to racial identity by dance ethnographer Anna Beatrice Scott:

> Now I pride myself on being a post-essentialist black person, but when I went to a *bloco afro* rehearsal in San Francisco intent upon doing some Black Atlantic research this past March only to discover that I was one of only five black people out of at least fifty participants, including the drummers and teacher, I was having a hard time controlling my proprietary and protective instincts regarding black culture. I stood amidst the collection of Anglo, Asian, and Latino participants in the room, questionnaires in hand, smile on face, and wondered to myself, 'Where are the black people?' Why did it matter to me? And why was everyone staring at *me*, the materialisation of the adjective in *bloco afro?*[2]

As 'post-essentialist', Scott wants to detach skin colour and other racial attributes from a mandated way of life, and as black, she wants to retain privileged access to a cultural heritage. Scott names this dilemma and even complicates it further by receiving critically the gaze directed at her as an 'authentic' representative of the *bloco afro* tradition. Is the gaze she receives directed not only at her black body but also at her feminine body? What is in her 'flesh and bones' that makes her dancing 'truer', more *bloco afro* than that of Anglo, Asian, or Latino bodies dancing alongside her?

De Lauretis offers an opportunity to think through these questions by identifying essential differences as those that result from a profound and enduring immersion in cultural and historical specificities. Yet essential differences often inflect and complicate one another, necessitating a theorisation not only of their historical and cultural specificity but also of their interconnectedness. As Yvonne Yarbro-Bejarano and many others have observed, this theorisation of gendered, racial, and sexual categories must incorporate the ongoing dynamics of their impact on one another: 'Notions of *simultaneous* oppressions are not entirely successful in capturing the ways these categories interact and interdefine one another, while conceptualising the *intersection* of these categories may communicate an excessively static, rather than a dynamic, understanding of the process.'[3] The task, then, in focusing on gender, as one category of essential difference, is to construct it in interrelation with racial and sexual configurations of identity. One of the purposes of this article is to suggest that the failure to develop de Lauretis's concept of essential difference and to conceptualise gender in dynamic relation with race and sexuality stems from the unexamined use of the term *performance*.

Is *performance* the most appropriate term to describe the sedimented layers and complex networks of behavioural responses that constitute masculine and feminine roles? Since there are different techniques and theories of performance – the performer can assimilate the character of the part to be played and allow that character's feelings and motivations to generate and guide the actions, or the performer can carefully approximate behaviours judged to be typical of the character to be rendered – does gender as performance also stipulate a particular approach to performing? Most crucially, if gender is performance, what script or score is being performed? For those of us in dance, theatre, and performance studies, the recent appropriation of *performance* and its cousin *performativity* as terms that would illuminate cultural and textual studies signals a potentially fruitful interdisciplinary inquiry, but one that calls for certain discipline-based knowledge about the functions of these terms.

Rather than appeal to knowledge bases generated in the fields of theatre, dance, and performance studies for answers to these questions, arguments for gender as performance typically acknowledge the work of speech-act theorist J. L. Austin[4] as a foundational approach. Austin's theory of the performativity of language, a radical opening out of language to social and political dimensions, posits that under certain conditions the speaking of a phrase might alter the status of the body performing the speaking. It does not make any claims for speech as a form of bodily articulation (something that the phrase 'speech acts' might suggest), nor does it explore action as an accomplishment of the body. For Austin, the body, fundamentally the passive executant of the subject, enunciates words in the direction of another body-subject with which it intends to communicate. Some of its communications, by contractual agreement within the sociolinguistic order, perform the work of reordering the speaker's relations to his or her surroundings, as in the often-cited example of 'I do' as the pivotal statement in the marriage ceremony. The allure of Austin's focus on linguistic performances for more general theories of performance presumably resides in the proposition that the enactment of a generalised cultural script will implicate the individual in juridical and political networks of meaning that exercise a determining effect on identity. But can such a framework of distinctions between performative and nonperformative linguistic utterances be extended to the full realm of behaviour within which certain gestures might be identified as gendered?

Judith Butler, whose *Gender Trouble*[5] is often the cited source for the notion of gender as performance, draws on Austin's theories to emphasise the sedimented networks of social norms through which the subject is constituted as gendered.[6] Butler's conception of performativity, not unlike de Lauretis's essential difference, focuses on the historically specific constellation of reiterative and citational patterns, the regulatory systems, and not on any single or deliberate acts of individuals, that interpellate the subject as a gendered subject.[7] But for Butler it is difficult to envision how either performance or performativity extends beyond the verbal realm into non-verbal dimensions of human action. Although in early versions of her theory of gender identity, Butler[8] mentions bodily gestures, movements, and enactments of various kinds, in *Bodies That Matter* she defines performative acts as 'forms of authoritative speech: most performatives, for instance, are statements that, in the uttering, also perform a certain action and exercise a binding power'.[9] In her only reading of a nonprinted text, the film *Paris Is Burning*, Butler notes the categories of character types that are performed at the drag balls and their costuming, but she never examines the eclectic movement vocabularies and the sequencing of those vocabularies through which social commentary is generated. She considers the relationship between pedestrian and stage identities without actually detailing the ranges of exaggerative and ironic gestures used in each site. Only by assessing the articulateness of bodies' motions as well as speech, I would argue, can the interconnectedness of racial, gendered, and sexual differences within and among these bodies matter.

Performativity for Butler not only lodges primarily in the verbal dimensions of human behaviour but also exercises its power through compulsory reiteration. In order for gender to appear as natural, as the inevitable product of the body's sex, the acts through which it is constituted are repeated so frequently and interminably as to foreclose any possible apprehension of their constructedness: 'Performativity is thus not a singular "act", for it is always a reiteration of a norm or set of norms, and to the extent that it acquires an act-like status in the present, it conceals or dissimulates the conventions of which it is a repetition.'[10] By defining gender identity as reiterative, as a stylised repetition of social norms through time, Butler is able to unmask the contingent status of those norms and their coercive effects.[11] Although Butler emphasises that performativity can be located only in multiple rather than single acts, the focus on reiteration stresses the repetition of acts more than the relationality among them. How are these 'acts' organised so as mutually to reinforce and/or expand on one another? How do acts not only reiterate social norms but also vary them so as to establish resonances among distinct categories of normative behaviour?

In this article I pursue a methodology designed to answer these questions through a focus on the example of dance. Dance illumines the issues at stake in an analysis of gender as performance not only because dance, like gender, consists largely of bodily actions rather than effects of speech, but also because it delineates a clear function for the performer. By examining the role of performance in dance and contrasting it with choreography, I hope to show that choreography is a far more useful rubric for understanding gender. Choreography, the tradition of codes and conventions through which meaning is constructed in dance, offers a social and historical analytic framework for the study of gender, whereas performance concentrates on the individual execution of such codes. Choreography resonates with cultural values concerning bodily, individual, and social identities, whereas performance focuses on the skill necessary to represent those identities. Choreography presents a structuring of deep and enduring cultural values that replicates similar sets of values elaborated in other cultural practices, whereas performance emphasises the idiosyncratic interpretation of those values. Like performativity, choreography consists in sets of norms and conventions; yet unlike performativity, or at least its general usage thus far, choreography encompasses corporeal as well as verbal articulateness. Choreography therefore serves as a useful intervention into discussions of materiality and body by focusing on the unspoken, on the bodily gestures and movements that, along with speech, construct gendered identity. Choreography also focuses attention on the interrelationality of various sets of codes and conventions through which identity is represented.

In what follows I present an analysis of both choreography and performance through a consideration of examples drawn from social and theatrical dance traditions. My purpose is to intervene in the general discussion of gender as performance and to examine critically key oppositions – between essentialism and deconstruction, the corporeal and the linguistic, and the textual and the performed – that underlie that discussion. At the same time, I hope to demonstrate the value of dance as a conceptual framework for sorting through these very complex issues. Focus on dance enables a more thorough understanding of the cultural constructedness of body and identity and a more far-reaching set of strategies for effecting social change.

THEORETICAL MOVES

In order to illuminate what is entailed by the choreographic process, I begin with the example of the lone female choreographer at work in the dance studio. This example traces its origin to the modern dance tradition in the United States, a tradition whose feminist underpinnings have been well documented.[12] This initiative, undertaken by white, bourgeois women at the turn of the century, constructed a new expressive practice focused at the site of the individual dancing body. These artists sought to overhaul body and soul in order to liberate individual creative impulses from the stranglehold of societal norms and aesthetic values. Their choreographic accomplishments, congruent with experimental philosophies of education during that period, provided the rationale for the entrance of dance into higher education.[13] Construed as a way of knowing, other than and outside of verbal knowledge, the professional world of modern dance and the university dance programme continue to privilege the individual creative process and its realisation in dancing and in the making of new dances.

In making a new dance, the choreographer often stands motionless, staring into space, perhaps a mirror's space, for an indeterminate period of time. Then she tries out a move: one arm flings on the diagonal from low front to high back; the body flows after it, motion-filled by its momentum. The leg, initially trailing behind as the last trace of the body's twisted turning, swings suddenly to the front, causing enough impetus to carry the body through a second turn. Exiting from the turn's wildness, the body folds at hip and knee joints, back gently curved, arms arching forward over the head. The choreographer stands back up and resumes her stare. Does the turn need an additional bend of the torso or gesture from the back foot? Should the contrast between first and second turns be heightened? Is the body's final shape too symmetrical? Too soft? Too familiar? This series of questions promulgates other levels of interrogation: Is the phrase delirious enough? Does it look like half-baked Trisha Brown? Will everyone see that it is a variation on the earlier theme? Can the dancer do it without wrenching her back? Should the arms scoop under (in which case it looks too much like supplication) or should they scoop over (in which case it looks like a five-year-old's rendition of waves crashing on the shore)? The choreographer wrestles with these and related questions in no prescribed order and, quite probably, without ever articulating the questions or their answers verbally. She is sorting through, rejecting and constructing physical images. Her choices make manifest her theorising of corporeality.

The choreographer constructs relationships of body to momentum, stasis, impulse, and flow and articulates relationships of the body's parts one to another. She engages the body's semiotic field – the connotations that head, hands, pelvis, or heels carry with them, the meanings evoked by tension, undulation, or collapse – and situates the body within the symbolic features of the performance space – the centre, side, high, and low that the architectural context designates. In so doing, she fashions a repertoire of bodily actions that may confirm and elaborate on conventional expectations for gendered behaviour, or she may contrive a repertoire that dramatically contravenes such expectations. In either case, dancing dramatises the separation between the anatomical identity of the dancer and its possible ways of moving. Part of dance's compelling interest derives from the kinds of links the choreography makes between sex and gender.

This is not to say that the anatomical body of the dancer is a natural body. That body exists along a continuum of attributes that define male or female sexual identity. Its shoulders may be unusually broad for a woman, its feet unusually flexible for a man. And this anatomy is not destiny. The dancer cultivates the body through training regimens that develop its strength, flexibility, endurance, and coordination.[14] It may acquire a massive muscularity uncharacteristic of the female body or a willowy flexibility uncharacteristic of the male body. This body, already codified in terms of its sex but appearing as one of two sexes, then presents itself to the viewer. Its movement will be seen as gendered, as putting into play various codes of gendered behaviour.

Thus the choreographer considers kinds of bodily stances (open or closed), bodily shapes (erect or curved), engagements with the surrounding space (direct or diffuse), timing of movements (slow or quick, continuous or abrupt), qualities of motion (restrained, sustained, undulating, bursting), and sequencing of body parts (random or sequential) characteristic of each gender's motion.[15] She stipulates a quality of focus for the dancer, projecting attentiveness to the connections between internal sensation and external motion, projecting awareness of external space and making contact with other dancers, or calling attention to the body's enunciations in space. She likewise designates a kind of motivation for the movement in which dancers can appear to be propelled by an imaginary force located out in space or to initiate movement from within their own bodies. She reckons with established codes of contact between female and male bodies: where the body of one sex can touch the body of the other sex, what kinds of shapes bodies of the two sexes can make together, who can give weight and who bear it, who initiates movement and who follows, who is passive and who active, who is to be looked at and who is doing the looking. She forges phrases of movement that construct groupings of dancers with gendered connotations – chaotic, convoluted, pristine, or geometric. When she does this for multiple bodies, she elaborates a theory not only of gendered corporeal identity but also of relations among gendered bodies.

Male and female bodies, bodies of different colour and racial attributes may or may not evidence vocabularies or styles of movement associated with their sexual or racial identities. These bodies gesture toward, touch, or support one another. They follow in one another's pathways, reiterate or vary one another's moves. They evidence a range of emotional responses toward one another, all the while oblivious to or interactive with the audience. They may distribute themselves so as to frame a soloist or to present multiple competing events. They may cite other dances or dance traditions as part of their danced argument. In the sustained development of their activities, they will appear to narrate events, to tell a kind of story, perhaps with characters, motivations, and responses to one another, or perhaps to speak of the weight, momentum, and agility of which bodies are capable. They may enunciate values and relationships characteristic of a particular ethnic identification, or they may present a series of affective states. Accumulating these choices concerning the behaviour of bodies, the choreography builds up an image of community, one that articulates both individual and collective identities.

Throughout the creative process of articulating these identities, the choreographer engages a tradition of representational conventions, knowledge of which is shared to a greater or lesser extent by both dance makers and dance viewers. To achieve the meaning she envisions, the choreographer selects from among these conventions, implementing, innovating, and even challenging aspects of the tradition. Viewers will, in turn, analyse the choreographic implementation of conventions in order to derive their own interpretation of the dance. However intuitive or inspired the creative process may seem, the choreographer is nonetheless labouring at the craft of dance making. However distinctive or gifted her dances may seem, she is working as one of a group of practitioners sharing a body of knowledge about how dances mean what they do. However immediate the dance's message may appear to viewers, their understanding of the dance will be based on their ability to decode the choreographic coding of meaning. Thus, the choreography may contribute innovations that will subtly alter the contents of its representational tradition, but these innovations can acquire their full meaning only through their situatedness within that tradition.

Dancers who enter the studio to translate choreography into performance begin by learning the movement, its timing, and its disposition for the body in space, as meticulously as is required by the aesthetic demands of the situation. Yet they also modify the movement so as to develop a personal relationship with it. In order to 'make it their own', they may alter movement to adapt to their bodily capacities so that they, and by extension the movement itself, achieve greater clarity in performance. They may imbue the movement with personal meanings in addition to those described by the choreographer so as to attain a greater fervency. They may elaborate a persona – an integrative conception of the body-subject who would move in the way specified in the choreography – and then use this concept to further refine stylistic features of their performance. They may also calculate the effect of their performance on viewers and calibrate effort, intensity, and focus so as to 'reach' the audience in a manner consonant with the choreography's theoretical goals. They may even connect to a history of performers or a traditional style of performance that informs their current project. Throughout the process of learning and presenting a dance, performers manifest these and other competencies, the product of years of arduous training.

Occasionally, dancers are asked to move beyond the bounds of their training as performers and to assume roles as cochoreographers of the dance. They may be asked to generate movement based on specific strictures or guidelines, to solve problems of sequencing, or even to engage critically, comment on, or select from among the representational strategies that the choreography deploys and that they embody in performance. The fact that dancers may assist in these choreographic projects, however, does not alter the distinctiveness of the two roles. Insofar as they are performers, they will be concerned primarily with these kinds of questions: How shall I phrase this section? Should I hold back here in order to provide more contrast with the intensity of that moment? Does my timing appear mannered? Can I be more focused? How can I look occupied with one action while actually waiting for the arrival of another body with whom I must appear to have a spontaneous interaction? What additional strength, flexibility, or endurance do I need to enhance the execution of the movement?

How the performer answers these questions will affect the overall impact of the choreography and may subtly alter its intent. Certainly, there is a sense in which the performance of any given dance stands as the most accurate presentation of its choreography (stands as the choreography) insofar as any given viewer has access to it. Still, throughout the viewing of a dance, one can perceive the guiding score for the action as distinct from the execution of that score. One can see the residue of strategic choices concerning representation as distinct from the bringing to liveness of those choices. And in this distinctiveness, the contrasting functions of choreography and performance are apparent: dance making theorises physicality, whereas dancing presents that theory of physicality.

[...]

CHOREOGRAPHING GENDER

The emphasis on the individual as elaborated thus far in performance and performance studies influences in subtle yet crucial ways the role that performance plays in the claim for gender as performance. Performance emphasises the transformative moment when the individual instantiates prescribed, prearranged patterns of movement, speech, or display. Gender as performance focuses on the unmasking of these 'natural' patterns as culture, or on the compulsory execution of these patterns. Analysis of the score or script to be executed matters less than the individual's adaptation of those scripts. This suppression of the script for the performance leads to models of social change based primarily on individual insubordination or transgression. Any body, discontented with the regimen of behaviours assigned to it, can alter its participation in the regimen but can hardly effect serious change in the content of the regimen itself. Furthermore, the focus on individual execution or enactment can deflect inquiry away from the historical and cultural specificities of the performance. Gender is being performed, but what is gender that it is being performed?

If performance as assimilated into cultural studies sometimes pursues the individual at the expense of the social, it also encapsulates an unexamined appropriation of the physical (read feminine) by the textual (read masculine). Both the corporeal and the feminine, as I have tried to show, share attributes of instability, ephemerality, and unknowability, whereas the textual, even in its deconstructed versions, maintains a solidity and rationality that aligns with the masculine. The vast majority of studies implementing the notion of performance have focused on written representations of gender rather than the orchestrated actions of moving yet nonspeaking bodies. They neglect the body and at the same time use body to inflect textuality with a new vitality. This enlivenment of language through a demonstration of its performative capabilities continues to rely on traditional notions of the text's solidity as contrasted with the less stable moment of its performance.[16] The choreographic dimensions of the performative act – the text's capacity to body forth a theoretical and political orientation – remain buried in the text, property of the linguistic order and its engagement with the social. Since the claim for gender as performance develops out of Austin's linguistic studies rather than theatre research, this lack of attention to repertoires of behaviour other than those of the text should come as no surprise. However, the perpetuation of verbal and nonverbal oppositionality implicit in the performative text limits the analysis of gender and may even perpetuate traditional gender inequalities.

Choreography challenges the dichotomisation of verbal and nonverbal cultural practices by asserting the thought-filledness of movement and the theoretical potential of bodily action. It names the necessarily collective practice of engagement with enduring yet historically specific conventions of representation and emphasises the connections that such conventions have to social and political structurings of power.[17] New conceptualisations of the script, developed in the wake of poststructuralist critiques of author and text, likewise summon up this theorisation of human action, yet the legacy of the dramatic text continues to infuse the script with a kind of permanence, whereas the notion of choreography as a theoretical premise underscores the changeability of events and their environs.[18] Choreography also disrupts the traditional divisions of labour between verbal and nonverbal acts by fusing the experiential and 'feminine' cultivation of bodily presence to the intellectual and 'masculine' analysis of representation.

To approach gender as choreography also suggests a potential bridge between academic and activist spheres of engagement with gender operations. It is precisely through a choreographic assessment of bodies, their behaviour, and their location that collective interventions such as 'Take Back the Night', 'Confront the Rapist at the Worksite', 'Same-Sex Kiss-Ins', or 'Guerrilla Girls at the Whitney Museum' acquire their perspicacity and charisma.[19] These theorised responses to choreographies of gender and power illustrate an ongoing engagement with systems of representation and an ability to restrategise as power alters the form of its appearance. Because of their canny analysis of body politics, these responses also move activist and scholarly realms of feminism toward one another. [...]

Body, as Susan Bordo has observed, should serve as a metaphor for the subject's locatability, for the finitude of experience rather than for its evanescence or universality: 'For the appreciation of difference requires the acknowledgement of some point beyond which the dancer cannot go. If she were able to go everywhere, there would *be* no difference, nothing that eludes. Denial of the unity and stability of identity is one thing. The epistemological fantasy of *becoming* multiplicity – the dream of limitless multiple embodiments, allowing one to dance from place to place and self to self – is another. What sort of body is it that is free to change its shape and location at will, that can become anyone and travel anywhere?'[20] Neither in performance nor in choreography is the body 'free' to change its shape and location, although, as I have argued here, the performing body, especially as that extension of the textual body that simply moves the text into action, might well appear as unlimited. In fact, performance places important and obvious strictures on the body's whereabouts, since a body can perform only in a given time and place. Yet, it is the choreography this body performs that articulates its connectedness to a specific surround.

Located yet connected, the choreographed body not only suggests an alternative to theory versus practice, it also undermines the oppositionality between essential and deconstructed versions of gendered identity. To analyse gender as choreography is to acknowledge as systems of representation the deeply embedded, slowly changing rules that guide our actions and that make those actions meaningful. Not biologically fixed but rather historically specific, these rules are redolent with social, political, economic, and aesthetic values. They impart to any body a specificity that must be acknowledged, yet they also connect that body to other cultural orchestrations of identity. To choreograph a change in these rules is to grapple with the intensely routinised patterns they have produced, but also with the rules themselves, their configuration and dynamism, and the alliances they create with other structurings of power. Such a change may be registered by a single body, but its choreographic call to action will reflect a theorisation of social as well as individual bodies.

In this choreographic response to the choreographies of gender, bodies are both active and reactive, generative and responsive, writing and written. Their actions are not an unmediated authentic expression, nor are they only the summation of all the discursive practices that contain and objectify them. Choreography relies on the inculcated capabilities, impulses, and preferences that years of practice produce, but it also leaves open the possibility for the unprecedented. Bodies change the world through their

persistent adherence to routinised action, but also by congregating precipit-
ously, stumbling, ducking, or striking a balance; by stretching or impostur-
ing; by standing defiantly or running deviantly; or by grasping others' hands.
These thought-filled actions defy strategies of containment and move us
toward new theorisations of corporeal existence and resistance.

Summaries and Notes

1. ERIN STRIFF, INTRODUCTION

1. Ronald J. Pelias and James VanOosting, 'A Paradigm for Performance Studies', *The Quarterly Journal of Speech*, 73:2 (May 1987), 219–231, 223.
2. Marvin Carlson, *Performance: A Critical Introduction* (New York and London, 1996), p. 6.
3. Dwight Conquergood, 'Of Caravans and Carnivals: Performance Studies in Motion', *The Drama Review*, 148 (Winter 1995), 137–8.
4. Richard Schechner, 'What Is Performance Studies Anyway?' ed. and introd. Peggy Phelan and ed. Jill Lane, *The Ends of Performance* (New York, 1998), pp. 357–62, p. 358.
5. Conquergood, 'Of Caravans and Carnivals', pp. 137–9.
6. Philip Auslander, 'Evangelical Fervor', *TDR*, 39:4 (1995), 178–83.
7. Schechner, 'A New Paradigm for Theatre in the Academy', *TDR*, 36:4 (Winter 1992), 7–10, 9.
8. Jill Dolan, 'Geographies of Learning: Theatre Studies, Performance, and the "Performative"', *Theatre Journal*, 45:4 (Dec. 1993), 417–41, 424.
9. W. B.Worthen, 'Disciplines of the Text/Sites of Performance', *TDR*, 39:1 (Spring 1995), 13–44, 14.
10. Dolan, 'Geographies of Learning', 420.
11. Auslander, 'Evangelical Fervor', 179–80.
12. Conquergood, 'Of Caravans and Carnivals', 137–8.
13. I am here indebted to Philip Auslander for pointing this out to me.
14. Erving Goffman, *The Presentation of the Self in Everyday Life* (London, 1971), pp. 28–9.
15. Marvin Carlson, *Performance: A Critical Introduction* (New York and London, 1996), p. 187.
16. Victor Turner, *From Ritual to Theatre: The Human Seriousness of Play* (New York, 1982), pp 53–5.
17. Andrew Parker and Eve Kosofsky Sedgwick, ed. and intro., *Performativity and Performance* (New York and London, 1995), p. 1.
18. Carlson, *Performance: A Critical Introduction*, p. 7.
19. Schechner, 'What Is Performance Studies Anyway?' 360.
20. Carlson, *Performance: A Critical Introduction*, p. 197.
21. Conquergood, 'Rethinking Ethnography: Towards a Critical Cultural Politics', *Communications Monographs*, 58 (June 1991), 179–94, 189.
22. Schechner, 'What Is Performance Studies Anyway?' 361.
23. J. L. Austin, *How to Do Things With Words*, 2nd edn, ed. J. O. Urmson and Marina Sbisà (Oxford and New York, 1962, 1975), p. 5.

2. SHARON MAZER, 'THE POWER TEAM: MUSCULAR CHRISTIANITY AND THE SPECTACLE OF CONVERSION'

(The author has abridged her own work, which originally appeared in *The Drama Review: A Journal in Performance Studies*, 38.4 (1994), 162–88.)

Summary

The John Jacobs Power Team are bodybuilders who perform feats of strength as a metaphor for their commitment to Christianity. The emphasis on physical strength also serves the purpose of rebutting any preconceptions that Christianity might be effeminate, a message designed to appeal to an audience with a large proportion of young men. The essay also considers the way the advertising, the price of the tickets, linked merchandising, and the venues in which the show is performed all contribute to the religious message. Audiences may be drawn to the spectacle of men breaking blocks of ice and concrete, but in return they must listen to Power Team members proselytise on behalf of their faith. This tightly constructed spectacle is designed to elicit a commitment to Christianity. Audience participation is unavoidable, Mazer argues, because the spectators are encouraged to dedicate or rededicate themselves to Christ at the performance finale, thereby entering into the spectacle themselves. Even the spectators who do not step forward at the end of the show provide an effective dramatic contrast to those who do.

Notes

1. Robert Bly, *Iron John: A Book About Men* (Reading, MA, 1990), p. 26.
2. Trinity Broadcasting Network (TBN), 'The Power Connection', 23 Nov. (1991).
3. John Jacobs Evangelistic Association (JJEA), 'John Jacobs and the Power Team: Touches the World', Promotional video-cassette (1991).
4. At the beginning of the twentieth century, Billy Sunday became the first evangelical preacher to employ the decision card consistently, although variants had appeared throughout the nineteenth century (Steve Bruce, *Pray TV: Televangelism in America* [London, 1990], p. 19). Bernard A. Weisberger notes: 'Once, the salvation of a soul had been a miracle, recorded for certain only in God's book of life. Now, it was a nightly crowd performance, registered on cards' (Bernard A. Weisberger, *They Gathered at the River* [Chicago, 1958], p. 271).
5. See Jeffrey K. Hadden and Anson Shupe, *Televangelism; Power and Politics on God's Frontier* (New York, 1988), pp. 43–4. For a statistical summary of the spread and effect of televangelism, see George Gallop, Jr, *Religion in America: Fifty Years: 1933–1985* (Princeton, NJ, 1985), pp. 148–64.
6. Hadden and Shupe, *Televangelism; Power and Politics on God's Frontier*, pp. 43–4.
7. Weisberger, *They Gathered at the River*, p. 230.
8. Meg Grant, 'John Jacobs and His Team of Muscular Christians Give New Meaning to the Power of Faith', *People Magazine*, 8 Feb. (1988), 111.
9. Charita M. Goshay, 'Team Has the Power of Faith: Weightlifters Show Strength of Scriptures', *The Repository*, 7 Aug., Canton, OH (1992), B3.
10. Tristam Korten, 'Satan and Concrete Beware: Power Team Wars on Devil', *Sunday Record*, 4 July (1993), p. 14.

11. Dave Yewman, 'Muscle-bound men of God giving devil hell in Dickinson', *Galveston Daily News*, 151, 16 Mar. (1993), pp. 1, 25. Brenda Pritts, ' "Powerful" Men with a Message', *He's Alive Today*, Nov. (1992), 8–9.

12. Pastor E.C. Damiani, Senior Pastor at Faith Assembly of God in Poughkeepsie, Personal communication, 29 June, New York (1991).

13. According to Hadden and Shupe: 'Sunday was a showman. He would skip, gyrate, slide, and do cartwheels. He would stand on chairs, peel off layers of clothing as he worked himself into a lather, and do burlesque-style imitations. He was bombastic, loud, abusive, rancorous.' Hadden and Shupe, *Televangelism; Power and Politics on God's Frontier*, p. 45.

14. Jacobs sometimes refers to God as 'The King who leads His people to victory', as such echoing the use of the term 'rex athleta Christi' – the king who is an athlete for Christ – in late medieval Europe (John M. Hobeman, *Sport and Political Ideology* [Austin, TX, 1984], p. 53).

15. Goshay, 'Team Has the Power of Faith: Weightlifters Show Strength of Scriptures', B3.

16. Anthony Wilson, 'Team's message packs a punch', *Abilene Reporter-News*, 21 Feb. (1992), pp. 1A, 8A.

17. Jeff Holland, ' "Power Team" Will Perform At RSHS', *Sunday Richmond County Daily Journal*, 62, 14 Apr. (1993), p. 182.

18. G.W. Brown, 'Move over Batman, God has a new team of Superheroes', *Putnam County Beacon News-Journal*, 14 July (1992), sec. 2, p. 2.

19. TBN, 'The Power Connection', 11 Jan. (1992).

20. JJEA, 'Ministry to Move a Generation', Promotional brochure (1988).

21. Goshay, 'Team Has the Power of Faith: Weightlifters Show Strength of Scriptures', B3. Holland, ' "Power Team" Will Perform At RSHS', 182.

22. Korten, 'Satan and Concrete Beware: Power Team Wars on Devil', 14.

23. TBN, 'The Power Connection', 14 Mar. (1992).

24. TBN, 'The Power Connection', 11 Jan. (1992).

25. Thanks for these insights to Mike Goldman and Tony the kickboxer.

26. Pritts, ' "Powerful" Men with a Message', 8. See also John Faught, 'Pure Power', *Permian Basin Today* (n.d.), 9–10A. In another version, Jacobs tells *People Magazine* that 'when as a student at Oral Roberts University he saw a karate expert dazzle an audience' he realised that the exhibition was appealing to non-Christians as well as to Christians. In his words: 'I liked that. I had gotten tired of all those all-Christian events, and I wanted to bring the sinners in' (in Grant, 'John Jacobs and His Team of Muscular Christians Give New Meaning to the Power of Faith', 111–12).

27. TBN, 'The Power Connection', 21 Dec. (1991).

28. The evangelical community visibly quantifies its work. For example, TBN holds frequent telethons to finance a crusade or to support its share of a broadcast satellite; the hosts often display a pair of toteboards, one showing the amount of dollars pledged, the other showing the 'Number of Souls Saved'. The Power Team cites the numbers to potential sponsors, as one testimonial claims: 'More than 1000 cards were filled out by converts with over 60 per cent in the adult age category' (Pastor Tony Scott, Cathedral of Praise Toledo, OH, Letter of recommendation dated 25 May, provided by the John Jacobs Evangelistic Association in its promotional materials (1993).

3.   BERNTH LINDFORS, 'ETHNOLOGICAL SHOW BUSINESS: FOOTLIGHTING THE DARK CONTINENT'

(From *Freakery: Cultural Spectacles of the Extraordinary Body*, ed. Rosemarie Garland Thomson [New York, 1996], pp. 207–18.)

Summary

In nineteenth-century Britain people of other races and cultures were put on display for commercial gain. These performing 'noble savages' are analysed in terms of cultural commentary of the time. Lindfors also traces the way in which the performers were viewed as a representation of 'otherness' and evidence of British cultural superiority. These displays coincided with the abolition of slavery and thus performed racism and imperialism in a socially acceptable manner. Lindfors suggests that in an era of burgeoning colonialism, these shows reveal more about the anxieties of the impresarios and audiences, and their need to assert their own racial and cultural superiority, than about the performers themselves.

Notes

1. Barbara Kirshenblatt-Gimblett, 'Objects of Ethnography', in *Exhibiting Cultures: The Poetics and Politics of Museum Display*, ed. Ivan Karp and Steven D. Lavine (Washington, DC, 1991), p. 402.
2. Ibid., p. 434.
3. London *Times*, 26 November 1810, p. 3.
4. Mrs Mathews, *Memoirs of Charles Mathews, Comedian* (London, 1839), 4, p. 137.
5. A Constant Reader, 'The Female Hottentot', *Examiner*, 14 October 1810, 653.
6. See, e.g., *Morning Chronicle*, 12 October 1810, p. 3, and *Examiner*, 28 October 1810, 681.
7. For an account of these proceedings, see Bernth Lindfors, 'Courting the Hottentot Venus', *Africa* (Rome), 40 (1985), 133–48.
8. Broadside reprinted in R. Toole-Stott, *Circus and Allied Arts: A World Bibliography, 1500–1962* (Derby, 1962), 3, p. 334.
9. *Mémoires du Museum d'Histoire Naturelle*, 3 (1817), 259–74.
10. Quoted in Percival R. Kirby, 'The Hottentot Venus', *Africana Notes and News*, 6 (1949), 60.
11. *Liverpool Mail*, 14 November 1846, p. 3.
12. Quoted on page 19 of *History of the Bosjesmans, or Bush People; the Aboriginals of Southern Africa* (London, 1847), a pamphlet sold at later shows. M. H. C. Lichtenstein's *Reisen im südlichen Afrika in den Jahren 1803, 1804, 1805 and 1806* (Berlin, 1811–1812), first published in English translation in London (1812–1815), was subsequently reissued in English by the Van Riebeeck Society in Cape Town (1928–1930).
13. Anthony Traill, 'The Languages of the Bushmen', in *The Bushmen: San Hunters and Herders of Southern Africa*, ed. Phillip V. Tobias (Cape Town and Pretoria, 1978), p. 138.
14. Ibid., p. 139, my emphasis.
15. *Liverpool Mail*, 14 November 1846, p. 3. Cf. *Liverpool Courier*, 18 November 1846, p. 6; and Dublin's *Saunders's News-Letter*, 16 December 1847, p. 2.
16. *Liverpool Chronicle*, 5 December 1846, p. 5.

17. *Birmingham Advertiser*, 6 May 1847, p. 2.
18. *Midland Counties Herald, Birmingham and General Advertiser*, 22 April 1847, p. 63.
19. *Glasgow Examiner*, 24 June 1848, p. 2.
20. *Douglas Jerrold's Weekly Newspaper*, 22 May 1847, p. 636. Cf. Dublin's *Evening Packet*, 28 December 1847, p. 3.
21. *Spectator*, 12 June 1847, 564.
22. *Era*, 6 June 1847, 11.
23. *Manchester Guardian*, 10 March 1847, p. 5.
24. *Glasgow Examiner*, 1 July 1848, p. 2.
25. *Manchester Express*, 9 March 1847, p. 3.
26. *Warder*, 22 January 1848, 5.
27. *Plymouth Times*, 3 August 1850, p. 3.
28. *Morning Post*, 19 May 1847, p. 6.
29. *Cork Southern Reporter*, 17 February 1848, p. 2.
30. *Observer*, 21 June 1847, p. 6.
31. David Livingstone, *A Popular Account of Missionary Travels and Researches in South Africa* (London, 1875), p. 35.
32. Charles Dickens, 'The Noble Savage', *Household Words*, 11 June 1853, 197–202. All quotations are from this source.
33. London *Times*, 16 May 1853, p. 4.
34. London *Times*, 18 May 1853, p. 8.
35. Irving Wallace, *The Fabulous Showman: the Life and Times of P. T. Barnum* (New York 1959), p. 111.
36. A poster for W. C. Coup's United Monster Shows at the Great Paris Hippodrome in Chicago in 1881 advertises 'Princess Amazulu, King Cetewayo's Daughter and Suite'. A newspaper advertisement for the same circus the following year bills 'Zulu Princess Amadage, daughter of King Cetewayo, and her maids of honor'; these women were also said to be 'the only Female Zulus who ever left Zululand and the only genuine Zulus in America' (Circus World Museum, Baraboo, Wisconsin).
37. William Cameron Coup, *Sawdust and Spangles: Stories and Secrets of the Circus* (Chicago, 1901), p. 166.
38. Thomas (Whimsical) Walker, *From Sawdust to Windsor Castle* (London, 1922), p. 130.
39. George Middleton, *Circus Memoirs, as Told to and Written by His Wife* (Los Angeles, 1913), p. 69.
40. Programme for P. T. Barnum with Great London Circus, Madison Square Garden, 17 April 1888 (Dyer Reynolds Circus Collection, Memphis State University).
41. J. G. Wood, 'Dime Museums as Seen from a Naturalist's Standpoint', *Atlantic Monthly*, 55 (June 1885), 760.
42. Samuel McKechnie, *Popular Entertainments through the Ages* (London, n.d.), p. 210.
43. For this information I am grateful to the late Robert Parkinson, formerly Research Director of the Circus World Museum, Baraboo, Wisconsin. The words are defined in a glossary appended to Esse Forrester O'Brien, *Circus: Cinders to Sawdust* (San Antonio, 1959), p. 260.

4. KATHERINE LIEPE-LEVINSON, 'STRIPTEASE: DESIRE, MIMETIC JEOPARDY, AND PERFORMING SPECTATORS'

(From *The Drama Review: A Journal in Performance Studies*, 42.2 (1998), 9–37.)

Summary

Liepe-Levinson considers the way spectators can become implicated within the performance of the striptease. She notes that female spectators seem more interested in eliciting the gaze of the stripper than objectifying the male object of the look, and that even when they do objectify him, this does not affect men's position of control in society. Male spectators, in contrast, take full opportunity to gaze at female bodies with impunity. However, Liepe-Levinson argues that the striptease does not simply reproduce traditional sex/gender roles. Other rituals in which the men must remain inert while women dance above and in front of them, suggest that sexual roles can be continually reified and denied in the strip show. Audiences may also shift the focus to themselves; once spectators tip a dancer to perform just for them, they too become performers, mimicking those on stage and watching themselves performing, while pretending that in their excitement they might 'lose control' or put themselves in a risky situation. Finally, Leipe-Levinson demonstrates that many theories of gender and representation overlook the possibility that the spectator is not helplessly manipulated by what he or she sees, but is knowingly and pleasurably swept away.

Notes

1. Jay Bildstein, 'How to Own, Manage, Run or Even Dance in a Topless Bar', lecture/workshop sponsored by the Learning Annex, 1 June, at the St. Moritz Hotel, New York City (1992).
2. The field research cities included New York, Houston, Washington, DC, San Francisco, Los Angeles, Chicago, Peoria, and Montreal. Other municipalities noted for these entertainments, including Windsor and Toronto in Canada and Kansas City, Miami, Boston, and New Orleans in the US, were considered for this project. They were eventually eliminated because the cities chosen offered similar or even more interesting events. I attended strip shows in the New York City area from the winter of 1990 through the winter of 1993. I reviewed strip events in Washington, DC, in half a dozen instalments from the winter of 1990 through the winter of 1992 and exotic dance acts in the other cities listed from January 1990 through August 1990. The historical time span of the three-plus years of field research is notable because it bookends the 1991 Supreme Court decision (*Barnes* v. *Glen Theatre*) that proclaimed live nude adult entertainments unprotected by freedom of expression. While this decision was a product of the unparalleled American proliferation of strip bars and clubs during the late 1980s, the ruling also followed on the heels of the 1989/1990 National Endowment of the arts debacle of denying funding to artists whose work represented their cultural and sexual positions through many means – including through the use of nudity.
3. I attended gay strip events in San Francisco, Los Angeles, Montreal, and New York City as well as transsexual strip events at Show World in New York City (located in a theatre in the basement of the Show World complex). Lesbian strip events, like many of those for straight women, tend to be subset within other events and entertainments (e.g., private parties, or dance clubs and bars not

exclusively devoted to strip shows). The subsetting aspect of strip events for females, straight and gay, coupled with my own heterocentric limitations, rendered lesbian performances less visible for me as a researcher. Adrienne Rich notes that, because our cultural imperatives repeatedly situate the phallus at the centre of sociosexual discourses while insisting that women cannot exist without men, it is 'small wonder that lesbians are reported to be a more hidden population than male homosexuals' (Adrienne Rich, 'Compulsory Heterosexuality and Lesbian Existence', *Powers of Desire*, ed. Ann Snitow, Christine Stowsell, and Sharon Thompson [New York, 1983], p. 200; see also pp. 189–90). Continuing along this line, Jill Dolan discusses the importance, but also the personal and political dangers, of publicly representing lesbian sexuality in this 'era of political intolerance and sexual prudence' (Jill Dolan, *The Feminist Spectator As Critic* [Ann Arbor, MI, 1988], p. 119). She also questions whether representations of lesbian sexuality and desire would become 'neutralised' if they were viewable as commodities 'consumable in a more mainstream economy' (ibid., p. 120). That is, heterosexual audiences usually do not consider the cultural differences in the production of meaning in these performances, nor do they contextualise them within the frame of social oppression. For another debate on this issue during the same time period see Sue-Ellen Case and Holly Hughes, 'A Case Concerning Hughes: Letters from Sue-Ellen Case and Holly Hughes', *TDR*, 33.4 (1989), 10–17. In addition to the party circuits and ad hoc performances in bars and clubs, strip events for lesbians researched in the initial stages of the study included New York City's Brooklyn dance club, Spectrum Disco, which featured the performances of one male and one female stripper on weekend nights for mixed audiences; Tracks, a gay club in Washington, DC, that presented a weekly event called 'Lesbo-A-Go-Go', an exotic dance show for lesbians that included stripping but no actual nudity (Jim Deely, Display art manager for the *Washington Blade*, telephone interview with author [Washington, DC, 13 November 1991]; 'Tony', an employee at Tracks, in telephone interview with author [Washington, DC, 13 November 1991]; Phil Donahue, 'Lesbo-A-Go-Go', *Phil Donahue Show* [ABC, 15 November 1991]; and Debi Sundahl's *Burleszk* show, which originated at the Baybrick in San Francisco and made a number of road tours (Debi Sundahl, interview with author [New York City, Winter, 1990], telephone interview with author [San Francisco, Spring, 1990]). See also 'Stripper', *Sex Work: Writings by Women in the Sex Industry*, ed. Frederique Delacoste and Priscilla Alexander (Pittsburgh, 1987), pp. 177–9).

4. The majority of spectators and performers involved in the strip events discussed in this essay are white and middle-class. Show World in New York City and the Colorado in Houston, Texas, offered the greatest diversity in terms of the race, class, and ethnicity of both dancers and spectators. All the bars, clubs, and theatres reviewed for this study are 'mainstream' in the sense that they freely advertise their whereabouts and generally attempt to abide by the municipal rules governing such events.

5. While Dolan notes that the relations between female strippers and male spectators are 'complex and subtle, as power circulates between the two positions', she ultimately posits that exotic dancing acts produce male spectator pleasure because they offer men the experience of control over women (Dolan, *The Feminist Spectator As Critic*, p. 65).

6. Ibid., pp. 64–5.

7. Erving Goffman, *Interaction Ritual: Essays on Face to Face Behavior* (Garden City, NY, 1967), p. 269.

8. Ibid., p. 268. For similar arguments see Richard Schechner, *The End of Humanism* (New York, 1982), pp. 28–9 and Susan Bennett, *Theatre Audience: A Theory of Producing and Reception* (New York, 1990), p. 114.

9. Goffman builds his theory of jeopardy and action in entertainment events on Michael Balint's concept of the 'thrill' (Michael Balint, *Thrills and Transgressions* [London, 1959], pp. 23–4).

10. Nelson Foote, 'Sex as Play', *Social Problems*, 1 (April 1954), 101.

11. Harmony Theatre house rules were explained by owner-manager 'Dominique' (interview with author, New York City, 28 May 1990). I also noted, when observing strip events in May 1990, the strict adherence to these rubrics at the Harmony.

12. While there is a tendency for female striptease spectators to behave 'aggressively' and a tendency for male striptease spectators to behave 'passively' in these events, there is no standardised patron behaviour or reason for attending strip shows. Some women sit quietly through the entire show. Some college boys, who infrequently visit strip events on weekend nights, are far more rowdy than the 'regulars'. And businessmen, here and there, may try to act in a more controlled fashion to impress their peers.

13. Keith McWalter, 'Couch Dancing', *New York Times Sunday Magazine* (6 December 1987), p. 138.

14. Clubs that feature table dancing performances for male patrons include Rick's, Caligula's, the Men's Club, and the Colorado in Houston; Big Alice's in Peoria; Cabaret Showgirls, Cabaret Penthouse, Le Sexe Scandal, and Le Super Sexe in Montreal; and Scores, Flash Dancers, Show World's Big Top Lounge, Stringfellows Presents Pure Platinum, and Goldfingers in New York City. La Bare in Houston and Club 281 and the Apollon in Montreal feature table dancing entertainments for female patrons.

15. Karl Toepfer, *Theatre, Aristocracy, and Pornocracy: The Orgy Calculus* (New York, 1991), p. 153.

16. *Showgirls*, dir. Paul Verhoeven, United Artists (1995).

17. Dolan, *The Feminist Spectator As Critic*, pp. 64–5.

18. Clubs that feature photo shoots as part of their strip events include Flash Dancers, New York Dolls, Chippendales, and Show World in New York City; Cabaret Showgirls in Montreal; Chippendales in Los Angeles; and the Sugar Shack II in Chicago.

19. Richard Schechner, *Between Theater and Anthropology* (Philadelphia, 1985), p. 279.

20. Barbara Freedman, 'Frame-Up: Feminism, Psychoanalysis, Theatre', *Performing Feminisms: Feminist Critical Theory and Theatre*, ed. Sue-Ellen Case (London, 1990), p. 74.

21. Ibid.

22. Rosalind Coward, *Female Desires: How They Are Sought, Bought and Packaged* (New York, 1985), p. 196.

23. Andrea Dworkin and Catherine McKinnon have long been at the forefront of an anti-pornography campaign that equates sexually explicit representations with actual physical violence against women. See Andrea Dworkin, *Pornography: Men Possessing Women* (New York, 1979), *Intercourse* (New York, 1987) and Catherine McKinnon, *Feminism Unmodified: Discourses on Life and Law* (Cambridge, MA, 1987).

24. Berkeley Kaite, 'The Pornographer's Body Double: Transgression is the Law', *Body In-vaders: Panic Sex in America*, ed. and intro. Arthur Kroker and Marilouise Kroker (New York, 1987), p. 155.

25. Williams quotes from Kate Millet's contradictory statement about pornography in the documentary film *Not a Love Story*, dir. Bonnie Sherr Klein, prod. Dorothy Todd Henaut and Kathleen Shannon, 68 min. Archive of the National Film Board of Canada (1981) in which Millet explains that explicitness can be useful because it may help us overcome the 'dreadful patriarchal ideas that sex is evil and that the evil in it is women'. Linda Williams, *Hardcore: Power, Pleasure, and the 'Frenzy of the Visible'* (Berkeley, CA, 1989), pp. 265–6.

5.   PHILIP AUSLANDER, 'THE SURGICAL SELF: BODY ALTERATION AND IDENTITY'

(From *From Acting to Performance* [New York and London, 1997], pp. 126–53.)

Summary

This essay theorises the performance of the medicalised body with respect to the performances of Orlan, who has plastic surgery as an artistic gesture, and Kate Bornstein, a post-operative male-to-female transsexual, whose performance pieces reflect the process of her changing body. Auslander considers the relationship between the self and its outward representation, the body, and how technological intervention alters this dichotomy. Orlan looks upon plastic surgery as an ideological practice, critiquing its use as an enhancement of conventional beauty. The surgical procedure itself becomes a performance, through Orlan's use of costumes, props, recording equipment, and her own artistic control over the surgeon's knife. Through her performances and critical writing, Bornstein attacks those who would say that she is not a 'real' woman, arguing that there is more to gender than biology. Both perform their physicality and their gender in a way that is antithetical to dominant ideologies of the body.

Notes

1. Sarah Kember, 'Medicine's New Vision?' *The Photographic Image in Digital Culture*, ed. Martin Lister (London and New York, 1995), pp. 95–114.
2. Maxine Sheets-Johnstone, 'Charting the Interdisciplinary Course', *Giving the Body Its Due*, ed. Maxine Sheets-Johnstone (Albany, NY, 1992), p. 3.
3. Andrew Murphie, 'Negotiating Presence: Performance and New Technologies', in Philip Hayward (ed.), *Culture, Technology, and Creativity in the Late Twentieth Century* (London, 1991), p. 210.
4. Ibid., p. 224.
5. Paula A. Moynahan, MD, *Cosmetic Surgery for Women* (New York, 1988), p. 203.
6. Leon Tcheupdjian, MD, *Liposuction: New Hope for a New Figure through the Art of Body Contouring* (Chicago, IL, 1988), p. 232.
7. Bernice L. Hausmann, 'Demanding Subjectivity: Transsexualism, Medicine, and the Technologies of Gender', *Journal of the History of Sexuality*, 3.2 (1992), 288–9.
8. Barbara Rose, 'Is it Art? Orlan and the Transgressive Act', *Art in America*, 81.2 (1993), 85.
9. Laura Cottingham makes the same observation in a more negative context. Referring to Burden's having had himself shot for one piece and crucified on a Volkswagen for another, she writes:

Neither of these actions collude in any way with actions considered normative in society; the same cannot be said for a woman undergoing facial surgery in an attempt to look like an idea of beauty. Similarly, Burden's acts were anarchic in the sense that he did not submit to any institutional authority. ... Orlan's performance, however, delivers her body to one of the most authoritative institutions in modern society – the medical establishment. (Laura Cottingham, 'Orlan', *Frieze International Art Magazine*, 14 (1994), 60.

I hope to make clear here that both the idea of beauty underpinning Orlan's project and the ways she delivers herself to the medical establishment are points of resistance to dominant discourses.

10. Craig Owens, 'The Allegorical Impulse: Toward a Theory of Postmodernism', in *Art After Modernism: Rethinking Representation*, ed. Brian Wallis (New York and Boston, 1984 [1980]), p. 235, original emphasis.
11. Orlan 'Philosophy' published and distributed by the artist (undated).
12. Anne Balsamo, 'On the Cutting Edge: Cosmetic Surgery and the Technological Production of the Gendered Body', *camera obscura*, 28 (1992), 209.
13. Ibid., p. 211.
14. Kathryn Pauly Morgan notes that this standardised ideal is embraced by many of the women who seek plastic surgery: Jewish women want smaller noses, Asian women want their eyes 'Westernised', African-American women want lighter skin. 'What is being created in all of these instances is not simply beautiful bodies and faces but white, Western, Anglo-Saxon bodies in a racist, anti-Semitic context' (Kathryn Pauly Morgan, 'Women and the Knife: Cosmetic Surgery and the Colonization of Women's Bodies', *Hypatia*, 6.3 [1991], 36). While it is true that individual women freely choose to have this 'elective' surgery, 'the reality is often the transformation of oneself as a woman for the eye, the hand, and the approval of the Other – the lover ..., the customers, the employers, the social peers' (ibid., p. 38).
15. Sylvia Rosenthal, *Cosmetic Surgery: A Consumer's Guide* (Philadelphia, PA, 1977), p. 11.
16. Kathryn Pauly Morgan, 'Women and the Knife: Cosmetic Surgery and the Colonization of Women's Bodies', p. 45.
17. Ibid., p. 46.
18. Lynda Nead, *The Female Nude: Art, Obscenity and Sexuality* (London and New York, 1992), p. 11.
19. Orlan 'History' published and distributed by the artist (undated).
20. Kathryn Pauly Morgan, 'Women and the Knife: Cosmetic Surgery and the Colonization of Women's Bodies', pp. 34, 35 (my emphasis).
21. These quotations cast doubt on the validity of Rose's claim that Orlan's 'programme also provides a devastating critique of the psychological and physical consequences of the distortions of nature implied in the advanced technologies discovered by scientific research, from microsurgery to organ transplants to potential genetic engineering'. Barbara Rose, 'Is it Art? Orlan and the Transgressive Act', p. 87.
22. Jeanie Forte, 'Focus on the Body: Pain, Praxis, and Pleasure in Feminist Performance', *Critical Theory and Performance*, ed. Janelle G. Reinelt and Joseph R. Roach (Ann Arbor, MI, 1992), pp. 250–4.
23. 'I searched for those circumstances in which the body is undeniable, when the body's material presence is a condition of the circumstance. Interestingly, one is that of pain, and another is that of live performance: two cases where the body must be acknowledged' (ibid., p. 251).

24. Mark Dery, *Escape Velocity: Cyberculture at the End of the Century* (New York, 1996), p. 241.
25. Carole Spitzack, 'The Confession Mirror: Plastic Images for Surgery', *Canadian Journal of Political and Social Theory*, 12, 1–2 (1988), 44.
26. Ibid., p. 38.
27. Tanya Augsburg, 'The Persistence of Subjectivity: On Medical Technology, Meta-Performance, and Feminism in Orlan's Surgical Performances'. Unpublished paper presented at Nexus Center for Contemporary Art, Atlanta, GA (15 April 1994).
28. It has been pointed out to me that inasmuch as the processes and results of plastic surgery are readily available for viewing on cable television and the Internet, it can hardly be seen any longer as a covert event in need of demystification. There is some truth to this. But I would point out, first of all, that the way plastic surgery is represented on television and the Internet is controlled by the surgeons, not their patients. Orlan presents the procedures and results of cosmetic surgery from a radically different perspective. Secondly, even though the technical procedures and effects of plastic surgery are much more publicly visible than in the past, the fact that an individual has had plastic surgery is still kept secret more often than not. For both these reasons, Augsburg's description remains valid and Orlan's intervention remains significant.
29. Sharon Waxman, 'Art by the Slice: France's Orlan Performs in the Surgical Theater', *Washington Post*, 2 May 1993, *NewsBank* Performing Arts 1993: fiche 76, grids G11 (1993).
30. Ibid., G10.
31. Barbara Rose, 'Is it Art? Orlan and the Transgressive Act', p. 85.
32. Hausmann, 'Demanding Subjectivity: Transsexualism, Medicine, and the Technologies of Gender', pp. 298–9.
33. I realise that many members of the transsexual community do not consider Hausmann's account of their subjectivity to be valid. My use of her theorisation is not intended as an endorsement of the accuracy of her claims. I employ her essay because I find that her concept of the polysurgical attitude sheds some light on the performance practice of Orlan, for whom transsexuality is a metaphor. When I return to Hausmann in my discussion of Kate Bornstein below, I use her work to establish the normative, institutional view of transsexuality against which Bornstein is reacting.
34. Kate Bornstein, *Gender Outlaw* (New York and London, 1994), p. 22; Judith Butler, *Bodies that Matter: On the Discursive Limits of Sex* (London and New York, 1993), pp. 7–8.
35. Bornstein, *Gender Outlaw*, p. 30.
36. Claudette Guillaumin, 'The Constructed Body', trans. Diane Griffin Crowder, *Reading the Social Body*, ed. Catherine B. Burroughs and Jeffrey David Ehrenreich (Iowa City, IA, 1993), p. 41.
37. Bornstein, *Gender Outlaw*, p. 45.
38. Hausmann, 'Demanding Subjectivity: Transsexualism, Medicine, and the Technologies of Gender', pp. 293–4.
39. It should be clear that, although I am suggesting a parallel between Bornstein's and Orlan's respective performance works at a political level, I am not suggesting that the tone of Bornstein's writing and performance partakes of the same postmodernist, posthumanist irony that informs Orlan's performance project. Bornstein is notable, in fact, for the open sincerity of her performance persona and the absence of irony in her work.

40. Bornstein, *Gender Outlaw*, p. 11.
41. Ibid., p. 191.
42. Ibid., p. 230.
43. Ibid., p. 8.
44. Ibid., pp. 228, 238.
45. Ibid., p. 94.
46. Ibid., p. 52.
47. Ibid., p. 210–13.
48. Ibid., p. 220.
49. Hausmann, 'Demanding Subjectivity: Transsexualism, Medicine, and the Technologies of Gender', p. 293.

6. LYNDA HART, 'RECONSIDERING HOMOPHOBIA: KAREN FINLEY'S INDISCRETIONS'

(From *Fatal Women: Lesbian Sexuality and the Mark of Aggression* [New York and London, 1994], pp. 89–103.)

Summary

Hart concentrates here on the performance artist Karen Finley, and her 1990 defunding by the National Endowment of the Arts along with three other performance artists who aligned themselves with queer politics. Hart argues that although Finley is heterosexual, her work became aligned with homosexuality, demonstrating the pervasiveness of homophobia. Hart argues that because Finley transgresses the boundaries of the body in performance by inserting food into bodily orifices, she is linked with 'unnatural' sexual practices and homosexuality. Simply by behaving as an aggressive woman Finley is seen to be performing lesbian acts, thereby eliciting a homophobic response. In addition, Hart reads Finley's work as focusing on women's devalued and abject role in society: Finley enacts roles from rape victims to housewives, railing against a system that ignores or devalues women's accomplishments and injuries they suffer.

Notes

1. Karen Finley, interview in *Angry Women*, ed. Andrea Juno and V. Vale (San Francisco, 1991), pp. 41 and 44.
2. C. Carr, 'The Sexual Politics of Censorship: War on Art', *Village Voice*, 5 June 1990, p. 28.
3. The anti-obscenity clause was replaced by a statement requiring works of art to meet 'general standards of decency and respect for the diverse beliefs of the American public', a requisite that could prove equally or more problematic.
4. David Leavitt, 'The Fears That Haunt a Scrubbed Nation', *New York Times*, August 19 1990, sec. 2, p. 1.
5. Simon Watney, *Policing Desire: Pornography, AIDS, and the Media* (Minneapolis, 1987), p. 16.
6. A special issue of *October* (61 [Summer 1992]), 'The Identity in Question', indicates the persistent difficulties of these debates.
7. Linda Alcoff, 'Cultural Feminism versus Post-Structuralism: The Identity Crisis in Feminist Theory', in *Reconstructing the Academy: Women's Education and*

Women's Studies, ed. Elizabeth Minnich, Jean O'Barr, and Rachel Rosenfeld (Chicago, 1988), p. 269.

8. Gayatri Spivak, 'Subaltern Studies: Deconstructing Historiography', in *In Other Worlds: Essays in Cultural Politics* (New York, 1987), p. 205.

9. Leavitt, 'Fears', p. 1.

10. Ibid.

11. Joseph Neisen, 'Heterosexism or Homophobia?' *Out/Look*, 10 (Fall 1990), 36–7.

12. Jonathan Dollimore, 'Masculine Sexuality – 1: Homophobia and Sexual Difference', *Oxford Literary Review*, 8. 1–2 (1986), 9.

13. Peggy Phelan, 'Serrano, Mapplethorpe, the NEA, and You: "Money Talks",' *Drama Review*, 34. 1 (1990), 14.

14. Homi K. Bhabha, 'Signs Taken for Wonders: Questions of Ambivalence and Authority under a Tree outside Delhi, May 1817', in *Race, Writing and Difference*, ed. Henry Louis Gates, Jr (Chicago 1986), pp. 168–72.

15. I take the phrase 'eccentric subject' from Teresa de Lauretis's 'Eccentric Subjects: Feminist Theory and Historical Consciousness', *Feminist Studies*, 16. 1 (1990), 115–50.

16. C. Carr, 'Unspeakable Practices, Unnatural Acts: The Taboo Art of Karen Finley', *Village Voice*, 24 July 1986, pp. 17–18, 86. This article is reprinted in *Acting Out: Feminist Performances*, ed. Lynda Hart and Peggy Phelan (Ann Arbor, MI, 1993).

17. 'Letters: The Yam Became a Hot Potato', *Village Voice*, 15 July 1986, pp. 4–6.

18. Eve Kosofsky Sedgwick, 'A Poem Is Being Written', *Representations*, 17 (Winter 1987), 129.

19. Guy Hocquenghem, 'Family, Capitalism, Anus', *Semiotext(e): Anti-Oedipus* 2. 3 (1977), 157.

20. Lauren Berlant, 'The Female Complaint', *Socialtext*, 19–20 (1988), 242.

21. Catherine Schuler, 'Spectator Response and Comprehension: The Problem of Karen Finley's *Constant State of Desire*', *Drama Review*, 32 (Spring 1988), 135.

22. Finley was dubbed the 'nude chocolate-smeared young woman' by Rowland Evans and Robert Novack, in 'The NEA's Suicide Charge', *Washington Post*, 11 May 1990, p. A27.

23. Julia Kristeva, *Powers of Horror: An Essay on Abjection*, trans. Leon S. Roudiez (New York, 1982), p. 3.

24. Ibid., p. 4.

25. Mary Douglas, *Purity and Danger: An Analysis of Concepts of Pollution and Taboo* (London, 1966), p. 5.

26. Elin Diamond, 'Brechtian Theory/Feminist Theory', *Drama Review*, 32–1 (1988), 90.

27. The published version, in *Shock Treatment* (San Francisco, 1990), reads slightly differently and does not indicate that Finley is gesturing over the wedding cake. I base my reading on a performance in Philadelphia at The Painted Bride in the spring of 1989. I use quotation marks to indicate transcription from notes I took during the performance. It should be kept in mind that some degree of improvisation is at work in Finley's performances and thus her words and gestures vary.

28. *The Theory of Total Blame* is unpublished. My notes are based on the performance at The Kitchen, New York City, 1989. For a fuller discussion of this play see my 'Motherhood According to Karen Finley: *The Theory of Total Blame*', *Drama Review* 36. 1 (1991), 124–34.

29. Juliet Mitchell, 'Introduction I', in *Feminine Sexuality*, p. 23.

30. Hélène Cixous and Catherine Clément, *The Newly Born Woman*, trans. Betsy Wing (Minneapolis, 1986), p. xii.
31. Quoted in ibid., p. 4.
32. Ibid., pp. 36–9.
33. Leo Bersani, 'Is the Rectum a Grave?' in *AIDS: Cultural Analysis, Cultural Activism*, ed. Douglas Crimp (Cambridge, MA, 1988), p. 211.

7. VIVIAN M. PATRAKA, 'SPECTACULAR SUFFERING:
PERFORMING PRESENCE, ABSENCE, AND WITNESS
AT THE US HOLOCAUST MEMORIAL MUSEUM'

(From *Spectacular Suffering: Theatre, Fascism, and the Holocaust* [Bloomington, IN, 1999], pp. 109–31. The original work from which this chapter is taken is entitled 'Spectacular Suffering: Performing Presence, Absence, and Witness at U.S. Holocaust Museums' and also considers the Beit Hashoah Museum of Tolerance in Los Angeles.)

Summary

Patraka invokes Michel de Certeau's reading of the difference between a place and a space in order to question whether it is possible to look at the United States Holocaust Memorial Museum in Washington, DC, as a space where subjects can project their own responses and experiences rather than a place where scripted responses of 'official' Holocaust memory are enacted. She looks at the museum as a site of performance, as well as reading its fund-raising mailings in order to define its ideological underpinnings. Her analysis of the Holocaust Memorial Museum involves, for example, examining the neo-classical facade that identifies it with the official government buildings that surround it, lending it official significance within a specifically American history. Patraka also looks at the way the museum portrays Jews as the feminised victim and the Americans as masculinised liberators, focusing on suffering rather than on strategies of resistance. As a Certeauian space where many competing discourses are made possible, the museum has the potential for broader significance.

Notes

1. For example, on 19 April 1993, three days before the United States Holocaust Memorial Museum actually opened, front-page news for the Bowling Green *Sentinel-Tribune* (and I'm sure many other local newspapers) included an article entitled 'Survey: One in 5 doubt Holocaust happened'. A Holocaust survey (referred to as 'the first systematic study of Americans' knowledge of the Nazi's extermination of 6 million Jews before and during World War II') done by the Roper Organization in the United States in November of 1992 and provided by the American Jewish Committee, sampled 992 adults. To the question 'Does it seem possible or does it seem impossible to you that the Nazi extermination of the Jews never happened?' 22 per cent said 'It seems possible' it never happened, 65 per cent said 'It seems impossible' it never happened, and 12 per cent replied with 'Don't know/ No answer'. These statistics were framed in a box next to the article.

Furthermore, the Roper Survey found 'that 38 per cent of adults and 53 per cent of high school students did not know the meaning of the term the Holocaust'. The information presented here, as well as its placement in time, constitutes a kind of self-evident rationale for an American Holocaust museum (though the museum is never directly mentioned) or for a Holocaust pedagogy in US public schools, potentially increasing a favourable reception among the four out of five who believe it is impossible that the Nazi extermination never happened.

2. Michel de Certeau, *The Practice of Everyday Life*, trans. Steven Rendall (Berkeley, CA, 1984), pp. 117–18.

3. As Jim Young notes in *The Texture of Memory*, 'Over time, the only "common" experience uniting an otherwise diverse, often fractious, community of Jewish Americans has been the vicarious memory of the Holocaust. Left-wing and right-wing Jewish groups, religious and secular, Zionist and non-Zionist may all draw different conclusions from the Holocaust. But all agree that it must be remembered, if to entirely disparate ideological ends' (James E. Young, *The Texture of Memory: Holocaust Memorials and Meanings* [New Haven, CT, 1993], p. 348).

4. Mieke Bal, 'Telling, Showing, Showing Off', *Critical Inquiry*, 18 (Spring 1992), 558.

5. Actually, the Washington Monument, by means of which the museum locates itself within a national landscape, was also privately sponsored on government land. For an analysis of the political and funding history of the Washington Monument, see Kirk Savage, 'The Self-made Monument: George Washington and the Fight to Erect a National Memorial', in *Critical Issues in Public Art: Content, Context, and Controversy*, ed. Harriet F. Senie and Sally Webster (New York, 1992), pp. 5–32.

6. Philip Gourevitch, 'Behold Now Behemoth: The Holocaust Memorial Museum: One More American Theme Park', *Harpers*, 287.1718 (1991), 55.

7. Mieke Bal, 'Telling, Showing, Showing Off', 560.

8. Over the years the museum has increased its efforts to depict the histories of Gypsies, homosexuals, Jehovah's Witnesses and the handicapped. For example, the spring 1997 special issue of 'Update: United States Holocaust Memorial Museum' contains the article 'Gay and Lesbian Campaign Passes $1 Million Mark'. These funds are to go to two activities: 'an endowment for the study of homosexuals in the Holocaust' and 'the further documentation of gay oral histories, location of artifacts for the permanent collection, lectures and special programmes' (Update, supplement 2). The museum also coordinated an exhibit of artifacts related to the 'experiences of homosexuals living under Nazism' during the time the NAMES Project Memorial Quilt was on display in Washington.

9. More interesting in terms of the use of computers in relation to the Holocaust is the display, within the exhibit, of the Hollerith, a very early data-processing device. This device enabled the Nazis to assert in 1934, 'We are recording the individual characteristics of every single member of the nation onto a little card', thus using technology as a means to impose and process the essentialised 'characteristics' used to constitute people into groups. While these data were used to persecute Jews and other groups, the reference to 'every single member of the nation' recollects the way in which persecution is interrelated with the regulation and containment of the population as a whole. Such reduction of the population to life-affirming or life-denying data ought to clarify the stakes for 'normative' groups in resisting genocidal actions.

10. Mieke Bal, 'Telling, Showing, Showing Off', p. 560.
11. Michael Berenbaum, *The World Must Know: The History of the Holocaust as Told in the United States Holocaust Memorial Museum* (Boston, 1993), p. 82.
12. Peggy Phelan, *Unmarked: The Politics of Performance* (New York, 1993), p. 147.

8. PEGGY PHELAN, 'HEARING ANITA HILL AND CLARENCE THOMAS'

(From *Mourning Sex: Performing Public Memories* [New York and London, 1992], pp. 95–116. The original work from which this chapter is taken is entitled 'Bloody Nose, Loose Noose: Hearing Anita Hill and Clarence Thomas' and makes references to Sigmund Freud and Wilhelm Fliess's patient Emma Eckstein and her symptom of a bloody nose, and also to Celia, a hanged slave woman Anita Hill invoked in the hearings, and to Nina Totenberg, a reporter who broke the Hill–Thomas story, who was discredited because of her past history of plagiarism.)

Summary

Peggy Phelan looks at the 1991 United States Senate Judiciary Committee hearings in which Clarence Thomas, who was seeking confirmation as a Supreme Court Justice, was accused by Anita Hill of sexual harassment. Phelan focuses particularly on how the legal system and psychoanalysis attempt to redress sexual injury, and could not be used to discover the underlying 'truth'. Neither a legal trial nor public psychotherapy, the hearings bore the hallmarks of both. They also provided a performance of two competing narratives, Hill's word against Thomas's, which then functioned as entertainment for the television audience. Asymmetrical social relationships create an atmosphere that fosters traumas, as the Hill–Thomas hearings demonstrate.

Notes

1. See Cathy Caruth (ed.), *Trauma: Explorations in Memory* (Baltimore and London, 1994).
2. For interesting new approaches to legal theory see: Iris Marion Young, *How to Throw Like a Girl and Other Essays in Feminist Philosophy and Social Theory* (Bloomington, 1990), Martha Minow, *Making All the Difference: Inclusion, Exclusion and American Law* (Ithaca, NY, 1990), and Patricia Williams, *The Alchemy of Race and Rights: Diary of a Law Professor* (Cambridge, MA and London 1991). For new critical approaches to law and culture see *Representations*, 30. Unfortunately, the valuable insights of these texts and critical studies more generally were nowhere in evidence at the Hill–Thomas hearings.
3. For a fascinating analysis of the law and delirium see Christopher Lane, ' "The Delirium of Interpretation": Writing the Papin Affair', *Differences*, 5. 2 (1993), 24–61.
4. No licensed psychologists were called as witnesses; legal experts in sexual harassment law were also prohibited witnesses. Unless otherwise stated all quotations come from *The New York Times'* transcripts of the trial published between 12 and 15 October 1991. For important analyses of the hearings see Toni Morrison, *Race-ing Justice, En-gender-ing Power: Essays on Anita Hill, Clarence Thomas, and the Construction of Social Reality* (New York, 1992); Timothy M. Phelps and

Helen Winternitz, *Capitol Games: Clarence Thomas, Anita Hill, and the Story of a Supreme Court Nomination* (New York, 1992); David Brock, *The Real Anita Hill: The Untold Story* (New York, 1993), and Robert Chrisman and Robert L. Allen (eds), *Court of Appeal: The Black Community Speaks Out on the Racial and Sexual Politics of Thomas vs. Hill* (New York, 1992).

5. Abortion is 'the most volatile legal issue in the country' (in Phelps and Winternitz, *Capitol Games*, p. 18). Therefore, controlling the Judicial body is central to controlling women's bodies.

6. Hill claimed that she was hospitalised for five days 'on an emergency basis' with stomach pains which she attributed to stress from Thomas' sexual pursuit of her.

7. William Schnieder, a fellow at the conservative American Enterprise Institute, remarked early on: 'The cynicism of this choice – the white man's Negro – may be transparent. It could backfire. Liberals will once again argue that the President is using race for political advantage and that he is not really committed to a civil rights agenda' (in Phelps and Winternitz, *Capitol Games*, p. 16). For a different analysis of the Marshall–Thomas connection see Brock, *The Real Anita Hill*, pp. 27–9). Brock argues that Thomas had been Bush's choice to succeed William Brennan who retired in 1990, but his advisors insisted that Thomas did not have enough experience on the federal courts.

8. In Phelps and Winternitz, *Capitol Games*, p. 15.

9. Quoted in Kendall Thomas, 'Beyond the Privacy Principle', *Columbia Law Review*, 92. 6 (1992), 1431.

10. For further illumination of Thomas' political beliefs see 'In Opposition to Clarence Thomas: Where we Must Stand and Why', Congressional Black Caucus Foundation, September 1991 (please note this report was written before the Anita Hill charges were made public) in Chrisman and Allen, *Court of Appeal*, pp. 231–54).

11. Kimberle Crenshaw, 'Whose Story is It Anyway? Feminist and Antiracist Appropriations of Anita Hill', *Race-ing Justice, En-gender-ing Power: Essays on Anita Hill, Clarence Thomas, and the Construction of Social Reality*, ed. Toni Morrison (New York, 1992), pp. 420–39).

12. In 'The Miscegenation Analogy' Andrew Koppleman (Andrew Koppleman, 'The Miscegenation Analogy: Sodomy Law as Sex Discrimination', *Yale Law Journal*, 98. 1 [1988], 145–64) begins his argument by noting: 'While enforcement of [sodomy] laws is sporadic at best, this is as poor a measure of the injury they inflict as the relative infrequency of lynching in the post-Civil War South.' Koppleman's essay appeared in *The Yale Law Journal*, and as alumnae, Thomas and Hill may have kept up with the *Journal*. Thomas told the Senate he had read a lot about the history of lynching and he may have had a personal interest in miscegenation analogies since he himself was married to a white woman. But my point is not so much that Thomas read Koppleman; but rather that the languages of lynching and privacy used so effectively by Thomas had been analysed by Koppleman in relation to the sodomy statutes. Both lynching and the sodomy laws do great symbolic injury, and Thomas wanted the historical weight of the injury of lynching to be on the white senators' minds.

13. It is important to point out that the Georgia Criminal Code does not make a distinction between homosexual and heterosexual sodomy, although the Supreme Court did. In Georgia, the statute simply reads: 'A person commits the offense of sodomy when he performs or submits to any sexual act involving the sex organs of one person and the mouth or anus of another.' In the lower courts, Michael Hardwick was joined in challenging the constitutionality of this

statute by John and Mary Doe, a heterosexual married couple. But the district court and the court of appeals agreed that the Does had no standing (they had not been arrested; Hardwick had). The Supreme Court opinion asserted that its decision only applied to homosexual sodomy and 'express[ed] no opinion on the constitutionality of the Georgia statute as applied to other acts of sodomy' (478 U.S. at 188n.l). For a brief polemic against the reasoning applied in *Bowers*, see Tom Stoddard, '*Bowers* v. *Hardwick*: Precedent by Personal Predilection', *University of Chicago Law Review*, 54 (1987), 648–56. For a thorough and brilliant deconstruction of the language and logic of the opinion see Thomas, 'Beyond the Privacy Principle' (1992) (and citations therein).

14. Phelps and Winternitz, *Capitol Games*, pp. 280–5.

15. See especially Morrison, *Race-ing Justice*, and Chrisman and Allen, *Court of Appeal*. When I say that we will never get to the 'truth' of what happened between Hill and Thomas, I do not mean anything remotely like Senator Alan Simpson who complained that the 'truth' was not recoverable in the Senate hearings but surely would be in a court of law: 'I'll tell you how to find the truth. You get into an adversarial courtroom, and everybody raises their hands once more, and you go at it with the rules of evidence, and you really punch around in it, and we can't do that. It's impossible to do that in this place' (quoted in Andrew Ross, 'The Private Parts of Justice', *Race-ing Justice, En-gender-ing Power: Essays on Anita Hill, Clarence Thomas, and the Construction of Social Reality*, ed. Toni Morrison [New York, 1992] p. 50).

16. No evidence supports the idea that watching pornography would make one a sexual harasser. But the perception of Thomas as a 'porn watcher' would not have helped his case. Nor for that matter would a public discussion of Hill's 'proclivities' have helped hers.

17. Even the obvious objection that Kathy Grace Thomas could easily say if he had beat her is disposed of neatly in this rumour. One of the conditions of her alimony, this story goes, is that she never accuse him of it. If she says he beat her, she would lose the money. (In fact, however, the legal documents only revealed a no-fault divorce. Clarence Thomas was granted custody of their son Jamal.) As Phelps and Winternitz point out, the rumour about the divorce began long before Anita Hill arrived in Washington: 'There was a rumour that something nasty had happened between the judge and his ex-wife, though there was absolutely nothing to substantiate it. The rumour had been unwittingly fuelled by *The Wall Street Journal*, which had championed Thomas on its editorial pages. In its initial story about the nomination, the newspaper had mentioned, but not explained, the existence of some concern in Republican circles about the divorce affecting the nomination. *The Journal* had said too much and too little, thus setting off the sort of manic speculation that happens all the time behind the often pretentious facade of the media' (Phelps and Winternitz, *Capitol Games*, pp. 68–9).

18. The lack of understanding about the distinction between genuine sexual abuse and seduction fantasies has made it possible, on occasion, for frivolous, but nonetheless extremely damaging, claims of sexual abuse to be too easily granted legal grounds for criminal accusation. (This seems to be especially true in cases involving child care workers and the testimony of large groups of children.) For further discussion see Lawrence Wright, 'Remembering Satan', *The New Yorker*, 17 (24 May, 1993).

19. In Arthur S. Hayes, 'Courts Concede the Sexes Think in Unlike Ways', *Wall Street Journal* (28 May 1991), B1.

20. Quoted in Hayes ('Courts Concede the Sexes Think in Unlike Ways', B1). While the new standard has been developed in relation to sexual harassment, it can be applied to negligence and self-defence cases as well.
21. It is useful to be cautious in claiming victories over these kinds of 'concessions'. They work to perpetuate essential gender differences, a reasonable man and a reasonable woman, that may not, in the long run, make law an ally in progressive struggle. Moreover as the lawyer for the plaintiff in the Jacksonville case pointed out, 'We have a male judge who thought the conduct was genuinely trivial. How is he going to think like a reasonable woman?' (in Hayes, 'Courts Concede the Sexes Think in Unlike Ways', B5).
22. In Elizabeth Kolbert, 'Most in National Survey Say Judge is More Believable', *New York Times* (15 October 1991), p. A1.
23. The shift may be due to the manner in which the poll was taken. Anthropologists in Detroit found the majority of women believed Hill. Of 101 interviews conducted three weeks after the hearings, 53 per cent were strong Hill supporters and 16 per cent supported Hill with some reservations. See Kate Darby Rauch, 'Interviews Find Different Take on the Hill–Thomas Controversy', *Washington Post* (7 December 1992), p. A3. For another interpretation of the polls and their bias, see Nancy Fraser, 'Sex, Lies and the Public Sphere: Some Reflections on the Confirmation of Clarence Thomas', *Critical Inquiry*, 18 (1992), 595–612.

9. RICHARD SCHECHNER, 'THE STREET IS THE STAGE'

(From *The Future of Ritual: Writings on Culture and Performance* [New York and London, 1993], pp. 45–93. The original work from which this chapter is taken also includes a discussion of American anti-war protests, as well as the rituals of Ramlila of Ramnagar, Mardi Gras, Gasparilla, and Spring Break in Daytona Beach, Florida.)

Summary

Official movements such as those by the military tend to be orderly and regimented, while unofficial demonstrations tend toward the chaotic. Schechner employs the Bakhtinian concept of carnival to consider the way demonstrations by 'the people' may bring about revolution and change, but are more frequently fundamentally conservative, ending with the old order restored. Unofficial movements may take over official public spaces, and are marked by excess, using theatrical techniques in order become more visible to the media.

Notes

1. Abbie Hoffman, *Woodstock Nation* (New York, 1969), p. 48.
2. Vice-President Agnew uttered these words in a speech before the Young Presidents Organization in Honolulu. In 1973 he was forced to resign as vice-president because of corruption and bribe-taking while holding office in Maryland where in the 1960s he was Baltimore County executive and governor. His Honolulu speech is quoted in Baxandall (1969), p. 52. Spiro Agnew, 'Honolulu address to the Young Presidents Organization, 2 May', in Lee Baxandall, 'Spectacles and scenarios: a dramaturgy of radical activity', *TDR, The Drama Review*, 13.4 (1969), 52–71.

3. Mikhail Bakhtin, *Rabelais and His World* (Bloomington, 1984), pp. 212–13.
4. Jerry Rubin, *Do It!* (New York, 1970), pp. 142–3.
5. Lee Baxandall, 'Spectacles and scenarios: a dramaturgy of radical activity', p. 65.
6. Bristol is echoing ideas first enunciated early in the twentieth century by Arnold Van Gennep, *The Rites of Passage* (Chicago, 1960) first published 1908 and Emile Durkheim, *The Elementary Forms of the Religious Life* (New York, 1915). See also Victor Turner, *The Forest of Symbols* (Ithaca, NY, 1967); *The Ritual Process* (Chicago, 1969); *Dramas, Fields, and Metaphors* (Ithaca, NY, 1974); 'Variations on a theme of liminality', in *Secular Ritual*, ed. Sally F. Moore and Barbara Myerhoff (Amsterdam, 1977); *From Ritual to Theatre* (New York, 1982); 'Body, brain, and culture', *Zygon*, 18.3 (1983), 221–45 for his emendations to Van Gennep and Durkheim as well as his own theories regarding liminality, the ritual process, and antistructure. (Michael Bristol, *Carnival and Theater* [London, 1985], p. 30).
7. See Chapter 7 of Richard Schechner, *The Future of Ritual* (New York, 1993) for a discussion of the relation between Girard's ideas and theatre. (René Girard, *Violence and the Sacred* [Baltimore, MD, 1977], p. 119.)
8. Bristol, *Carnival and Theater*, p. 33.
9. Girard, *Violence and the Sacred*, p. 120.
10. Roger Caillois, *Man and the Sacred* (Glencoe, NY, 1959), pp. 125–6.
11. Ibid., p. 123.
12. See Marvin Carlson, *Places of Performance* (Ithaca, NY, 1989) and Sally Harrison-Pepper, *Drawing a Circle in the Square* (Jackson, MS, 1990).
13. See Turner, 'Variations on a theme of liminality', *From Ritual to Theatre*, and 'Are there universals of performance in myth, ritual, and drama?' in *By Means of Performance*, ed. Richard Schechner and Willa Appel (Cambridge, 1990) for distinctions between the liminal and the liminoid.
14. See Richard Schechner, 'Last exit from Shanghai', *American Theater*, 6.8 (1989), 24ff. and 'Tales of a few cities', *New Theatre Quarterly*, VII. 28 (1991), 315–24.
15. Chiu Yu Mok and J. Frank Harrison (eds), *Voices from Tiananmen Square* (Montreal–New York, 1990), pp. xi–xii.
16. Jonathan D. Spence, *The Gate of Heavenly Peace* (New York, 1981), p. 17.
17. Ibid., pp. 17–18.
18. Charles Tilly, *From Mobilization to Revolution* (Reading, MA, 1978).
19. Joseph W. Eshcrick and Jeffrey N. Wasserstrom, 'Acting out democracy: political theater in modern China', *The Journal of Asian Studies*, 49.4 (1990), 835–66, 839.
20. Ibid., p. 841.
21. Ibid.
22. Ibid., pp. 844–5, 848.
23. See Turner, *The Ritual Process*, and *From Ritual to Theatre*. Schechner, 'From ritual to theatre and back: the structure/process of the efficacy-entertainment dyad', *Educational Theatre Journal*, 26.4 (1974), 455–81 and *Performance Theory* (London and New York, 1988).
24. The statistics and anecdotes are taken from Robert D. McFadden, 'The Berlin Wall: a monument to the cold war, triumphs and tragedies', *The New York Times*, 10 November 1989, A15. See also Peter Clay Schmidt's *The Fall of the Berlin Wall*, video (1990).
25. A 'domino effect' swept through the world from China in May 1989, Germany in August, and then to Czechoslovakia, Romania, the USSR, Albania, Yugoslavia, and South Africa. Although extremely disparate at one level, the demands in all these places were similar at the level of wanting more representation within, or independence from central authorities.

26. Ferdinand Protzman, 'Thousands swell trek to the West by East Germans', *New York Times*, 12 September 1989, pp. A1, 14.
27. Serge Schmemann, 'Exodus galls East Berlin', *New York Times*, 14 September 1989, p. A14.
28. Schmemann, 'Sour German birthday', *New York Times*, 6 October 1989, p. A8.
29. Schmemann, 'Gorbachev lends Honecker a hand', *New York Times*, 7 October 1989, p. A5.
30. Henry Kamm, 'East Berliners march for democracy', *New York Times*, 22 October 1989, p. A16.
31. Schmemann 'Another big rally in East Germany', *New York Times*, 31 October 1989, p. A17.
32. Schmemann, 'East Germany opens frontier to the West', *New York Times*, 10 November 1989, pp. A1, 14.
33. Berlin Wall chunks soon found their way into the 'collectibles' market. Americans sent away for 'genuine' fragments of the Wall, mounted and placarded. Of course, who was to say if the chunk of concrete someone paid $50 for was really from the Wall? Do you think the distributor, faced with a shortage of Wall amidst a frenzy of money, would hesitate to 'simulate' a little piece of the Wall? Would this simulation, should it have occurred, be considered forgery or theatre or both?
34. All quoted examples of celebrating are taken from accounts reported in *The New York Times* on 10, 11, and 12 November 1989.
35. Craig R. Whitney, with David Binder, and Serge Schmemann, 'Party coup turned East German tide', *New York Times*, 19 November 1989, p. A27.

10.   JOSEPH ROACH, 'CULTURE AND PERFORMANCE IN THE CIRCUM-ATLANTIC WORLD'

(From *Performativity and Performance*, ed. Eve Kosofsky Sedgwick and Andrew Parker [New York and London, 1995], pp. 45–63.)

Summary

This article focuses on funerals and the performance of collective memory across cultures. According to Roach, written literature is not the only way to transmit culture, and he considers the significance of other cultural forms such as dance, storytelling and speech. Invoking Certeau's theories regarding the 'practice of everyday life', he considers the way spectators may become actors in these cultural rituals. Roach elaborates on performance as a 'non-identical repetition', that always functions as a variation on that which came before it. The essay also considers the way that communities can attempt to define their own culture by actively selecting what they will transmit through performance. Using examples of cultural exchange from Northern Europe, Africa and the Americas, Roach notes the way in which funerals employ a variety of performative methods, such as poetry, music, and dramatic ceremonies. Roach also considers the practice of cultural appropriation, particularly focusing on surrogation, a term he uses to describe the practice of substituting one person for another in performance. He argues that the trade in culture in the Circum-Atlantic world is not always evenly balanced.

Notes

1. Anna Deavere Smith, interviewed by John Lahr, quoted in 'Under the Skin', *The New Yorker* (28 June 1993), 92.
2. Ngugi wa Thiong'o, interviewed by Bettye J. Parker, *Critical Perspectives on Ngugi wa Thiong'o*, ed. G. D. Killam (Washington DC, 1984), p. 61; Kwame Anthony Appiah, *In My Father's House: Africa in the Philosophy of Culture* (New York and Oxford, 1992), p. 132.
3. Michel de Certeau, *The Practice of Everyday Life*, trans. Stephen F. Rendall (Berkeley and Los Angeles, 1984), pp. 91–110.
4. John W. Kronik, 'Editor's Note', *PMLA*, 107 (1992), 425.
5. Richard Schechner, *Between Theater and Anthropology* (Philadelphia, 1985), pp. 35–116.
6. Henry Louis Gates, Jr, *The Signifying Monkey: A Theory of Afro-American Literary Criticism* (New York, 1988), pp. 63–88; Margaret Thompson Drewal, *Yoruba Ritual: Performers, Play, Agency* (Bloomington, 1992), pp. 4–5.
7. For the material in this paragraph, I am variously indebted to John J. MacAloon, *Rite, Drama, Festival, Spectacle: Rehearsals Toward a Theory of Cultural Performance* (Philadelphia, 1984); Paul Connerton, *How Societies Remember* (New York, 1989); and Maurice Halbwachs, *On Collective Memory*, ed. Lewis A. Coser (Chicago and London, 1992).
8. Joseph Roach, 'Slave Spectacles and Tragic Octoroons: A Cultural Genealogy of Antebellum Performance', *Theatre Survey*, 33 (1992), 169.
9. Jonathan Arac, *Critical Genealogies: Historical Situations for Postmodern Literary Studies* (New York, 1987), p. 2.
10. Michel Foucault, *Discipline and Punish: The Birth of the Prison*, trans. Alan Sheridan (New York, 1979), p. 31.
11. Paul Gilroy, *'There Ain't No Black in the Union Jack': The Cultural Politics of Race and Nation* (Chicago, 1987), p. 157.
12. J.S. Bromley, *The New Cambridge Modern History*, Vol. VI, *The Rise of Great Britain and Russia* (Cambridge, 1971), p. 571; for a view of the larger context, see Fernand Braudel, *The Mediterranean and the Mediterranean World in the Age of Philip II*, 2 vols (New York, 1972–73).
13. See Paul Zumthor, *Oral Poetry: An Introduction*, trans. Kathryn Murphy-Judy (Minneapolis, 1990).
14. See Sidney Mintz, *Sweetness and Power: The Place of Sugar in Modern History* (New York, 1985).
15. Barbara Kirshenblatt-Gimblett, 'Objects of Ethnography', in *The Poetics and Politics of Museum Display*, ed. Ivan Karp and Steven D. Lavine (Washington and London, 1991), p. 430.
16. Angus Calder, *Revolutionary Empire: The Rise of the English-Speaking Empires from the Fifteenth Century to the 1780s* (New York, 1981), p. 347.
17. For several commentaries, see Curtis Price's critical edition, *Dido and Aeneas, an Opera* (New York and London, 1986).
18. Henry Purcell and Nahum Tate, *Dido and Aeneas* (1689; facs. rpt Boosey & Hawkes, n.d.), p. 8.
19. John Dryden, *Virgil: The Aeneid Translated by John Dryden* (New York, 1944), p. 126.
20. Thomas Walker, 'Ciaccona and Passacaglia: Remarks on Their Origin and Early History', *Journal of the American Musicological Society*, 21 (1968), 300–20.

21. James Clifford, *The Predicament of Culture: Twentieth-Century Ethnography, Literature and Art* (Cambridge, MA and London, 1988), p. 15.

22. Chief Logan, quoted in Jay Fliegelman, *Declaring Independence: Jefferson, Natural Language, and the Culture of Performance* (Stanford, CA, 1993), p. 98.

23. Thomas Jefferson, quoted in Fliegelman, ibid., p. 192.

24. Eric Lott, 'Love and Theft: The Racial Unconscious of Blackface Minstrelsy', *Representations*, 39 (1992), 23–50.

25. Joseph Roach, 'Mardi Gras Indians and Others: Genealogies of American Performance', *Theatre Journal*, 44 (1992), 461–83; see Judith Bettelheim and John W. Nunley, *Caribbean Festival Arts: Each and Every Bit of Difference* (St. Louis, 1988).

26. Victor Turner, *Schism and Continuity: A Study of Ndembu Village Life* (Manchester, 1957), p. 93.

27. Victor Turner, *Celebration: Studies in Festivity and Ritual* (Washington, DC, 1982), p. 16.

28. See Richard Huntington and Peter Metcalf, *Celebrations of Death: The Anthropology of Mortuary Ritual* (Cambridge and New York, 1979).

29. Marjorie Garber, *Vested Interests: Cross-Dressing and Cultural Anxiety* (New York, 1993), p. 33.

30. Richard Steele, *The Tatler*, ed. Donald F. Bond (Oxford, 1987), II, p. 423.

31. Judith Milhous, 'An Annotated Census of Thomas Betterton's Roles, 1659–1710', *Theatre Notebook*, 29 (1975), Part I, 33–45; Part II, 85–94.

32. Steele, *Tatler*, II, 423–4.

33. bell hooks, *Black Looks: Race and Representation* (Boston, 1993), p. 180.

34. Appiah, *In My Father's House*, p. 191.

35. Willie Pajaud: in file, Funeral and Music: General, William Ransom Hogan Jazz Archive, Tulane University.

36. Joseph Charles Augustus, Obituary, *New Orleans Times-Picayune* (12 October 1992), p. B8, Hogan Jazz Archive.

37. Malcolm Rebennack (Dr. John): in Joseph August, 'Mr. Google Eyes', Memorial Service Program, Hogan Jazz Archive.

38. See Jack Vincent Buerkle and Danny Barker, *Bourbon Street Black: The New Orleans Black Jazzman* (New York, 1973), and William J. Schafer and Richard B. Allen, *Brass Bands and New Orleans Jazz* (Baton Rouge and London, 1977); 'Nelson' could also be used as a verb to describe the distinctive motion of the grand marshal (see Archie Carey: in file, Funeral and Music: Grand Marshall, Hogan Jazz Archive).

39. Gwendolyn Midlo Hall, *Africans in Colonial Louisiana: The Development of Afro-Creole Culture in the Eighteenth Century* (Baton Rouge and London, 1992), pp. 50, 372.

40. James C. Scott, *Domination and the Arts of Resistance: Hidden Transcripts* (New Haven and London, 1990).

41. Claude C. Robin, *Voyage to Louisiana*, trans. Stuart O. Landry (New Orleans, 1966), p. 248.

42. Richard Allen: in file, Funeral and Music: Local, Hogan Jazz Archive.

43. Robert Tallant, *Voodoo in New Orleans* (1946; rpt Gretna, Louisiana, 1983), pp. 33–6.

44. Joe August, Obituary.

11. PAUL GILROY, ' "JEWELS BROUGHT FROM BONDAGE": BLACK MUSIC AND THE POLITICS OF AUTHENTICITY'

(From *The Black Atlantic: Modernity and Double Consciousness* [London, 1993], pp. 73–110. The original work from which this chapter is taken concludes with discussion of the Fisk University Jubilee Singers, musical criticism, soul music, and digital simulation in music.)

Summary

Gilroy is interested in the doubleness of cultural forms and relates these ideas to black music. Since slaves were denied access to the written word, music was one of the few modes of cultural expression made available to them, and is therefore seen as reflecting the slave experience. Gilroy then looks at the particular example of black culture and music in the United Kingdom. He makes the point that black communities in Britain have arrived relatively recently, and have therefore drawn upon black Caribbean and American culture, and by extension, their musical traditions. Consequently, black music in the United Kingdom, while incorporating the British experience, is replete with traditions and experiences of other black subgroups. Gilroy also argues that the diaspora and cultural exchange that makes these musical forms possible over time goes beyond individual cultures and contributes to a new, hybridised cultural creation.

Notes

1. Andrew Bowie, *Aesthetics and Subjectivity* (Manchester, 1990), p. 68.
2. These views are echoed by Richard Wright's insistence on the blues as merely the sensualisation of suffering.
3. 'The threshold between Classicism and modernity ... had been definitely crossed when words ceased to intersect with representations and to provide a spontaneous grid for the knowledge of things.' Michel Foucault, *The Order of Things* (London, 1974), p. 304.
4. Frederick Douglass, *Narrative of the Life of Frederick Douglass, an American Slave, Written by Himself* (Cambridge, MA, 1960), p. 46.
5. St. Clair Drake, *Black Folks Here and There*, Afro-American Culture and Society Monograph Series no. 7 (Los Angeles, 1987).
6. Edouard Glissant, *Caribbean Discourse*, trans. J. Michael Dash (Charlottesville, VA, 1989), p. 248; John Baugh, *Black Street Speech* (Austin, TX, 1983).
7. Robert Farris Thompson, *Flash of the Spirit* (New York, 1983) and 'Kongo Influences on African-American Artistic Culture', in J. E. Holloway (ed.), *Africanisms in American Culture* (Bloomington and Indianapolis, 1990).
8. bell hooks and Cornel West, *Breaking Bread* (Boston, 1991).
9. We may follow Kristeva too into the idea that the condition of exile which partially defines the experience of these artists also compounds their experience of dissidence. 'A New Type of Intellectual: The Dissident', in Toril Moi (ed.), *The Kristeva Reader* (Oxford, 1986).
10. Robert Proctor, *Value-Free Science? Purity and Power in Modern Knowledge* (Cambridge, MA, 1991); Donna Haraway, 'Manifesto For Cyborgs', in Linda Nicholson (ed.), *Feminism/Postmodernism* (New York and London, 1990).
11. Ralph Ellison, *Shadow and Act* (New York, 1964), p. 234.
12. C. L. R. James, *Notes on Dialectics* (London, 1980).

13. C. L. R. James, 'The Mighty Sparrow', in *The Future in the Present* (London, 1978); Kathy Ogren, '"Jazz Isn't Just Me": Jazz Autobiographies as Performance Personas', in Reginald T. Buckner et al. (eds), *Jazz in Mind: Essays on the History and Meanings of Jazz* (Detroit, 1991).
14. Kobena Mercer, 'Black Art and the Burden of Representation', *Third Text*, 10 (Spring 1990), and 'Looking for Trouble', *Transition*, 51 (1991).
15. This concept is suggestively explored by Glissant in *Caribbean Discourse* and by St. Clair Drake in his two-volume study *Black Folk Here and There* (1987 and 1990).
16. Judith Butler, *Gender Trouble* (New York and London, 1990); Jane Flax, *Thinking Fragments* (Berkeley and Oxford, 1990); E. Spelman, *Inessential Woman* (Boston, 1988); Sandra Harding, 'The Instability of Analytical Categories in Feminist Theory', in S. Harding and J. O'Barr (eds), *Sex and Scientific Enquiry* (Chicago, 1988).
17. These processes have been examined in Gurinder Chudha's film *I'm British But* (British Film Institute, 1988).
18. On Apache Indian see John Masouri, 'Wild Apache', *Echoes* (1 February 1992), 11; Laura Connelly, 'Big Bhangra Theory', *Time Out* (19–26 February 1992), 18; and Vaughan Allen, 'Bhangramuffin', *The Face*, 44 (May 1992), 104–7.
19. For example Malkit Singh, *Golden Star (U.K.)*, 'Ragga Muffin Mix 1991', remixed by Bally Sagoo, Star Cassette SC 5120. Thanks to Chila Kumari Burman for this reference.
20. I am thinking here of the way in which the street funk experiments of the Los Angelino band War paved the way for modernist reggae experiments. Play War's 'Slippin' into Darkness' back to back with the Wailers' 'Get Up Stand Up' and you will see what I mean.
21. Dennis Wepman et al., *The Life: The Lore and Folk Poetry of the Black Hustler* (Philadelphia, 1976).
22. Henry Louis Gates, Jr, 'Rap Music: Don't Knock It If You're Not onto Its "Lies"', *New York Herald Tribune*, 20 June 1990.
23. Eric Berman, 'A Few Words with Eric B. and Rakim', *Crossroads Magazine*, 4 (December 1990), 10.
24. Cornel West, 'Black Culture and Postmodernism', in B. Kruger and P. Mariani (eds), *Re-Making History* (Seattle, 1989).
25. Trey Ellis's piece 'The New Black Aesthetic (N.B.A.)', *Callaloo*, 12. 1 (Winter 1989), 233–47, exemplified the perils of casual, 'anything goes' postmodernism for black cultural production. It was striking how, for example, profound questions of class antagonism *within* the black communities were conjured out of sight. Apart from his conflation of forms which are not merely different but actively oppose one another, Ellis did not seriously consider the notion that the N.B.A. might have a very particular and highly class-specific articulation within a small and isolated segment of the black middle class which has struggled with its dependency on the cultural lifeblood of the black poor.
26. Edward Said, 'Travelling Theory', in *The World, the Text and the Critic* (London, 1983).

12.   JUDITH BUTLER, 'CRITICALLY QUEER'

(From *Bodies That Matter: On the Discursive Limits of 'Sex'* [New York and London, 1993], pp. 223–42.)

Summary

Butler refers to J. L. Austin's use of the term 'performative' for a speech act which enacts that which it articulates, such as a legal sentence or a baptism. The performative can be seen as a way of asserting authority, and by extension, of insisting on cultural norms. Butler draws upon Eve Kosofsky Sedgwick's theories of queer performativity, and focuses particularly on the performative of the marriage ceremony. The 'I pronounce you...' carries with it assumptions of the heterosexual norm, and is contrasted with the performative 'queer', which, used as an insult, keeps the 'guilty' party outside hegemonic discourse. Butler's argument is that though our gender is assigned, we never fit the role perfectly, and are therefore always performing the gender we wish to be associated with. Gender, therefore, can only be cited or impersonated; it can never be an essential core of one's makeup. As one example of performativity, drag possesses the potential to question heterosexual hegemony. Queer activism has utilised theatricality as a political act.

Notes

This essay was originally published in *GLQ*, 1.1 (Fall 1993). I thank David Halperin and Carolyn Dinshaw for their useful editorial suggestions. This chapter is an altered version of that essay.

1. This is a question that pertains most urgently to recent questions of 'hate speech'.
2. Friedrich Nietzsche, *On the Genealogy of Morals*, trs. Walter Kaufman (New York, 1969), p. 77.
3. Michel Foucault, *The History of Sexuality, Volume One*, trs. Robert Hurley (New York, 1978), pp. 92–3.
4. See Eve Kosofsky Sedgwick's 'Queer Performativity' in *GLQ*, 1.1 (Spring 1993). I am indebted to her provocative work and for prompting me to rethink the relationship between gender and performativity.
5. It is, of course, never quite right to say that language or discourse 'performs', since it is unclear that language is primarily constituted as a set of 'acts'. After all, this description of an 'act' cannot be sustained through the trope that established the act as a singular event, for the act will turn out to refer to prior acts and to a reiteration of 'acts' that is perhaps more suitably described as a citational chain. Paul de Man points out in 'Rhetoric of Persuasion' that the distinction between constative and performative utterances is confounded by the fictional status of both: '... the possibility for language to perform is just as fictional as the possibility for language to assert' (p. 129). Further, he writes, 'considered as persuasion, rhetoric is performative, but considered as a system of tropes, it deconstructs its own performance' (pp. 130–1, in *Allegories of Reading* [New Haven, CT, 1987]).
6. In what follows, that set of performatives that Austin terms illocutionary will be at issue, those in which the binding power of the act *appears* to be derived from the intention or will of the speaker. In 'Signature, Event, Context', in *Limited, Inc.* (Evanston, IL, 1988), Jacques Derrida argues that the binding power that Austin attributes to the speaker's intention in such illocutionary acts is more properly attributable to a citational force of the speaking, the iterability that establishes the authority of the speech act, but which establishes the non-singular character of that act. In this sense, every 'act' is an echo or citational chain, and it is its citationality that constitutes its performative force.
7. 'Signature, Event, Context', p. 18.

8. The historicity of discourse implies the way in which history is constitutive of discourse itself. It is not simply that discourses are located *in* histories, but that they have their own constitutive historical character. Historicity is a term which directly implies the constitutive character of history in discursive practice, that is, a condition in which a 'practice' could not exist apart from the sedimentation of conventions by which it is produced and becomes legible.

9. My understanding of the charge of presentism is that an inquiry is presentist to the extent that it (a) universalises a set of claims regardless of historical and cultural challenges to that universalisation or (b) takes a historically specific set of terms and universalises them falsely. It may be that both gestures in a given instance are the same. It would, however, be a mistake to claim that all conceptual language or philosophical language is 'presentist', a claim which would be tantamount to prescribing that all philosophy become history. My understanding of Foucault's notion of genealogy is that it is a specifically philosophical exercise in exposing and tracing the installation and operation of false universals. My thanks to Mary Poovey and Joan W. Scott for explaining this concept to me.

10. Theatricality is not for that reason fully intentional, but I might have made that reading possible through my reference to gender as 'intentional and non-referential' in 'Performative Acts and Gender Constitution', an essay published in Sue-Ellen Case (ed.), *Performing Feminisms* (Baltimore, MD, 1991), pp. 270–82. I use the term 'intentional' in a specifically phenomenological sense. 'Intentionality' within phenomenology does not mean voluntary or deliberate, but is, rather, a way of characterising consciousness (or language) as *having an object*, more specifically, as directed toward an object which may or may not exist. In this sense, an act of consciousness may intend (posit, constitute, apprehend) an *imaginary* object. Gender, in its ideality, might be construed as an intentional object, an ideal which is constituted but which does not exist. In this sense, gender would be like 'the feminine' as it is discussed as an impossibility by Drucilla Cornell in *Beyond Accommodation* (New York, 1992).

11. See David Román, '"It's My Party and I'll Die If I Want To!": Gay Men, AIDS, and the Circulation of Camp in U.S. Theatre', *Theatre Journal*, 44 (1992) 305–27; see also by Román, 'Performing All Our Lives: AIDS, Performance, Community', in Janelle Reinelt and Joseph Roach (eds), *Critical Theory and Performance* (Ann Arbor, MI, 1992).

12. See Larry Kramer, *Reports from the Holocaust: The Making of an AIDS Activist* (New York, 1989); Douglas Crimp and Adam Rolston (eds), *AIDSDEMO-GRAPHICS* (Seattle, 1990); and Doug Sadownick, 'ACT UP Makes a Spectacle of AIDS', *High Performance*, 13 (1990), 26–31. My thanks to David Román for directing me to this last essay.

13. Judith Butler, *Gender Trouble: Feminism and the Subversion of Identity* (New York, 1990), pp. 57–65. See also her 'Melancholy Genders, Refused Identifications', in *Psychoanalytic Dialogues* (forthcoming).

14. I thank Laura Mulvey for asking me to consider the relation between performativity and disavowal, and Wendy Brown for encouraging me to think about the relation between melancholia and drag and for asking whether the denaturalisation of gender norms is the same as their subversion. I also thank Mandy Merck for numerous enlightening questions that led to these speculations, including the suggestion that if disavowal conditions performativity, then perhaps gender itself might, be understood on the model of the fetish.

15. See 'Freud and the Melancholia of Gender', in Butler, *Gender Trouble*.

16. This is not to suggest that an exclusionary matrix rigorously distinguishes between how one identifies and how one desires; it is quite possible to have overlapping identification and desire in heterosexual or homosexual exchange, or in a bisexual history of sexual practice. Further, 'masculinity' and 'femininity' do not exhaust the terms for either eroticised identification or desire.
17. See Douglas Crimp, 'Mourning and Militancy', *October*, 51 (Winter 1989), 97–107.

13. SUSAN LEIGH FOSTER, 'CHOREOGRAPHIES OF GENDER'

(From *Signs*, 24.1 (1998), 1–33. The original work from which this chapter is taken also considers choreography in light of cultural values, dance studies' exclusion from feminist discourse, and a consideration of the term 'performance'.)

Summary

Returning to J. L. Austin's performative speech acts, Foster notes the way in which physical embodiment is absent from these performative articulations. She argues that gender can be understood more effectively as choreography than performance, since gender is ultimately dependent on the use of the body, its gestures and appearance. In addition, Foster asks who, if gender is a performance, has written the script that is being performed? She makes the link between the way choreography is dependent on and responds to a series of rituals and conventions, whereas performance can be read as the individual ability to enact such a script. The performance of the dance itself is based on particular cultural and historical moments and depends on working through gendered connotations of certain movements and body types.

Notes

1. Teresa de Lauretis, 'Upping the Anti *(sic)* in Feminist Theory', *Conflicts in Feminism*, ed. Marianne Hirsch and Evelyn Fox Keller (New York and London, 1990), p. 244.
2. Anna Beatrice Scott, 'Spectacle and Dancing Bodies That Matter: Or, If It Don't Fit, Don't Force It', *Meaning in Motion*, ed. Jane Desmond (Durham, NC and London, 1997), p. 259.
3. Yvonne Yarbro-Bejarano, 'Expanding the Categories of Race and Sexuality in Gay and Lesbian Studies', *Professions of Desire*, ed. George Haggerty (New York, 1995), p. 128.
4. J. L. Austin, *How to Do Things with Words* (Cambridge, MA, 1962).
5. Judith Butler, *Gender Trouble: Feminism and the Subversion of Identity* (New York and London, 1990).
6. See, e.g., the following incidental references to Butler and to gender as performance. Chosen randomly, they suggest the wide impact of the notion of gender as performance on cultural studies generally: Israel Burshatin, 'Playing the Moor: Parody and Performance in Lope de Vega's "El primer Fajardo"' in 'Special Topic: Performance', ed. Kimberly Benston, *PMLA*, 107.3 (1992), 578; Erik MacDonald, *Theater at the Margins: Text and the Post-Structured Stage* (Ann Arbor, MI, 1993), p. 123; Laurence Senelick, Introduction to *Gender in Performance: The Presentation of Difference in the Performing Arts*, ed. Laurence

Senelick (Middletown, CT, 1992), p. xi; Clare Hemmings, 'Resituating the Bisexual Body: From Identity to Difference', *Activating Theory*, ed. Joseph Bristow and Angelia R. Wilson (London, 1993), pp. 118–38.; Paula Rabinowitz, 'Soft Fictions and Intimate Documents: Can Feminism Be Posthuman?' *Posthuman Bodies*, ed. Judith Halberstam and Ira Livingston (Bloomington, 1995), p. 102; Jocelyn Robson and Beverly Zalcock, 'Looking at "Pumping Iron II": The Women', *Immortal, Invisible*, ed. Tamsin Wilton (New York and London, 1995), pp. 185–6; Emily Apter, 'Acting out Orientalism', *Performance and Cultural Politics*, ed. Elin Diamond (New York and London, 1996), pp. 15–34, esp. 27; Nancy Duncan, 'Introduction: (Re)placings', *Body Space*, ed. Nancy Duncan (New York and London, 1996), p. 5; Kathryn R. Kent, ' "No Trespassing": Girl Scout Camp and the Limits of the Counterpublic Sphere', *Women and Performance*, 8.2 (1996), 191.

7. For Butler's discussion of interpellation and its relation to Althusser, see Judith Butler, *Bodies That Matter: On the Discursive Limits of Sex* (New York and London, 1993), p. 121.

8. Judith Butler, 'Performative Acts and Gender Constitution: An Essay in Phenomenology and Feminist Theory', *Performing Feminisms*, ed. Sue-Ellen Case (Baltimore, MD, 1990), p. 270.

9. Judith Butler, *Bodies That Matter: On the Discursive Limits of Sex*, p. 225.

10. Ibid., p. 12.

11. Butler also makes this point in 'Performative Acts and Gender Constitution: An Essay in Phenomenology and Feminist Theory' (Butler, *Performing Feminisms*, p. 271).

12. See Nancy Lee Chalfa Ruyter, *Reformers and Visionaries: The Americanization of the Art of Dance* (Brooklyn, NY, 1979); Elizabeth Kendall, *Where She Danced: The Birth of American Art Dance* (Berkeley and Los Angeles, 1984); Ann Daly, *Done into Dance* (Bloomington, 1996) and Linda Tomko, *Dancing Class* (Bloomington, 1999).

13. See Sali Ann Kriegsman, *Modern Dance in America: The Bennington Years* (Boston, 1981) and also Tomko, *Dancing Class*.

14. I have elaborated on this argument in Susan Leigh Foster, 'Dancing Bodies', in *Incorporations*, ed. Jonathan Crary and Sanford Kwinter, *Zone*, 6 (1992), 480–95.

15. The kinds of movement qualities, spacing, and timings I describe here are meant to be suggestive of categories of movement analysis rather than as systematic or exhaustive lists of gendered characteristics. They take inspiration from but do not claim the kind of comprehensiveness argued for by the early twentieth-century movement theorist Rudolph Laban. A description of his system for analysing gendered movement can be found in Irmgard Bartinieff, *Body Movement, Coping with the Environment* (New York, 1980), pp. 58–9, 92–3. An alternative and very thoughtful systemisation of gender in relation to movement styles is provided in Iris Marion Young, *How to Throw Like a Girl and Other Essays in Feminist Philosophy and Social Theory* (Bloomington, 1990).

16. Sue-Ellen Case, 'Performing Lesbian in the Space of Technology, Part I', *Theatre Journal*, 47.1 (1995), 1–18 has pointed to the prejudices entailed in the focus on the textual in studies of performativity.

17. Katie King argues in support of this notion of choreography as theory when she describes 'the whole of the many forms theorising takes: acting, thinking, speaking, conversation, action grounded in theory, action producing theory, action suggesting theory, drafts, letters, unpublished manuscripts, stories in writing and

not, poems said and written, art events like shows, readings, enactments, zap actions such as ACT UP does' (Katie King, 'Producing Sex, Theory, and Culture: Gay/Straight Remap-pings in Contemporary Feminism', *Conflicts in Feminism*, ed. Marianne Hirsch and Evelyn Fox Keller [New York and London, 1990], p. 89).

18. This notion of choreography shares much with Elizabeth Grosz's notion of signature. See Elizabeth Grosz, *Space, Time, and Perversion* (New York and London, 1995), pp. 21–3.

19. For a lucid account of the cultural work performed by Queer Nation's kiss-ins in shopping malls, see Lauren Beriant and Elizabeth Freeman, 'Queer Nationality', *Fear of a Queer Planet: Queer Politics and Social Theory*, ed. Michael Warner (Minneapolis and London, 1993), pp. 193–229).

20. Susan Bordo, *Unbearable Weight* (Berkeley and Los Angeles, 1993), pp. 228–9).

Suggestions for Further Reading

Auslander, Philip, 'Evangelical Fervor', *The Drama Review*, 39.4 (1995), 178–83.
——, *From Acting to Performance: Essays in Modernism and Postmodernism* (New York and London, 1997).
——, *Liveness: Performance in a Mediatized Culture* (New York and London, 1999).
Austin, J. L., *How to Do Things With Words*, 2nd edn, ed. J. O. Urmson and Marina Sbisà (Oxford and New York, 1962, 1975).
Butler, Judith, *Gender Trouble: Feminism and the Subversion of Identity* (New York and London, 1990).
——, *Bodies that Matter: On the Discursive Limits of 'Sex'* (New York and London, 1993).
Carlson, Marvin, *Performance: An Introduction* (New York and London, 1996).
Case, Sue-Ellen, Philip Brett and Susan Leigh Foster (eds), *Decomposition: Post-Disciplinary Performance* (Bloomington and Indianapolis, 2000).
——, *Cruising the Performative: Interventions into the Representation of Ethnicity, Nationality, and Sexuality* (Bloomington and Indianapolis, 1995).
Case, Sue-Ellen (ed.), *Performing Feminisms: Feminist Critical Theory and Theatre* (Baltimore and London, 1990).
Cohen-Cruz, Jan (ed.) and introd., *Radical Street Performance: An International Anthology* (New York and London, 1998).
Conquergood, Dwight, 'Of Caravans and Carnivals: Performance Studies in Motion', *The Drama Review*, 39:4 (1995), 137–41.
——, 'Rethinking Ethnography: Towards a Critical Cultural Politics', *Communications Mongraphs* 58 (June 1991), 179–94.
Diamond, Elin (ed.), *Performance and Cultural Politics* (New York and London, 1996).
Dolan, Jill, 'Geographies of Learning: Theatre Studies, Performance, and the "Performative"', *Theatre Journal*, 45:4 (Dec. 1993), 417–41.
Foster, Susan (ed.), *Choreographing History* (Bloomington and Indianapolis, 1995).
——, *Corporealities: Dancing, Knowledge and Power* (New York and London, 1996).
Garber, Marjorie, *Vested Interests: Cross-Dressing and Cultural Anxiety* (New York and London, 1993).
Goffman, Erving, *The Presentation of the Self in Everyday Life* (London, 1971).
Hart, Lynda and Peggy Phelan (eds), *Acting Out: Feminist Performances* (Ann Arbor, MI, 1993).
Hart, Lynda, *Fatal Women: Lesbian Sexuality and the Mark of Aggression* (New York and London, 1994).

Liepe-Levinson, Katherine, *Strip Show: Performances of Gender and Desire* (New York and London, 2002).

Lindfors, Bernth (ed.), *Africans on Stage: Studies in Ethnological Show Business* (Bloomington and Indianapolis, 1999).

Lucas, Ian, *Impertinent Decorum: Gay Theatrical Manoeuvres* (London, 1994).

MacAloon, John (ed.), *Rite, Drama, Festival, Spectacle: Rehearsals Toward a Theory of Cultural Performance* (Philadelphia, 1984).

Mckenzie, Jon, *Perform or Else: From Discipline to Performance* (New York and London, 2001).

Parker, Andrew and Eve Kosofsky Sedgwick (eds) and introd., *Performativity and Performance* (New York and London, 1995).

Patraka, Vivian M., *Spectacular Suffering: Theatre, Fascism and the Holocaust* (Bloomington and Indianapolis, 1999).

Pelias, Ronald J. and James VanOosting, 'A Paradigm for Performance Studies', *The Quarterly Journal of Speech*, 73:2 (May 1987), 219–31.

Phelan, Peggy, *Mourning Sex: Performing Public Memories* (New York and London, 1997).

——, *Unmarked: The Politics of Performance* (New York and London, 1993).

Phelan, Peggy (ed.) and introd., Jill Lane (ed.), *The Ends of Performance* (New York, 1998).

Read, Alan, *Theatre and Everyday Life: An Ethics of Performance* (London and New York, 1993).

Reinelt, Janelle G. and Joseph R. Roach (eds), *Critical Theory and Performance* (Ann Arbor MI, 1992).

Roach, Joseph, *Cities of the Dead: Circum-Atlantic Performance* (New York, 1996).

Román, David, *Acts of Intervention: Performance, Gay Culture, and AIDS* (Bloomington and Indianapolis, 1998).

Schechner, Richard, 'A New Paradigm for Theatre in the Academy', *The Drama Review*, 36:4 (Winter 1992), 7–10.

——, *Between Theatre and Anthropology* (Philadelphia, 1985).

——, *The Future of Ritual: Writings on Culture and Performance* (New York and London, 1993).

——, *Performance Studies: An Introduction* (New York and London, 2002).

——, *Performance Theory*, rev. edn (New York and London, 1988).

Sedgwick, Eve Kosofsky, *Queer Performativity: Henry James's* 'The Art of the Novel' *GLQ*, 1 (Spring, 1993), 1–16.

Turner, Victor, *From Ritual to Theatre: The Human Seriousness of Play* (New York, 1982).

——, *The Anthropology of Performance*, preface by Richard Schechner (New York, 1986).

Worthen, W. B., Jill Dolan (reply); Joseph Roach (reply); Richard Schechner (reply); Phillip B. Zarrilli (reply). 'Disciplines of the Text/Sites of Performance', *The Drama Review*, 39:1 (Spring 1995), 13–44.

Notes on Contributors

Philip Auslander is Professor of the School of Literature, Communication, and Culture at the Georgia Institute of Technology. He is the author of *The New York School Poets As Playwrights: O'Hara, Ashbery, Koch, Schuyler and the Visual Arts* (1989), *Presence and Resistance: Postmodernism and Cultural Politics in Contemporary American Performance* (1992), *From Acting to Performance: Essays in Modernism and Postmodernism* (1997) and *Liveness: Performance in a Mediatized Culture* (1999).

Judith Butler is Maxine Elliot Professor in the Departments of Rhetoric and Comparative Literature at the University of California, Berkeley. She is the author of *Subjects of Desire: Hegelian Reflections in Twentieth-Century France* (1987), *Gender Trouble: Feminism and the Subversion of Identity* (1990), *Bodies That Matter: On the Discursive Limits of 'Sex'* (1993), *The Psychic Life of Power: Theories of Subjection* (1997), *Excitable Speech* (1997), as well as numerous articles and contributions on philosophy, feminist and queer theory. Her most recent work on Antigone and the politics of kinship is entitled *Antigone's Claim: Kinship Between Life and Death* (2000).

Susan Leigh Foster is Professor in Dance at University of California, Riverside. She is the author of *Reading Dancing* (1986), the editor of *Choreographing History* (1995) and *Corporealities* (1996), and the author of *Choreography and Narrative* (1996). Her most recent book is entitled *Dances that Describe Themselves*.

Paul Gilroy is Professor of Sociology and African American Studies at Yale University. His publications include *'There Ain't No Black in the Union Jack': The Cultural Politics of Race and Nation* (1987), *The Black Atlantic: Modernity and Double Consciousness* (1993), *Small Acts: Thoughts on the Politics of Black Cultures* (1993) and *Between Camps: Nations, Culture and the Allure of Race* (2000).

Lynda Hart was Professor of English at the University of Pennsylvania at the time of her death from breast cancer in 2000. She was the author of *Sam Shepard's Metaphorical Stages* (1987), and editor of the collection of essays on Feminist Theatre, *Making a Spectacle: Feminist Essays on Contemporary Women's Theatre* (1989), and co-editor (with Peggy Phelan) of its sequel, *Acting Out: Feminist Performances* (1993). Her book *Fatal Women: Lesbian Sexuality and the Mark of Aggression* (1994) won the Alice Paul Award and was nominated for the Callaway Prize. She authored *Between the Body and the Flesh: Performing Sadomasochism* (1998) and edited *Of All the Nerve: Deb Margolin Solo* (1999).

Bernth Lindfors is Professor of English and African Literature at the University of Texas, Austin. He is the author of *African Textualities: Texts, Pre-texts and*

Contexts of African Literature (1997), *The Blind Men and the Elephant and Other Essays in Biographical Criticism* (1999), editor of *Africans on Stage: Studies in Ethnological Show Business* (1999) and co-editor (With Hal Wylie) of *Multiculturalism and Hybridity in African Literatures* (2000).

Katherine Liepe-Levinson has worked as a professional dancer, actor, choreographer, director, and playwright in the United States and Europe. She has taught for the High School of Performing Arts in New York City, Colgate University, Hunter College, Empire College, and City College. She has published articles on cultural studies and arts education for journals such as *ET CETERA* and *TDR*. She is the author of *Strip Show: Performances of Gender and Desire* (2002). She is currently working as a freelance writer and arts education consultant in New York City.

Sharon Mazer is Head of the Department of Theatre and Film Studies at the University of Canterbury in Christchurch, New Zealand. She is the author of *Professional Wrestling: Sport and Spectacle* (1998).

Vivian M. Patraka is Professor of English and Theatre at Bowling Green State University. She currently serves as Director of the Institute for the Study of Culture and Society. Most recently, she edited and introduced a collection of Joan Schenkar's plays, *Signs of Life: Comedies of Menace by Joan Schenkar* (1998), and authored *Spectacular Suffering: Theatre, Fascism, and the Holocaust* (1999). Her work on Holocaust theatre, performance, and museums and Feminist theatre and performance has appeared in numerous journals and anthologies.

Peggy Phelan is the Ann O'Day Maples Chair in the Arts, Stanford University. She is the author of *Unmarked: The Politics of Performance* (1993) and *Mourning Sex: Performing Public Memories* (1997). With Helena Reckitt, she is the author of *Art and Feminism* (2001). She is the co-editor (with Lynda Hart) of *Acting Out: Feminist Performance* (1994) and (with Jill Lane) *The Ends of Performance* (1998).

Joseph Roach is the Charles C. and Dorathea S. Dilley Professor of Theater at Yale University. He is the author of *The Player's Passion: Studies in the Science of Acting* (1985), winner of the Barnard Hewitt Award, co-editor, with Janelle Reinelt, of *Critical Theory and Performance* (1992) and author of *Cities of the Dead* (1996) which was awarded the James Russell Lowell Prize and the Joe A. Callaway Prize.

Richard Schechner is Professor of Performance Studies at New York University. He is the author of *Environmental Theater* (1973), *Performance Theory* (1985), *Between Theater and Anthropology* (1985) and *The Future of Ritual: Writings on Culture and Performance* (1993). Schechner is also a theatre director whose work has been seen in the USA, Europe, Africa, and Asia. His most recent production was *Hamlet* (1999).

Index

212